Smart Talent Management

Smart Talent Management

Managing People as Knowledge Assets

SECOND EDITION

Edited by

Vlad Vaiman

Professor and Associate Dean, School of Management, California Lutheran University, USA

Charles Vance

Professor Emeritus, Loyola Marymount University, USA

Ling Ju

Founder, CEO and Director, 917 Fine Arts Corporation, USA

Edward Elgar
PUBLISHING

Cheltenham, UK • Northampton, MA, USA

Published by
Edward Elgar Publishing Limited
The Lypiatts
15 Lansdown Road
Cheltenham
Glos GL50 2JA
UK

Edward Elgar Publishing, Inc.
William Pratt House
9 Dewey Court
Northampton
Massachusetts 01060
USA

Paperback edition 2024

A catalogue record for this book
is available from the British Library

Library of Congress Control Number: 2023933739

This book is available electronically in the **Elgar**online
Business subject collection
http://dx.doi.org/10.4337/9781802202717

ISBN 978 1 80220 270 0 (cased)
ISBN 978 1 80220 271 7 (eBook)
ISBN 978 1 0353 3902 0 (paperback)

Printed and bound by CPI Group (UK) Ltd, Croydon, CR0 4YY

Contents

Figures

Tables

Contributors

Torben Andersen is Associate Professor, PhD (CBS and University of Warwick), at the Department of Business Development and Technology (Herning), Aarhus University, Denmark. His research has been concentrating on structural, strategic and change aspects of HRM and International HRM. He has been a visiting professor at San Francisco State University (2000), University of Auckland, New Zealand (2005) and Bamberg University (2016). He teaches in a variety of countries including Iceland, Germany, UK, China, New Zealand and the USA.

Saša Batistič is an Assistant Professor in the Department of Human Resource Studies at Tilburg University, the Netherlands. His research interests include human resource management, social networks, work relationships, socialization of organizational newcomers, and employability.

Françoise Cadigan is an Assistant Professor of Human Resource Management at MacEwan University in Edmonton, Alberta, Canada. Her research interests include talent management, decision-making and manager preferences for different types of employees, and the effects of artificial intelligence on HRM decision making.

Yunhyung Chung is a Full Professor of Management and Human Resources at the University of Idaho, USA. She received her PhD from the School of Management and Labor Relations at Rutgers University. Her research interests include workplace diversity and faultlines, social networks, strategic human resource management, and retirement security. She has published in journals such as *Academy of Management Journal, Journal of Management, Strategic Management Journal, Small Group Research*, and *Research in Personnel and Human Resource Management* among others.

Saba Colakoglu is a Lecturer of Organizational Behavior at the Scheller College of Business, Georgia Institute of Technology, USA. She received her PhD from the School of Management and Labor Relations at Rutgers University. Her research interests include strategic human resource management with an international focus, MNC subsidiary staffing, and global careers. She won the International Human Resource Management Scholarly Research Award from the Academy of Management in 2016. Her research has appeared in such journals as *Academy of Management Journal, Journal of International*

Business Studies, *Journal of Organizational Behavior*, and *International Journal of Human Resource Management*, among others. She is currently serving as the Vice President of Women in the Academy of International Business.

Kieran M. Conroy is an Associate Professor in Global Strategy at Queen's University Belfast, UK. His research concentrates on the evolution of corporate strategies and strategic leadership in multinationals, with central themes including headquarter–subsidiary relationships, knowledge orchestration, global mobility flows, and global human capital development. His work has been published in *Journal of World Business*, *Global Strategy Journal*, *Journal of International Management*, and *British Journal of Management*, among others. He serves on the Editorial Review Board of *Academy of Management Perspectives* and *Journal of World Business* among others.

Colette Darcy is Dean of the School of Business at National College of Ireland and a Senior Lecturer in Human Resource Management. She is a former Government of Ireland Scholar and was awarded the European Foundation for Management Development/Emerald Outstanding Doctoral Thesis Award for her research examining employee fairness perceptions and claiming behavior. Her research interests extend to organizational justice, work-life balance and career theory. She has published her work in several academic journals including *Human Resource Management Review*, *European Management Journal*, and others. She has also collaborated on several texts in HR and organizational behavior.

Nicky Dries is a Full Professor of Organizational Behavior at KU Leuven and BI Norwegian Business School. Her research interests are careers, talent management, and the future of work. Nicky was an Associate Editor at *Applied Psychology* until 2019 and is or was on the editorial boards of *Journal of Vocational Behavior*, *Journal of World Business*, and *European Journal of Work and Organizational Psychology*. Since 2016, she is featured on AcademiaNet, the European database of leading women in science. In 2019, she was listed as one of the world's top-100,000 scientists. In 2021, she was selected for Belgium's inaugural '40 under 40' cohort, a think tank for the nation's most promising young societal leaders. Nicky has been an active member of the two largest cross-cultural projects in career studies, i.e., the Career Adaptability/Life Design project (2008–2013) and 5C (Consortium for the Cross-Cultural Study of Contemporary Careers; 2011–ongoing).

Thomas Garavan is Professor of Leadership Practices and Visiting Research Professor, CUBS, University College Cork and Visiting Research Professor, National College of Ireland, Dublin. He is a leading researcher worldwide in learning and development, HRD, leadership development and workplace learning. He is Editor of the *European Journal of Training and Development* and Associate Editor of *Personnel Review*. He is a member of the Editorial Board of *Human Resource Management Journal*, *Human Resource Development Quarterly*, *Human Resource Development Review*, *Advances in Developing Human Resources*, and *Human Resource Development International*. His research interests include CSR and transformational leadership, cross-cultural dimensions of diversity training, tacit knowledge in manufacturing, international human resource management standards and human resource management.

Ying Hong is an Associate Professor in the Leading People and Organizations area at the Gabelli School of Business, Fordham University, USA. She received her PhD in industrial relations/human resources from Rutgers University. She specializes in research on the strategic role of human resource management and its linkage with service excellence. Her work has appeared in peer-reviewed journals such as the *Academy of Management Journal* and the *Journal of Applied Psychology*. She received the Scholarly Achievement Award from the human resources division of the Academy of Management and the 2016/2018 Dean's Award for Excellence in Research from the Gabelli School of Business.

Stefan Jooss is a Senior Lecturer at UQ Business School, The University of Queensland, Australia. His main research interest and focus is in the areas of talent management, global mobility, and the future of work. His work has been published in *Human Resource Management Journal*, *Human Resource Management Review*, *The International Journal of Human Resource Management*, and *International Journal of Contemporary Hospitality Management*, among others.

Ling Ju is the founder and CEO of 917 Fine Arts Corp, an art advisory and exhibition business based in south Florida, USA. She received an MBA degree from Loyola Marymount University in Los Angeles and other degrees and certificates from universities across various countries. Besides pursuing her strong interest in management research, Ling spends her time in real estate investment and building a global education platform for art and design.

Konstantin Korotov is Professor of Organizational Behavior at ESMT Berlin, Germany. His research interests are leadership development, executive coaching, executive education and careers. He has authored, co-authored and co-edited multiple academic articles, books, book chapters, and case studies on these topics. He is the founder of the ESMT annual coaching colloquia—a series of academic and practitioner events for exploration of nascent themes in the field of executive coaching and development. In addition to his academic work, Konstantin has held positions of the Faculty Lead of the

ESMT Executive MBA, Associate Dean of Executive Education, and Director of the Center for Leadership Development Research. His portfolio of executive education programs includes, among others, Allianz, Bosch, Daimler, Deutsche Telekom, Deutsche Bank, EY, European Parliament, Merz Pharma, Siemens, TÜV Nord, etc.

Marina Latukha is a Doctor of Economics and Professor in HRM at Leonard de Vinci Pole University, EMLV Business School. She has graduated from postdoctoral programs in the Harvard Business School, the Haas School of Business, the London Business School, and worked as Professor at St. Petersburg State University, Graduate School of Management. Her research interests focus on global talent management, international and strategic human resource management, talent diversity, and emerging multinationals. She is the author of a number of academic articles published in top-ranked academic journals, such as the *International Journal of Human Resource Management, Journal of Business Research, Thunderbird International Business Review*, and others. Marina is the author of *Talent Management in Emerging Market Firms: Global Strategy and Local Challenges* (2015) and has edited *Talent Management in Global Organizations: A Cross-Country Perspective* (2018) and *Diversity in Action: Managing Diverse Talent in a Global Economy* (2022).

Mark L. Lengnick-Hall is Professor Emeritus of Management in the Alvarez College of Business at The University of Texas at San Antonio, USA. He received a PhD in Organizational Behavior and Human Resource Management from Purdue University. Dr. Lengnick-Hall has written over 50 articles and 3 books on various human resource management topics. His primary research interests have been strategic human management, the employment of people with disabilities, and volunteers and nonprofit organizations.

Clíodhna MacKenzie is a Lecturer in the Department of Management & Marketing at Cork University Business School at University College Cork, Ireland. Clíodhna holds a PhD in business from the University of Limerick. She has previously worked for both US multinationals and global IT consultancy firms. Clíodhna has international experience in the IT and telecoms fields and has worked in the USA, EMEA and APAC. Her academic research focuses on organizational and leadership failures, risk-taking, governance, ethics and social responsibility and has published in several leading HR journals.

Maria Laura MacLennan is an Adjunct Professor in Business at Centro Universitario FEI in Brazil. She holds a PhD in Business Studies from the University of Sao Paulo (USP), where she conducted research on international HRM and strategy. She is an active member of the Academy of International Business and European Academy of International Business. Her main research interest is to conduct interdisciplinary studies bounding HRM and strategy including international business and international strategy.

Anthony McDonnell is Full Professor of Human Resource Management, Deputy Dean, Head of the Department of Management and Marketing and co-Director of the HR Research Centre at Cork University Business School, University College Cork, Ireland. He is Chair of the Irish Academy of Management and has held appointments at Queen's University Belfast, University of South Australia and University of Newcastle (Australia).

Andrea R. Neely is an Assistant Professor of Management in the Rollins College of Business at the University of Tennessee at Chattanooga, USA. She received her PhD from The University of Texas at San Antonio in Organizational Behavior and Human Resource Management. Her research interests broadly consist of relationships, roles, and resources. She has interest in social capital, reciprocity, CSR, and volunteers. Her most recent publication is 'A process model of volunteer motivation' in *Human Resource Management Review* with Mark L. Lengnick-Hall and Michelle D. Evans. Her active projects include HR in a volunteer context, employee perceptions on Zoom, CSR work roles, and reciprocity.

Rob F. Poell is Professor of Human Resource Development in the Department of Human Resource Studies at Tilburg University, the Netherlands. His research interests include workplace learning; employee learning-path strategies; knowledge hiding; future roles of HRD practitioners; learning networks; and interactions among employees, managers and HRD practitioners.

Anne Roefs is an organization consultant focusing on HR & People Analytics at GalanNXT, Utrecht, the Netherlands. She holds an MSc degree in Human Resource Studies from Tilburg University, the Netherlands.

Vlad Vaiman is Professor and the Associate Dean at the School of Management of California Lutheran University, USA and a visiting professor at several premier universities around the globe. He has published seven books on managing talent in organizations and at a country level, as well as a number of academic and practitioner-oriented articles and book chapters on talent management and International HRM. His work appeared in *Academy of Management Learning and Education, Human Resource Management, International Journal of Human Resource Management, Human Resource Management Review, Journal of Business Ethics,* and many others. He is also a founding editor and the Chief Editorial Consultant of the *European Journal of International Management,* and an editorial board member of several academic journals, such as *Human Resource Management, European Management Review,* and *Human Resource Management Review,* among others. He is a founder, organizer, and a leading chair of the EIASM Workshop on Talent Management, as well as the editor of the Emerald book series on Talent Management.

Marian van Bakel is Associate Professor with the Department of Business and Management of the University of Southern Denmark, where she conducts research in international human resource management, particularly expatriation. Her main research interests are the social context of expatriation, expatriate-HCN interactions both in and outside the organization, intercultural competence and intercultural mentoring. She received her PhD in international business communication at Radboud University Nijmegen, the Netherlands, while also working as in-house communication consultant at Radboud University Nijmegen Medical Centre. She serves on the editorial review boards of the *International Journal of Human Resource Management* and the *Journal of Global Mobility*.

Charles Vance is Emeritus Professor at Loyola Marymount University in Los Angeles. For nearly 30 years his research has examined the host country national as an important yet often-neglected player in the foreign subsidiary and expatriate management context. He is the author of over 100 scholarly publications and creative works, as well as three books, including *Managing a Global Workforce* (2015) and *Mastering Management Education* (1993). He also has been very active as a guest instructor and consultant in numerous countries related to training development, leadership, and global talent management.

Anand van Zelderen is a PhD student at the KU Leuven, Faculty of Economics and Business, Belgium. Financed by the Research Foundation Flanders (i.e., FWO Aspirant grant), his doctoral research focuses on the unequal treatment of employees and its impact on their well-being and the organization at large. Furthermore, Anand has a keen interest in seeing Virtual Reality (VR) being used to its fullest potential in academic research and is currently working on a long-term project to recreate fictional organizations in virtual space to conduct various controlled virtual experiments that cannot readily be recreated in actual organizations.

Foreword

David Collings

When the first edition of *Smart Talent Management* was published some 15 years ago, research on talent management was very much in its infancy. Thus, Vlad Vaiman and Charles Vance were very much in the vanguard in building the theoretical foundations of the emerging area of talent management. Talent management has been described as a bridge field reflecting the fact that it draws so significantly on theories from other fields to build its own theoretical foundations. Vaiman and Vance were amongst the first to identify the value of a knowledge management lens to inform our understanding of the emerging area of talent management. The value of such efforts should not be underestimated. At that time the area was struggling for legitimacy in the academic community and volumes such as this one were hugely important in terms of providing outlets for authors with an interest in the emerging area and building the knowledge base of the area.

There is no doubt that organizations continue to struggle with many of the same talent challenges as they did when the original volume was published, albeit in a different and highly volatile context. The pandemic has shifted expectations around how and where talent work, with many reflecting on why they work. It has also accelerated many of the trends in the future of work which were already in train with high demand for skills in areas such as digitization, robotics and the like. Equally, the increased focus on remote and hybrid working means leaders and managers require new skill sets to manage in these new contexts. The #metoo movement and the global reaction to George Floyd's murder bring diversity, equality, and inclusion questions to the fore, while the war in Ukraine and the pandemic have focused organisations to re-evaluate operating models and altered global supply chains in many sectors. These and other trends put talent management front and centre for organizations globally and reinforce the importance of a volume such as this.

The current volume builds on the ambition of the first edition with the overarching purpose to present a valuable fusion of these two important areas of emphasis for current research and practice in management. It reflects the developments in our understanding of the area in the past decade and a half, combined with the external dynamics mentioned above, and presents a much more nuanced and rich discussion of these key topics in the chapters. There is also more critical tone in the contributions, reflecting more light and shade in the discussions in the chapters. Indeed, one of the most impressive elements of the volume for me is the calibre of the contributors. They bring a real international perspective to the volume and approach the area from a range of core backgrounds. This makes for a diverse and well researched set of chapters covering a really important array of topics.

I am excited to see this new volume, and Vaiman, Vance and new colleague Ling Ju have done a wonderful job of curating this set of new and updated chapters. This collection, while moving forward our understanding of key questions at the intersection of talent management and knowledge management, also offers several very important suggestions for where research needs to go to further advance our understanding of the interaction between these important areas. There is no doubt that the volume will be valuable to researchers in both talent management and knowledge management, as well as students and reflective practitioners looking for the most up to date discussion of these critical areas. Congratulations to the editors and contributors on this timely and important collection.

David Collings
Chair of Sustainable Business
Trinity College Dublin, Ireland

1. Smart talent management: the productive fusion of talent and knowledge management

Vlad Vaiman, Charles M. Vance and Ling Ju

INTRODUCTION

Nearly 15 years ago saw the release of the first edition of this book—one of the first beginning to examine talent management as distinct from traditional human resource management. And particularly unique in the growing discussion of talent management was our assertion, which we still hold today, of the value of combining talent management (TM) and knowledge management (KM) to form a powerful conceptual and practical amalgamation contributing to an organization's success in our competitive global marketplace. For want of a more precise and scientific label, we call this combination simply 'smart talent management.' Among other major outcomes of the recent COVID-19 pandemic, where employees have been physically absent due to remote work requirements and forcing the focus upon knowledge contribution, an organization's human talent is seen more clearly as possessing key knowledge that requires effective management.

Following our first edition there have been several important publications that examine the KM/TM combination paradigm related to knowledge management and strategic HRM, leadership support and managerial involvement, organizational learning, human capital, and KM integration with individual HR functions (e.g., see Khaligh & Ranjbarian, 2022; Rezaei, Khalilzadeh, & Soleimani, 2021; Antunes & Pinheiro, 2020; Pellegrini et al., 2020; Sumarsi, 2020; Muhammed & Zaim, 2020; Nisar, Prabhakarb, & Strakovaa, 2019; Shujahat et al., 2019; Milton & Lambe, 2019; Whelan & Carcary, 2011). We hope that this second edition of our book will continue to prompt further examination of the benefits of this combined attention to talent and knowledge management, focusing not only on the establishment of useful definitions, but also on the development and empirical exploration of the smart talent management paradigm. Just like in our first edition, therefore, we define our concept of smart talent management as the combined use of the distinctly different concepts of knowledge management and talent management to resolve human performance problems and to achieve organizational objectives.

There is one important distinction between our previous conceptualizations and current thinking on talent management, however, that somewhat augments our understanding of smart talent management. This change is prompted by an explosive development of the field of talent management in the past decade. In the previous edition of the book, smart talent management (STM) referred to the effective (i.e., 'smart') integration of knowledge management into the TM paradigm, where STM meant the smart or effective management of *all human resources*, who embody an organization's knowledge capital and capability in generating, acquiring, storing, transferring, and applying knowledge in support of company goals and objectives (competitive advantage). The more recent developments in the area of TM demonstrated that this approach is just 'one color' on a full spectrum of different approaches to TM.

TM is currently a rapidly growing discipline with an increasing consensus on TM definitions, theoretical frameworks, and levels of analysis. Among several important themes in the TM literature, the debate on *exclusive* versus *inclusive* TM approaches has received a significant amount of attention. This discussion revolves around the question of whether TM efforts in an organization should concentrate on all employees or only on those select few identified as talent, i.e., individuals who possess unique skills or show the highest potential for superior performance and organizational contribution. In more detail, the exclusive approach is aimed at *key employees in key positions* (organizational elite, so to speak), and it helps to (1) better differentiate TM from HRM, (2) support workforce differentiation and disproportionate investment (given the reality of limited resources) in individuals with high levels of human capital, (3) and ensure competitive advantage.

On the other hand, the inclusive approach is focused on *all employees*, where management believes that everyone in the organization has potential to create added value; it promotes increased diversity and heterogeneity of talent pools and requires a different understanding of the meaning of 'talent.' While this debate in both academia and practice still presses on, most experts (e.g., Daubner-Siva et al., 2018; Thunnissen and Gallardo-Gallardo, 2017; Gallardo-Gallardo & Thunnissen, 2016) agree that the exclusive approach is prevailing in contemporary TM studies. However, we submit that one should not look at this exclusive vs. inclusive dichotomy as an irreconcilable divide but rather as a continuum, where some organizations undoubtedly use an 'exclusive extreme' that is characterized by a disproportionate investment in highly talented individuals, with a greater focus on talent attraction and acquisition, while others utilize an 'inclusive extreme' embodied by an equal resource allocation and investment in low performers to balance up performance, with a greater concentration on talent development and retention. Most companies, however, operate somewhere in between these two extremes and do their best to invest in all levels of human capital development (Morris, Snell, & Bjorkman, 2016). So, as opposed to accepting a fully inclusive approach in this book, we will treat TM as a more complex phenomenon.

Despite changes in our understanding of TM, 'Smart' in STM still corresponds to our emphasis of the strategic role of knowledge management in today's organizations, and particularly within TM, which is part of strategic human resource management (SHRM) efforts of an organization. Our continued use of 'knowledge assets' in our book's title provides an explicit reference to the essential role of knowledge management tied to the human factor, building upon the past use of 'human capital' as a strategic tool for competitive advantage.

Thus, the overarching purpose of our book is to present a valuable fusion of two important areas of emphasis for current research and practice in management: talent management and knowledge management. The significance of knowledge management to competitive advantage and organizational success in our rapidly changing global knowledge-based economy is immense (Islam et al., 2022; Rialti et al., 2020; Paoloni et al., 2020). The generation/acquisition of ideas and knowledge, their internal transfer and application throughout the organization and across its various operations, cross-border transfer of knowledge, and so on, have all become an integral and important part of contemporary management, both domestic and international. But what many knowledge management scholars have missed in their predominantly theoretical perspective is the fact that effective knowledge management in practice is largely dependent upon the management of human talent, and especially upon such practical components as recruitment of talent, training, facilitated knowledge sharing, coaching and mentoring, performance management, succession planning, development of global leadership competencies, global alignment, and retention management, among others.

Talent management is quite different in the world of practice, especially when it comes to multinational enterprises (MNEs). As Vaiman and Collings (2015) have noted, one of the most important roles of the global talent function in practice relates to facilitating knowledge creation and knowledge sharing in the MNE, which is increasingly seen as a critical source of competitive advantage on the global stage. On the other hand, despite a tremendous increase in existing scholarly publications on talent management, most fail to adequately recognize human talent as repositories of potentially valuable knowledge—both tacit and explicit. This shortcoming of current academic perspectives in talent management is evident in a recent remark by a TM executive of a large US defense contractor, who indicated that their organization emphasizes retention efforts within the overall TM strategy, since a lot of valuable knowledge is unfortunately leaving the company due to inadequate attention to effective knowledge management.

TALENT MANAGEMENT: STRENGTHS AND LIMITATIONS

With our conceptual admixture in 'smart talent management,' this second edition updates our novel look at human talent in organizations, with employees at all levels representing potentially key agents of knowledge management in acquiring, transferring, and applying important knowledge for competitive advantage. Like 'human capital' and the more broad, generic term 'human resource management,' talent management is grounded predominantly in resource-based theory of organizations (Collins, 2021; Barney, 1991), where organizations can gain competitive advantage to the extent that their assets and resources with which they compete and pursue organizational objectives are valuable, rare, and difficult to imitate. Organizations that are able to attract human talent consistently and effectively, as well as develop and update, deploy where needed, obtain commitment to organization goals, build social capital, elicit ideas for ongoing improvement, and retain this talent will fare well in the long term in the global marketplace compared with other organizations that neglect such attention to human talent. As mentioned above, in the past 15 years since the release of the first edition of this book, there have been quite a few developments in the area of talent management, both in academia and practice. However, many of the same challenges that were identified early on have either persisted or reemerged after the 2007–2009 global recession, including tight labor markets, more complex talent demands in terms of incumbents' knowledge, skills, and ability, more complex technology and organizational structures, and increasing job mobility (Vaiman, Collings, & Cascio, 2021). Another major challenge that has surfaced rather recently is TM in times of crisis. This has been brought about by the COVID-19 pandemic, which caused not only human suffering on a massive global scale, but also major disruptions that resulted in profound changes in the way individuals and organizations live, work, and function. From a talent perspective, there is definitely a silver lining, as this challenge created multiple opportunities in terms of more flexible working arrangements, which are associated with increased employee satisfaction, productivity, and retention (Wang & Heyes, 2020; Baeza, Gonzalez, & Wang, 2018), and the potential to access more geographically diverse talent pools.

Another trend emerging from the COVID-19 pandemic is that many people have experienced remote work and have been quite successful after the initial set-up period. Consequently, organizations are talking about keeping many of their normally office-bound employees working from their homes or in a hybrid format (i.e., letting them work sometimes from home and the rest on-site). This is not only happening in the domestic setting but globally—for example, McKinsey (2021) estimates that up to 25% of the workforce in the developed world and about 10% in developing countries will continue working from home even after the pandemic. The increase in online and hybrid work has facilitated employee connections globally, reducing the need for physical global mobility in the 'new normal' following the pandemic. As the pandemic subsides, many employers are getting ready to welcome their employees back to in-person presence. Most understand, however, that there is no going back to 'business as usual,' and that the 'new normal' will be hybrid, requiring greater remote work arrangement flexibility. The question for organizations is how to manage and prosper from these developments. As work becomes increasingly remote and hybrid, talent management strategies need to adjust in line with this approach, creating dispersed rather than concentrated talent pools, shifting the best talent into most critical roles, moving away from a traditional performance management system, and creating the best employee experience possible, among other actions.

Importantly, many remote and hybrid employees are experiencing burnout, which they also attribute to a lack of open and sometimes unambiguous communication on the part of their management. Both anxiety and burnout usually lead to voluntary turnover, which may immediately affect both organization's availability of talent and TM strategy. To effectively address these serious issues, organizational leadership should develop clear policies that deal with communication technology, working hours, expectations for collaboration, available support, among many other factors. These guidelines, approaches, and expectations should be communicated clearly and frequently, and HR experts need to help managers to facilitate and reinforce these messages. There is still much work to do on this front, as apparently, most organizations are only starting to develop the specifics of hybrid working arrangements. As mentioned above, with the post-pandemic trend of increasing remote work flexibility, there is growing awareness of the need to focus less upon physically present employee performance management and more upon employee knowledge management—the knowledge assets that employees hold or should acquire.

In the world of academia, five key conceptualizations of TM have been revealed in the past 15 years. The first three have been identified by Lewis and Heckman (2006). First was about simply replacing the label HRM with TM, which did not go well with fellow academics who started looking at TM as just a new moniker for the existing function. The second conceptualization helped to shift the succession planning discussion from a somewhat static organizational chart-based approach to a more dynamic one based on predicting staffing needs and developing corresponding talent pools to meet these needs in the future (Cappelli and Keller, 2014). The third theme focused on the management of so-called 'A' players, i.e., employees who consistently demonstrated higher performance in comparison to 'B' (average performers) and 'C' (poor performers) players. The chief idea behind this was to reward A-players, while forcing C-players 'up or out.' Even though this approach had its own proponents (not least of whom was Jack Welch of GE), the idea of forced distribution upon which this approach was based garnered quite a lot of criticism, due to its negative effect on employees involved, cooperation and teamwork, organizational culture, etc. (Collings, Vaiman, & Scullion, 2022). The fourth theme has been brought up in 2009 by Collings and Mellahi, who identified an important direction in TM literature premised on the differentiation of key (or critical, pivotal) job roles in organizations. These roles are differentiated by their ability to generate a disproportional value—expressed in both quantity and quality of output—that contributes to the strategic intent (i.e., mission, vision, strategy, etc.) of the organization. Collings (2017) noted that this literature stream helped to shift the debate on differentiation in TM from employee inputs to outputs, which was a significant change in TM theorization. A later, fifth theme that emerged in the conceptualization of TM focused on the role of big data and people analytics in making more informed decisions on investments in talent (see Vaiman, Collings, & Scullion, 2012).

As mentioned earlier in this chapter, the academic literature has evolved mainly along two paths in terms of TM's conceptual foundations. The first, most prevailing focus is undoubtedly on *exclusive TM* which underscores the disproportionate contribution of high performing and high potential individuals often employed in critical roles. In line with this approach, Collings and Mellahi (2009) define talent management as 'activities and processes that involve the systematic identification of key positions which differentially contribute to the organisation's sustainable competitive advantage, the development of a talent pool of high potential and high performing incumbents to fill these roles, and the development of a differentiated human resource architecture to facilitate filling these positions with competent incumbents and to ensure their continued commitment to the organisation' (Collings & Mellahi, 2009: 305). Even though the above is not the only acceptable definition of TM in the literature, it is by far the most cited and used, emphasizing the tendency of academics to prefer a more exclusive approach to TM.

The second focus is on a more *inclusive approach* to TM, which accentuates the strengths (in terms of knowledge, skills, ability, expertise, etc.) that individual employees bring to the workplace and how organizations can build upon those strengths (Swailes, 2013, 2020). Inclusive TM is conceptualized as the understanding and acceptance that all employees in an organization should be viewed as talent, that everyone is capable of contributing something important to their organization, and that each and every employee should be provided with the opportunity to develop and be deployed in positions in which they may benefit their organization the most. Unlike the exclusive approach, this focus does not over-emphasize individual performance, which may be beneficial to collaboration and team-based contributions. Although this approach has its definite benefits and supporters among TM scholars, it remains somewhat more aspirational, both in academia and practice.

There is no doubt that TM as a discipline is as important and relevant now as it was when it first surfaced from the world of management consulting in early 2000s (see Michaels, Handfield-Jones, & Axelrod, 2001) in response to persistent challenges which companies around the world were facing in attracting and retaining key employees. Despite some critical issues—some of which were discussed above—talent shortages remain a critical issue for organizations globally, and global leaders continue to cite talent challenges as the most important issue that impacts their ability to deliver on both short- and long-term organizational objectives (Collings, Vaiman, & Scullion, 2022).

KNOWLEDGE MANAGEMENT: STRENGTHS AND LIMITATIONS

Besides the distinctly different emphases that we place on the term 'talent,' our addition of the conceptual discipline of knowledge management to the picture takes talent management to a more strategic level, where the human talent at all levels represents potentially important sources, transmitters, and implementers of knowledge essential to competitive advantage. Consistent with the maxim 'knowledge is power,' the competitive advantages of organizations are derived from core competencies, capabilities, and 'know-how' that are developed within them over time (Rehman, Mohamed, & Ayoup, 2019; Prahalad & Hamel, 1990). This collective knowledge is held explicitly within the set of documented policies, practices, directions, instructions, and so on, and implicitly or tacitly within developed routines of organizational life, as well as the conscious and unconscious experience base of employees at all levels (Nonaka & Takeuchi, 1995).

To a significant extent, employees embody the knowledge in use within the organization. According to the knowledge-based view of the firm (Grant & Phene, 2022; Grant, 1996), this employee know-how that greatly contributes to a firm's human core competencies potentially provides a strategic resource to assist the firm in adapting and competing in its market environments (Haesli & Boxall, 2005). Clearly, when all employee talent (including both regular and contingent employees) are seen as current and potential sources and purveyors of knowledge and know-how for beneficial application and utilization within the firm, the perceived role of human resource management policies and practices to attract, develop, motivate, facilitate knowledge exchange interactions within the organization, and retain this talent grows dramatically in importance (Zaim, Muhammed & Tarim, 2019). Besides increasing the perceived importance of HR policies and practices to the organization, knowledge management also provides a common, unifying purpose and link to integrate and coordinate these policies and practices more effectively within the various HR functions.

Despite the valuable potential contributions of knowledge management, there are potential shortcomings that limit its value and utility in improving organizational performance. Many efforts in knowledge management have focused on hardware and software database applications (e.g., expert systems) with apparently little regard for human dimensions affecting both the entry and retrieval of experience-based knowledge and information, which can become even more problematic due to cultural differences within our global organizations (Paik & Choi, 2005). Much work that does focus on human organizational issues in knowledge management remains at a rather abstract, theoretical, and fairly macro level, with little reference to specific HR policies, practices, and procedures for guiding and bringing knowledge management to the micro level of local firm operations (Cohen & Levinthal, 1990; Gupta & Govindarajan, 2000; Bhagat et al., 2002).

Nonaka and Takeuchi (1995) presented the concept of the 'knowledge spiral,' which examines four modes of knowledge transformations, involving knowledge creation and transfer between tacit knowledge (i.e., know-how or experience-based knowledge that is difficult to document) and explicit knowledge (i.e., more easily communicated or shared) at different levels within the firm. Hansen, Nohria, and Tierney (1999) provide a simpler way of envisioning links between knowledge management and the human dimension by distinguishing major approaches of knowledge management: the 'personalization' and 'codification' of knowledge. In the personalization approach, tacit or experience-based knowledge remains closely tied to the individuals who create or discover it from external sources and transmit this knowledge primarily through person-to-person contact. In contrast, the codification approach attempts to make knowledge more explicit and facilitate its transfer through entry onto databases and into operations manuals and employee training plans for wider company dissemination. The application of the personalization knowledge management approach appears to work most favorably in unique, novel situations, while the codification approach works best in situations involving fairly predictable conditions and routine organizational practices. However, despite their contributions to theory development, these approaches to knowledge management still fail to make a close link to specific HR functional practices for guiding local operations—such as in specific staffing, training and development, and various communications efforts and activities for creating and moving both explicit and tacit knowledge through the organization. There is still a relatively limited understanding of specific ways in which knowledge management and human resource practices may interact to support competitive advantage (Jyoti & Rani, 2017; Donate & Guadamillas, 2011). More details and recommendations promoting this productive interaction are a major contribution of this book.

Another limitation of knowledge management and related management of knowledge workers is the predominant focus on cerebral and cognitive, intellectual processes, and more impersonal big data and technical systems (Shujahat et al., 2019). There continues to be relatively little attention directed at individual learning and skill development in areas critical for individual, group, and organizational performance within the affective (e.g., feelings, emotions) and psychomotor (e.g., skills) domains (Malik, 2021; Rashid, Tout, & Yakan, 2021; Yang, Zheng, & Viere, 2009). Although discussions about implicit or tacit knowledge can relate to the largely unconscious and internalized knowledge aspects of the psychomotor domain, again they tend to lack sufficient detail about how this form of knowledge can be effectively developed.

Considerable work in emotional intelligence, creativity, and nonlinear thinking also points to the need to look beyond strictly cognitive dimensions of rational data-gathering and logical analysis of knowledge and information for achieving and maintaining high levels of performance (Groves & Vance, 2015; Kahneman, 2013). In a departure from the nearly complete focus on the cognitive domain, past work analyzing individual learning benefits of knowledge-sharing groups (both within and across organizations) has identified important forms of learning in the affective domain, such as increased confidence in problem solving, reduced anxiety caused by feelings of isolation, or an increased awareness of and accompanying sense of urgency in addressing a potential future problem (Vance et al., 1991).

VALUE OF THE TALENT/KNOWLEDGE MANAGEMENT HYBRID

A combined conceptualization of talent management and knowledge management in smart talent management considers that which employees can bring of value to the organization (i.e., their personal talent attributes) as extending far beyond only the cognitive domain. The power of the concept of talent includes its relevance to other essential domains of human development and performance besides an individual's store of rational information and cerebral knowledge. The concept of valued skills and competencies held by an experienced employee provides a more vivid picture, and strengthens the meaning of deep, hard to articulate, tacit knowledge, thereby directing it closer to the influence of specific HR practices for identifying, surfacing and capturing, and spreading this tacit knowledge within the organization. The valued personal attribute of talent also reaches into the affective domain, such as with emotional intelligence and the ability to read and manage one's own feelings in a constructive fashion, and to influence others in doing the same (Goleman, 1995, 1998).

We can see very successful global organizations today operating with the TM/KM hybrid model. One such organization is igus, GmbH of Germany, a leading manufacturer of energy chain systems that support industrial automation and robotics. The active involvement of all managers at all levels in HR practices in combining TM and KM is quickly apparent in a visit to the headquarters manufacturing facility in Cologne. As symbolized by the lower-case letters in its name, igus promotes a strong culture of humility, continuous learning, empowerment, and equality. With operations in 35 countries, the company heavily invests in training and talent development worldwide. Its open office space and furniture design supports an egalitarian atmosphere and facilitates the sharing of information. Everyone can contact anyone else in the company directly. A good example of this combined TM/KM smart talent management model in action, which here merges an empowerment approach with knowledge management, is the igus common maxim: 'First decide, then inform.'

As another good example, the multinational giant Procter & Gamble has been extremely successful in attracting, developing, and retaining its managerial talent worldwide. P&G's combined TM/KM effectiveness in disseminating key knowledge, skills, and abilities throughout its worldwide operations has resulted in the distinct competitive advantage of decision-makers who share a common mindset and alignment that supports an integrated and coordinated global business strategy. This TM/KM merger affecting specific HR practice is evident in the work of P&G's one East Asia regional senior HR executive called 'knowledge-based leadership.' The purpose of P&G's knowledge-based leadership approach is to enable all employees to perform at their peak by ultimately providing opportunities to make decisions in their area of responsibilities. In implementing knowledge-based leadership, P&G employees participate in various forms of training and development to master their three critical areas of knowledge/understanding: (1) the specific technical expertise involved in their work, (2) successful P&G business strategies and approaches, and (3) the Procter & Gamble PVP model that makes up the core fabric of their culture: *purposes* (e.g., company mission), *values* (e.g., core personal and interpersonal values held by each employee such as integrity, trust, passion for success, ownership), and *principles* of business practice linked to company success (e.g., 'mutual interdependency is a way of life,' 'innovation is the cornerstone of our success'). Once employees demonstrate that they have gained sufficient knowledge and clear understanding (including internalized commitment—learning in the affective domain) in these three primary areas, they are fully empowered to make decisions on their own to accomplish their work performance objectives.

The TM/KM hybrid merges the strengths of each individual approach, yet in combination is also able to surmount the limitations of each. From the above discussion we can summarize the distinct strengths of the combined TM/KM model in smart talent management as follows:

1. With its merger with knowledge management, talent management becomes much more than just a catchy euphemism to replace 'human resource management,' and is clearly raised to a strategic level of vital consideration, where employees are seen as holders of critical knowledge for the organization. The care and retention of such human talent are of great importance, for employee loss through turnover also can involve the loss of priceless tacit and transferable knowledge and social capital, including loss of future knowledge acquisition through terminated external professional networks.

2. Knowledge management provides a common purpose and focus to help unify and integrate HR functional efforts and activities and broaden the link with HR and organizational strategy.

3. The term 'talent' has a potent meaning that may convey the current or potential value of each employee within the organization—including contingent employees. Thus, the acquisition, development, deployment, and retention of such talent gains a greater investment imperative for the organization.

4. Following a more inclusive path, the TM/KM model has sound theoretical grounding, yet is positioned within the realm of specific HR functional practices, where all managers and supervisors perceive they have an important, central role.

5. The broad view of talent extends knowledge management beyond primarily a conscious, cognitive dimension to include deeper tacit and affective dimensions.

The intent of this book is to present the TM/KM conceptual hybrid, smart talent management, as a valuable multi-faceted direction for managerial action leading to organizational improvement and enhanced competitiveness. However, the idea of building a stronger connection between knowledge management and key HR practices is still in its infancy. We hope that our selection of papers will serve to enhance our understanding of this potentially powerful union and spur further theoretical and applied developments.

OVERVIEW OF THIS BOOK

Following this first (introductory) chapter, this book comprises nine exemplary contributions from top international scholars working in the areas of talent and knowledge management. In the second chapter, titled 'Conceptualizing and Operationalizing "Inclusive" Talent Management: Four Different Approaches,' the authors Françoise Cadigan, Nicky Dries, and Anand van Zelderen identify four different approaches to inclusive TM—a concept that is advocated more and more for by both academics and practitioners, and which has thus far lacked conceptual clarity and practical actionability. The four approaches are (1) focusing on potential and strengths rather than talent, (2) increasing the size of the talent pool, (3) defining a broader range of talent domains, and (4) top-grading the entire organization. The authors propose that exclusive and inclusive TM (co)exist on a continuum rather than as dichotomies and develop a decision tree for organizations and researchers to determine which custom approach might best fit their talent philosophy.

The third chapter, authored by Thomas Garavan, Clíodhna MacKenzie, and Colette Darcy and called 'In the War for Talent: Just Who is Worthy of Development? Talent Development in Organizations,' explores talent development as a critical pillar of the firm's overall talent management strategy. The authors position talent development as an inclusive process of developing all organizational talent that works synergistically with talent acquisition and retention to enhance employee and organizational outcomes. They specifically explore current debates within talent development including its contribution to knowledge management, the types of development strategies that organizations can use, the significance of generational differences for talent development, the role of cross-cultural factors, and the use of high potential development programs.

In the following chapter, 'Accelerated Development of Organizational Talent and Executive Coaching: A Knowledge Management Perspective,' Konstantin Korotov explores the practice of executive coaching as an instrument of accelerated talent development in organizations. Executive coaching, following a more exclusive TM perspective, has become a popular stand-alone developmental intervention or an enhancer in other efforts to develop employees. This chapter considers coaching as an intervention guiding an individual executive's efforts in obtaining tacit knowledge, turning implicit organizational knowledge into explicit for the executive concerned, and developing insights into reasons for various events happening in the organization. The chapter provides an opportunity to look at a particular coaching intervention example by exploring coaching notes from an accelerated development intervention. It further elaborates on how coaching helps an executive develop knowledge about job expectations, stakeholder landscape, organizational culture, self and identity, and group functioning.

The fifth chapter of our book is titled 'Employee Learning and Development from the Perspective of Strategic HRM,' and its authors Saba Colakoglu, Yunhyung Chung, and Ying Hong develop conceptual arguments suggesting that HR systems targeted at enhancing employees' ability, motivation, and opportunities for learning and knowledge creation (that are part of TM systems) are critical for effective knowledge management. Based on the assumption that the knowledge base of an organization lies within the minds of its talent pool, the authors argue that effective talent and HR management processes facilitating employee learning and development can create social climates for knowledge management, which in turn impact individual-level learning, organizational-level knowledge depositories, and consequently critical firm outcomes such as innovation and performance. This chapter offers practical talent management recommendations such as the need to identify learning-related skills and attributes among talent and ensuring talent management processes target those qualities, as well as assessing the social climate regularly to ensure it is conducive for effective knowledge management.

In the subsequent chapter 'Talent Staffing Systems for Effective Knowledge Management,' Mark L. Lengnick-Hall and Andrea R. Neely discuss the role of knowledge management and its impact on talent management. The authors provide their conceptualization of talent, include a discussion of knowledge management and how it applies, discuss talent staffing systems and how they impact both processes. Then, Lengnick-Hall and Neely describe the role of talent staffing systems and how they relate specifically to knowledge management systems, followed by the conversation about artificial intelligence as an emerging trend in talent and knowledge management. Finally, they use the Mayo Clinic as an example of talent and knowledge management integration. Although there are significant challenges given the dynamic environment, the authors contend that knowledge management should be incorporated with talent management for the well-being of all stakeholders.

Chapter 7 is titled 'Leveraging Firms' Absorptive Capacity by Talent Development.' The authors, Marina Latukha and Maria Laura MacLennan, discuss the interplay between talent development and a firm's absorptive capacity in different country-specific settings by focusing on the largest emerging markets: Russia (pre-Ukraine invasion), Brazil, and China. They elaborate on how talent development may increase the overall level of absorptive capacity (AC), namely knowledge acquisition, assimilation, transformation and exploitation, and how the context may impact the intensity and scale of this effect. The authors show how emerging market contexts shape a diverse organizational environment, whereas talent development acts as a booster for AC. They suggest the necessary conditions for talent management, specifically for talent development, to leverage acquisition, assimilation, transformation and exploitation of knowledge.

The eighth chapter of our book 'Employee Knowledge Hiding: The Roles of Protean Career Orientation, HR System and Relational Climate' by Anne Roefs, Saša Batistič, and Rob F. Poell is dedicated to an overlooked but critical human dysfunction of knowledge hiding. The authors contend that despite various efforts to encourage knowledge sharing among talented employees in organizations, hiding knowledge from peers still occurs. Therefore, to ensure success of their talent management efforts, organizations need to understand why and when their workers hide knowledge. Roefs, Batistič, and Poell identify three categories of reasons why knowledge hiding happens: (1) organization-related reasons; (2) job-related reasons; and (3) inter- and intra-personal reasons. The consequences of knowledge hiding can be substantial, as besides financial implications, it also brings risks of damaging relationships and causing distrust among employees. The chapter addresses specifically how personal characteristics as well as organizational practices (e.g., talent system and relational climate) can affect the incidence of knowledge hiding.

In the ninth chapter called 'The Unrealized Value of Global Workers: The Need for Global Talent Management,' Anthony McDonnell, Stefan Jooss, and Kieran M. Conroy highlight the pivotal positions that many global workers play. Specifically, they unpack the role of global workers as key boundary spanners, navigating relational, knowledge, and cultural boundaries across the organization. The chapter also argues that the full value of global workers remains unrealized given the lack of planning and integration of these workers in terms of knowledge management processes, talent management strategies, and global mobility functions. Specifically, the authors point to the lack of strategic and practical oversights from corporate HR functions and how this may be impacting upon both global workers' experiences and organizational efforts to maximize value.

The final chapter of the book entitled 'Upward Global Knowledge Management: A Review and Preliminary Field Validation of the Host Country National Local Liaison Role Model' and authored by Charles M. Vance, Marian van Bakel, Torben Andersen, and Vlad Vaiman examines five key role components and talent management practices of a proposed host-country national liaison (HCNL) model affecting foreign subsidiary knowledge management namely, (1) cultural interpreter, (2) communication manager, (3) information resource broker, (4) talent manager, and (5) internal change agent. The authors then present their preliminary field research to begin to validate this model before making recommendations for further research in understanding and employing appropriate talent management practices involving HCNLs for improved KM and organizational performance.

We hope you will enjoy this new edition of *Smart Talent Management*!

REFERENCES

Antunes, H.J.G. & Pinheiro, P.G. (2020). Linking knowledge management, organizational learning and memory. *Journal of Innovation and Knowledge*, **5**(2): 140–149.

Baeza, M.A., Gonzalez, J.A. & Wang, Y. (2018). Job flexibility and job satisfaction among Mexican professionals: A socio-cultural explanation. *Employee Relations*, **40**(5): 921–942.

Barney, J. (1991). Firm resources and sustained competitive advantage. *Journal of Management*, **17**(1): 99–120.

Bhagat, R.S., Kedia, B.L., Harveston, P.D. & Triandis, H. (2002). Cultural variations in the cross-border transfer of organizational knowledge: An integrative framework. *Academy of Management Review*, **27**(2): 204–221.

Cappelli, P. & Keller, J.R. (2014). Talent management: Conceptual approaches and practical challenges. *Annual Review of Organizational Psychology and Organizational Behavior*, **1**(1): 305–331.

Cohen, W.M. & Levinthal, D.H. (1990). Absorptive capacity: A new perspective in learning and innovation. *Administrative Science Quarterly*, **35**(1): 128–152.

Collings, D.G. (2017). Workforce differentiation. In Collings, D.G., Mellahi, K., and Cascio, W.F. (eds), *The Oxford Handbook of Talent Management*. Oxford: Oxford University Press, pp. 299–317.

Collings, D.G. & Mellahi, K. (2009). Strategic talent management: A review and research agenda. *Human Resource Management Review*, **19**(4): 304–313.

Collings, D.G., Vaiman, V. & Scullion, H. (eds) (2022). *Talent Management: A Decade of Developments*. Bingley: Emerald Publishing.

Collins, C.J. (2021). Expanding the resource based view model of strategic human resource management. *The International Journal of Human Resource Management*, **32**(2): 331–358.

Daubner-Siva, D., Ybema, S., Vinkenburg, C.J. & Beech, N. (2018). The talent paradox: Talent management as a mixed blessing. *Journal of Organizational Ethnography*, **7**(1): 74–86.

Donate, M.J. & Guadamillas, F. (2011). Organizational factors to support knowledge management and innovation. *Journal of Knowledge Management*, **15**(6): 890–914.

Gallardo-Gallardo, E. & Thunnissen, M. (2016). Standing on the shoulders of giants? A critical review of empirical talent management research. *Employee Relations*, **38**(1): 31–56.

Goleman, D. (1995). *Emotional Intelligence: Why it Can Matter More Than IQ*. New York: Bantam Books.

Goleman, D. (1998). *Emotional Intelligence at Work*. New York: Bantam Books.

Grant, R. (1996). Towards a knowledge-based theory of the firm. *Strategic Management Journal*, **17**(Winter special issue): 109–122.

Grant, R. & Phene, A. (2022). The knowledge-based view and global strategy: Past impact and future potential. *Global Strategy Journal*, **12**(1): 3–30.

Groves, K.S. & Vance, C.M. (2015). Linear and nonlinear thinking: A multidimensional model and measure. *Journal of Creative Behavior*, **49**(2): 111–136.

Gupta, A.K. & Govindarajan, V. (2000). Knowledge flows within multinational corporations. *Strategic Management Journal*, **21**(4): 473–496.

Haesli, A. & Boxall, P. (2005). When knowledge management meets HR strategy: An exploration of personalization-retention and codification-recruitment configurations. *International Journal of Human Resource Management*, **16**(11): 1955–1975.

Hansen, M.T., Nohria, N. & Tierney, T. (1999). What's your strategy for managing knowledge? *Harvard Business Review*, March–April: 106–116.

Islam, T., Zahra, I., Rehman, S.U. & Jamil, S. (2022). How knowledge sharing encourages innovative work behavior through occupational self-efficacy: The moderating role of entrepreneurial leadership. *Global Knowledge, Memory and Communication*, forthcoming.

Jyoti, J. & Rani, A. (2017). High performance work system and organisational performance: Role of knowledge management. *Personnel Review*, **46**(8): 1770–1795.

Kahneman, D. (2013). *Thinking, Fast and Slow*. New York: Farrar, Straus & Giroux.

Khaligh, G. & Ranjbarian, R. (2022). The effect of organizational talent and knowledge management on job satisfaction. *Journal of Human Capital Empowerment*, **4**(4): 275–287.

Lewis, R.E. & Heckman, R.J. (2006). Talent management: A critical review. *Human Resource Management Review*, **16**(2): 139–154.

Malik, S. (2021). The nexus between emotional intelligence and types of knowledge sharing: Does work experience matter? *Journal of Workplace Learning*, **33**(8): 619–634.

McKinsey & Company (2021). Grabbing hold of the new future of work. Organizational Practice. https://www.mckinsey.com/capabilities/people-and-organizational-perfor mance/our-insights/grabbing-hold-of-the-new-future-of-work.

Michaels, E., Handfield-Jones, H. & Axelrod, B. (2001). *The War for Talent*. Boston, MA: Harvard Business School Press.

Milton, N. & Lambe, P. (2019). *The Knowledge Manager's Handbook: A Step-by-Step Guide to Embedding Effective Knowledge Management in Your Organization*. London: Kogan Page.

Morris, S., Snell, S. & Björkman, I. (2016). An architectural framework for global talent management. *Journal of International Business Studies*, **47**: 723–747.

Muhammed, S. & Zaim, H. (2020). Peer knowledge sharing and organizational performance: The role of leadership support and knowledge management success. *Journal of Knowledge Management*, **24**(10): 2455–2489.

Nisar, T.M., Prabhakarb, G. & Strakovaa, L. (2019). Social media information benefits, knowledge management and smart organizations. *Journal of Business Research*, **94**: 264–272.

Nonaka, I. & Takeuchi, H. (1995). *The Knowledge-Creating Company*. New York: Oxford University Press.

Paik, Y. & Choi, D. (2005). The shortcomings of a standardized global management system: The case study of Accenture. *Academy of Management Executive*, **19**(2): 81–84.

Paoloni, M., Coluccia, D., Fontana, S. & Solimene, S. (2020). Knowledge management, intellectual capital and entrepreneurship: A structured literature review. *Journal of Knowledge Management*, **24**(8): 1797–1818.

Pellegrini, M.M., Ciampi, F., Marzi, G. & Orlando, B. (2020). The relationship between knowledge management and leadership: Mapping the field and providing future research avenues. *Journal of Knowledge Management*, **24**(6): 1445–1492.

Prahalad, C.K. & Hamel, G. (1990). The core competence of the corporation. *Harvard Business Review*, May–June: 79–91.

Rashid, A.S., Tout, K. & Yakan, A. (2021). The critical human behavior factors and their impact on knowledge management system-cycles. *Business Process Management Journal*, **27**(6): 1677–1702.

Rehman, S., Mohamed, R. & Ayoup, H. (2019). The mediating role of organizational capabilities between organizational performance and its determinants. *Journal of Global Entrepreneurship Research*, **9**(1): 1–23.

Rezaei, F., Khalilzadeh, M. & Soleimani, P. (2021). Factors affecting knowledge management and its effect on organizational performance: Mediating the role of human capital. *Advances in Human-Computer Interaction*, 2021: 1–16.

Rialti, R., Marzi, G., Caputo, A. & Mayah, K.A. (2020). Achieving strategic flexibility in the era of big data: The importance of knowledge management and ambidexterity. *Management Decision*, **58**(8): 1585–1600.

Shujahat, M., Sousa, M.J., Hussain, S., Nawaz, F., Wang, M. & Umer, M. (2019). Translating the impact of knowledge management processes into knowledge-based innovation: The neglected and mediating role of knowledge-worker productivity. *Journal of Business Research*, **94**: 442–450.

Sumarsi, S. (2020). Role of servant leadership, talent management, knowledge management and employee performance. *International Journal of Social and Management Studies*, **1**(1): 123–133.

Swailes, S. (2013). The ethics of talent management. *Business Ethics: A European Review*, **22**(1): 32–46.

Swailes, S. (ed.) (2020). *Managing Talent: A Critical Appreciation*. Bingley: Emerald Publishing.

Thunnissen, M. & Gallardo-Gallardo, E. (2017). *Talent Management in Practice: An Integrated and Dynamic Approach*. Bingley: Emerald Publishing.

Vaiman, V. and Collings, D. (2015). Global talent management. In Collings, D., Wood, G. T., and Caligiuri, P. (eds), *Routledge Companion to International Human Resource Management*. London: Routledge, pp. 210–225.

Vaiman, V., Collings, D. & Cascio, W. (2021). The shifting boundaries of talent management. *Human Resource Management*, **60**(2): 253–257.

Vaiman, V., Collings, D. & Scullion, H. (2012). Talent management decision making. *Management Decision*, **50**(5): 925–941.

Vance, C.M., Boje, D.M., Mendenhall, M.E. & Kropp, H.R. (1991). A taxonomy of learning benefits from external knowledge-sharing meetings. *Human Resource Development Quarterly*, **2**(1): 25–35.

Wang, W. & Heyes, J. (2020). Flexibility, labour retention and productivity in the EU. *The International Journal of Human Resource Management*, **31**(3): 335–355.

Whelan, E. & Carcary, M. (2011). Integrating talent and knowledge management: Where are the benefits? *Journal of Knowledge Management*, **15**(4): 675–687.

Yang, B., Zheng, W. & Viere, C. (2009). Holistic views of knowledge management models. *Advances in Developing Human Resources*, **11**(3): 273–289.

Zaim, H., Muhammed, S. & Tarim, M. (2019). Relationship between knowledge management processes and performance: Critical role of knowledge utilization in organizations. *Knowledge Management Research & Practice*, **17**(1): 24–38.

2. Conceptualizing and operationalizing 'inclusive' talent management: four different approaches

Françoise Cadigan, Nicky Dries and Anand van Zelderen

INTRODUCTION: THE TREND TOWARD INCLUSIVE TALENT MANAGEMENT

The origins of the term talent, its etymology and usage in the gifted education and sports literatures, and its first mentions in the field of talent *management* (cf. the 'war for talent' book by McKinsey consultants Michaels, Handfield-Jones, & Axelrod, 2001) all clearly demonstrate that talent has historically been defined as a scarce resource. In this type of approach, only a small percentage (e.g., between 1 and 20%) of any population is considered as having the potential to exhibit true talent (e.g., Collings & Mellahi, 2009; Gagné, 2000; Gelens et al., 2013; Ulrich & Smallwood, 2012). In companies, talent is typically equated to being an 'A-player'—i.e., a high-performing, high-potential employee who contributes disproportionally to the bottom line of their organization (Pepermans, Vloeberghs, & Perkisas, 2003; Silzer & Church, 2010; Slan-Jerusalim & Hausdorf, 2007).

Collings and Mellahi (2009) and Iles and colleagues (Iles, Chuai, & Preece, 2010; Iles, Preece, & Chuai, 2010) added that talent management should focus on getting these talented people into critical roles, defined as those that disproportionately contribute to an organization's strategic objectives. For instance, sales roles are critical at high-end retail organizations such as Nordstrom, whereas logistics roles are critical at large supply chain organizations such as Costco (Huselid, Beatty, & Becker, 2005). Getting high-performing, high-potential employees into these roles will thus provide the best return on investment (ROI) towards meeting strategic objectives—justifying higher investments in this specific subset of employees. In contrast, an accountant at either of these organizations may play an important role, but is not critical to achieving their strategic goals, and thus should not be included in their so-called 'talent pool.' Exclusive approaches to talent management, such as these, are argued to optimize costs by investing specifically in confirmed talent working in the most strategic roles (Lepak & Snell, 1999, 2002; Smart & Smart, 1997). It is estimated that between 40 and 60% of global companies have such 'high potential' programs in place for the management of their most talented employees (Pepermans et al., 2003; Silzer & Church, 2009a, 2009b; Slan-Jerusalim & Hausdorf, 2007).

Critics of so-called 'exclusive' talent management say it is elitist and exclusionary, as it creates and reproduces unequal treatment of employees (Bonneton, Festing, & Muratbekova-Touron, 2020; Swailes, 2013), which may harm their morale, engagement, collaboration, trust in leadership, and productivity (Pfeffer & Sutton, 2006; Sparrow, Scullion, & Tarique, 2014; Swailes & Blackburn, 2016). These scholars argue that the negative effects on those left out of high potential or talent programs, including withdrawal and disengagement (O'Connor & Crowley-Henry, 2019), outweigh these programs' possible benefits (e.g., Marescaux, De Winne, & Sels, 2013). Furthermore, according to the literature on knowledge management all employees, regardless of position, have the potential to hold valuable explicit and tacit knowledge that is critical to an organization's functioning and success (Vaiman & Vance, 2008), especially as this knowledge develops over time (Prahalad & Hamel, 1990).

As a result, less exclusive forms of talent management—focusing on the strengths and capabilities of all employees—are gaining traction both in the academic literature and in organizational practice (Swailes, Downs, & Orr, 2014) with empirical studies reporting that at least 50% of HR managers adhere to an inclusive talent philosophy (Leigh, 2009; Meyers et al., 2020; Peters, 2006). Although the arguments in favor of inclusive TM are certainly valid from a phenomenological point of view—i.e., many practitioners do not like the exclusive approach, and many organizations do not want to 'do' talent management in this way—the problem remains that it is a contradiction in terms when we consider the conceptual and theoretical origins of the term 'talent' both in the TM literature and beyond (Gallardo-Gallardo, Dries, & González-Cruz, 2013).

In this chapter we examine whether the existing tensions between exclusive and inclusive TM can be resolved, or at least clarified. Specifically, we set out to more explicitly conceptualize and operationalize what inclusive TM could look like in practice such that it becomes more concrete and actionable for organizations that wish to adopt this philosophy. In addition, we also aim to provide more construct clarity for researchers interested in the topic of inclusive TM, building extensively on the foundational work of Swailes (2013; Swailes et al., 2014). To date, inclusive TM has mostly been branded as 'anti-exclusive,' while it is much less clear what inclusive TM *itself* would look like. We perceive this as a risk, especially for the vulnerable employee groups inclusive TM scholars are specifically focused on protecting (Malik & Singh, 2014; O'Connor & Crowley-Henry, 2019); the risk being that organizations are quick to state that 'everyone has talent,' without having specific inclusive practices in place to back up this claim. We argue that a targeted approach is needed to ensure that the lofty goals of inclusive TM are met, and to make sure that this term is not appropriated or abused purely as a form of window-dressing or employer branding (Dries, 2013). So, if inclusive talent management is here to stay, we need better operationalizations of what is meant by 'inclusive,' and clearer pathways from concepts to practices. Throughout this chapter we argue that representing inclusive as *all employees*, and exclusive as a *small group of employees* may be somewhat of a false dichotomy. We propose four different approaches, summarized in Table 2.1, to inclusive talent management that can each rightfully claim to fit this construct.

The four approaches are: (1) focusing on potential and strengths rather than talent and gifts, (2) increasing the size of the talent pool, (3) defining a broader range of talent domains (i.e., the *talent for what?* question), and (4) topgrading the entire organization. In the following section, we explore each approach in detail. We end the chapter with a discussion on how these different theoretical/ conceptual approaches might translate into a logical set of TM practices.

FOUR APPROACHES TO INCLUSIVE TALENT MANAGEMENT

First Approach: Focusing on Potential and Strengths rather than Talent and Gifts

The first approach involves how talent is defined and operationalized and focuses on constructs other than talent. For instance, Nijs et al. (2014) operationalized 'talent' as a multidimensional concept comprising both an ability and an affective component such that to achieve excellence—the ultimate criterion for talent—an employee can either perform better than others (i.e., interpersonal excellence) or perform consistently at their personal best (i.e., intrapersonal excellence), in activities they like, find important, and in which they want to invest energy. Focusing on intrapersonal excellence and on the affective component of talent (i.e., liking what one does), these authors argued, will translate into a more inclusive TM approach than focusing on interpersonal excellence and on the ability component (i.e., being the best). Other authors, however, have stated that it is undesirable from a scientific point of view to define the same construct in different ways (Dries, 2013). An alternative approach is to use different terminology for interpersonal and intrapersonal constructs—i.e., talent and gifts for the former, and potential and strengths for the latter (Dries, 2022; Gallardo-Gallardo et al., 2013). This is

Table 2.1   *Four different approaches to inclusive talent management: overview and characteristics*

Approach characteristics	First approach: Focusing on potential and strengths rather than talent and gifts	Second approach: Increasing the size of the talent pool	Third approach: Defining a broader range of talent domains	Fourth approach: Topgrading the entire organization
Key concepts	*Potential:* Latent capabilities—representing the gap between a person's current level of functioning within a given performance domain and what he or she is maximally capable of—that can develop into strengths or talents but are not yet utilized or seen. *Strengths:* Patterns in attitudes, behaviors, and feelings developed through experience, that are manifested in episodes of personal excellence, capturing someone at their best.	*Threshold approach:* Comparing an employee's performance to a standard that is considered 'good enough,' rather than requiring him or her to outperform coworkers (i.e., forced ranking). The threshold for inclusion in a talent pool thus becomes absolute rather than relative.	*Conjunctive approach:* Talent is defined and measured as being excellent at X and Y and Z. A talented employee is expected to be better than most others in all different aspects of their job. *Disjunctive approach:* Talent is defined and measured as being excellent at X or Y or Z. A talented employee is expected to be better than most others in at least one specific aspect of their job.	*Topgrading:* An elite, 'ivy league' approach to TM where only the best people in the labor market are hired into the organization.
Who (or what) is a talent?	Etymologically (and statistically) speaking, not everyone can have 'talent,' but everyone *does* have the potential to develop strengths in domains they like, find important, and in which they want to invest energy.	Everyone who meets a preset standard of performance, regardless of the performance of comparable others. If everyone meets the threshold, everyone is a talent.	A talent is someone who is excellent (i.e., better than most others) in a given talent domain—for instance analytical, communicative, or leadership.	A talent is an A-player who is top in his or her field, as compared to similar profiles in the labor market—not just in his or her current organization.

Approach characteristics	First approach: Focusing on potential and strengths rather than talent and gifts	Second approach: Increasing the size of the talent pool	Third approach: Defining a broader range of talent domains	Fourth approach: Topgrading the entire organization
Definition of inclusion	While the definition of 'talent' requires performing better than others (cf. interpersonal excellence), the constructs potential and strength allow for all employees to be included, as they represent performance at a personal-best level (cf. intrapersonal excellence).	Inclusion does not necessarily mean that *everyone* is in a talent pool, but rather that everyone has the opportunity to qualify. Being excluded due to not making a preset 'cutoff percentage' does not happen in this approach. There should be clear criteria for how to improve one's performance in order to meet the threshold.	The more different talent domains are acknowledged as important by the organization, the higher the odds that any given employee will be excellent in at least one of them, thus allowing more employees to be included in a talent pool.	If everyone in the organization is top in their field, by definition everyone in the organization is a talent—this approach is thus highly elitist and inclusive at the same time since all employees are considered talents. The exclusivity occurs prior to entry, but much less so after.

Approach characteristics	First approach: Focusing on potential and strengths rather than talent and gifts	Second approach: Increasing the size of the talent pool	Third approach: Defining a broader range of talent domains	Fourth approach: Topgrading the entire organization
Advantages/Strengths	This is the only approach that allows for all employees to be included, as it does not require forced ranking or interpersonal comparison; each employee is regarded in their own right. Employees tend to like this approach as it values their unique contributions and customizes career paths around them—when done right.	This approach is least likely to trigger feelings of unfairness or psychological contract breach. It does not compare employees to each other and provides clear standards that need to be achieved in order to be included. It encourages employees to improve themselves and reinforces self-efficacy and self-esteem. The risk of misidentifying people as talents is lower than in a more exclusive, forced-ranking approach which tends to be more subjective and political.	This approach has the potential to form the ideal 'hybrid' approach, mixing exclusive and inclusive TM elements together. It allows people to be recognized and differentiated for excellent performance, while still including a much larger proportion of employees since more *types* of talent are recognized.	Some of the most successful and ambitious organizations in the world are known to use topgrading, which attracts the most hard-working and high-performing people in their industry. It has a strong reputation effect. Everyone working in this type of organization knows that their colleagues are also highly competent, and the relatively higher salary cost is expected to be offset by the return on investment (ROI) thereof.

Approach characteristics	First approach: Focusing on potential and strengths rather than talent and gifts	Second approach: Increasing the size of the talent pool	Third approach: Defining a broader range of talent domains	Fourth approach: Topgrading the entire organization
Disadvantages/Pitfalls	This approach does not allow for strategic workforce differentiation, where the most high-performing, high-potential people are put in the most pivotal positions and are disproportionally invested in following a return on investment (ROI) logic. This may mean that it is less cost-efficient and less optimal in terms of organizational performance and competitiveness. The lack of emphasis on interpersonal excellence may frustrate high performers.	Research shows that high performers tend to prefer forced-ranking approaches. High and average performers are not differentiated between in this approach, meaning that the best performers in the organization may feel under-rewarded.	When an overly narrow set of talent domains is seen as important by the organization, or when they are not sufficiently different from each other, the same type of people will be chosen again and again as talents. It is important to identify and reward talent in uncorrelated talent domains, and then apply a disjunctive approach to talent identification. Another pitfall is that there often still are (unspoken) hierarchies between talent domains, that show up in promotions and pay.	May create an elitist and arrogant organization, characterized by selection biases and 'management cloning.' It puts a lot of pressure on the selection process, knowing that it is quite difficult to assess the potential performance of (especially junior) new hires without ever having seen them in action in the context of the organization. It is not cost-efficient; in that it is not necessary to have the best people in the labor market for every single position (cf. differentiated HR architecture).

Approach characteristics	First approach: Focusing on potential and strengths rather than talent and gifts	Second approach: Increasing the size of the talent pool	Third approach: Defining a broader range of talent domains	Fourth approach: Topgrading the entire organization
Implications for TM practice	Measure performance often and look for indicators of untapped potential in performance fluctuations: when was it 'better'? in what team, on what project, under what supervisor? And can we replicate those 'personal best' contextual conditions? Train people on their strengths, rather than their weaknesses. Put them in roles that capitalize on their strengths and assemble teams of people with complementary strengths and weaknesses. Emphasize and reward team performance over individual performance.	Lowering the threshold employees need to meet to enter a talent program, thus giving the opportunity to more people. This can be done by increasing the (arbitrary) percentage of people who can be included in a talent pool, accepting everyone who meets an absolute threshold, or even affirmative action. Consider different qualitative criteria for inclusion altogether, such as motivation over performance, and knowledge over education. Rather than classifying employees as poor performers (cf. 'rank and yank'), actually help them improve and meet the threshold set by the organization.	Identify the different talent domains that are important to the organization and assess each employee on each talent domain using performance appraisals and forced ranking. Assess to what extent employees' scores are correlated between talent domains; if they are highly correlated, add talent domains that are more distinct. Use the data to evaluate in which talent domains the organization has many talented incumbents, and which are potentially lacking. In the long term, monitor whether certain talent domains are more appreciated by the organization in terms of promotion, pay, and quit rates.	Talents are identified (using the interpersonal excellence criterion) *prior* to organizational entry, which is less sensitive than differentiating between employees already working together. To attract these people, typically pay should be higher than the market rate, and/or the organization needs to have a good reputation. New staff are typically put on fixed contracts first, such that hires who fail to live up to expectations can be identified quickly and either improved through training or oriented to a position outside of the organization.

an interesting approach as it orients researchers and practitioners to different literatures and practices than the 'traditional' TM approach.

Potential

Potential is defined as latent capabilities that can develop into strengths or talents but are not yet utilized or seen. In other words, potential is the gap between a person's current level of functioning in a given performance domain, and what he or she is maximally capable of (De Boeck, Dries, & Tierens, 2019). Potential denotes possibilities, promise, and latent action (Altman, 1997). Scheffler (1985) describes potential as a *capacity* via critical periods and plasticity, *propensity* via development, and *capability* via choice to reach a specified goal. By definition, potential cannot be detected from current performance in an area that a person already knows well (Roussillon, 2002). Attributes that signal potential include curiosity, accepting responsibility for learning and change, adventuresomeness, effective learning from experience, getting results under tough conditions, and seeking and using feedback (Altman, 1997; McCall, 1994; Spreitzer, McCall, & Mahoney, 1997). The emphasis is on how individuals learn and act when they are at their best and discovering which conditions help them naturally to access this mastery (Lombardo & Eichinger, 2000). Potential connects to the knowledge-based view of the firm (Grant, 1996) in that as employees gain tenure with their organization, they also gain valuable explicit and tacit knowledge (i.e., absorptive capacity; Cohen & Levinthal, 1990) that help an organization compete in its market environment (Haesli & Boxall, 2005).

Potential assessments tend to be important both in exclusive and inclusive TM practice (Meyers & van Woerkom, 2014). However, in exclusive TM, typically a set percentage of employees is identified as having high potential (mostly 1–20%) annually, based on interpersonal comparison and forced ranking of employees—mirroring the principle of interpersonal excellence (Church et al., 2015). In inclusive TM, there is no forced ranking, and each employee is developed to achieve their 'best self' in the position(s) most suited to their potential and interests while also building valuable knowledge for the firm and their job. In addition, it is useful to reflect on how organizations might go about uncovering employees' *untapped* potential. One suggestion is to move away from a focus on assessing people's average performance, and instead look for fluctuations in performance over time (Dries, 2022). If a person has a mediocre (or even bad) performance, and if managers believe these employees may in fact have potential (cf. the 'nine-box' method of crossing performance and potential ratings; Philpot & Monahan, 2017), the following indicators may be of interest to managers: When was the performance 'better'? On which project, on which team, with what type of job tasks, at which point in time or career stage, and under which supervisor did this person perform better than they currently do? What is the degree of variability in performance between the formal appraisal periods (especially if these take place only once a year)? What is the best performance this employee has demonstrated across that entire period, and what were the circumstances of this 'personal-best' performance episode? Do other sources of variance play a role in the performance ratings—is everyone on that team poorly rated? Is the supervisor lenient or strict in his or her ratings? How are the team relationships? Is the person chronically under-stretched or bored? Does he or she have passions outside of the workplace that could be utilized, in one way or another, to enhance their engagement?

Thus, inclusive TM provides work opportunities that allow employees to demonstrate potential, growth, and learning new skills (Silzer & Church, 2009a). Helping employees reach their potential may further help them find meaning in work (Mitroff & Denton, 1999) such that people move beyond the present and anticipate possible scenarios in the future, reflecting their hopes and aspirations for the future in relation to work (Strauss, Griffin, & Parker, 2012). Connecting present work activities to one's future work self creates a sense of purpose and motivates employees to approach the desired end-states that their future work selves entail (Strauss et al., 2012). A recent longitudinal study found that as employees perceive themselves to be fulfilling more of their potential, their perceived work meaningfulness increases (De Boeck et al., 2019).

Strengths

Strengths represent an inclusive TM construct—like potential—the difference being that potential is latent, while strengths are presently visible in an employee's behavior. More specifically, strengths are defined as patterns in attitudes, behaviors, and feelings (Linley & Harrington, 2006) developed through experience, that are manifested in episodes of personal excellence, capturing someone at their best (e.g., Roberts et al., 2005; Wood et al., 2011). The strengths-based approach to TM aligns with the inclusive/developable talent philosophy described by Meyers and Van Woerkom (2014), which holds that anyone can develop potential into strengths through training and development, knowledge gain and learning (Briscoe, 2008).

Renzulli (2005) argues that everyone can contribute to societal improvement and that it is the duty of organizations to offer opportunities, resources, and the encouragement required to achieve each employee's full potential through maximization of their involvement and motivation. This approach relates to the positive psychology and vocational psychology literatures. For instance, positive psychologists Buckingham and Clifton (2001) assert that everyone possesses a certain set of strengths (e.g., adaptability, discipline) and that it is the specific cocktail of strengths that contributes to everyone's uniqueness. This approach is believed to generate psychological and physical health, which increase productivity.

Some scholars argue that the strengths-based approach restores social and ethical considerations in that exclusion from talent programs may signal that non-talented employees are inferior (Downs & Swailes, 2013). In this way, the strengths approach supports Swailes et al.'s (2014) ideas for fully inclusive talent management (FITM) described as a focus on capabilities and the creation of the conditions in which abilities may flourish (Nussbaum, 2012), which contribute to feelings of competence, self-worth, respect, appreciation, well-being (Ghielen, van Woerkom, & Meyers, 2018), and job related performance (Buckingham & Clifton, 2001; van Woerkom & Meyers, 2015). In FITM, those employees who need help receive it rather than those who are already advantaged or considered talented. In this way, no employee is excluded, rather each employee is helped in ways that benefit them and, in turn, their organizations via positive feelings explained by positive psychology (Seligman, 2002), and knowledge enhancement (Vaiman & Vance, 2008).

Overall, the strengths-based approach prioritizes employee welfare over profits, and provides opportunity via participation (Downs & Swailes, 2013). Van Woerkom, Meyers, and Bakker (2022) further propose that individual strength use, and collective strength use by teams are reciprocally related such that a strengths-based climate is positively related to collective strengths use, and a strengths-based climate strengthens the positive relationship between individual and collective strengths use. One idea is to shift the focus of TM away from individual performance and instead focus on composing complementary teams, in which members have strengths and weaknesses that cancel each other out, allowing for an optimal division of tasks (Dries, 2022). Vance et al. (1991) find that the learning benefits of knowledge-sharing groups include increased confidence in problem-solving, reduced isolation, and better ability to identify future problems.

Overall, this first approach rests on the assumption that people can thrive and succeed in the right context. This approach involves organizations making genuine efforts to elicit the potential and strengths of each employee, shifting the emphasis toward learning. The organizational challenge then becomes one of fitting all employees into jobs that they enjoy and which enable each individual's potential and strengths (Swailes et al., 2014) that also benefit the organization. This approach also constructively helps underperforming employees, or those whose strengths and potential do not benefit the organization, to exit the organization.

Second Approach: Increasing the Size of the Talent Pool

The second approach involves including a higher percentage of employees into the talent pool, which is a commonly suggested practice for inclusive TM (e.g., Sparrow et al., 2014). Similar to the first approach, this approach moves away from a competitive, winner versus loser mentality inherent in the global 'war for talent' paradigm and moves toward a more cooperative approach. In general, a key difference of this approach is between relative versus absolute performance evaluations. Relative performance evaluations are typically used for talent identification in exclusive TM, as a form of forced ranking using social comparison. In contrast, a 'threshold' approach looks at each individual's absolute performance compared to a standard of 'good enough,' but not compared to coworkers. A study by Blume, Rubin, and Baldwin (2013) compares employee preferences for performance management systems that either use a forced distribution system (FDS) where employees are compared against each other versus a non-comparative standards system where employees must meet a certain threshold. These scholars find that respondents with the highest cognitive ability or the ones who are the most 'talented,' by proxy, report the forced distribution system as fairer whereas everyone else prefers the standards-based or threshold approach.

A forced distribution system may employ a sorting effect, giving applicants the impression that the organization is serious about rewarding high performers and is intolerant to poor performance. The respondents in the study with the highest cognitive ability may expect to perform well and may view FDS as an indicator that the company values high achievement and will be more likely to offer opportunities for promotion. Further, such individuals may be more willing to work in a competitive environment where they believe they will rank highly when compared with others and be rewarded accordingly (Trank, Rynes, & Bretz, 2002). These findings support a key reason why organizations implement FDS, namely, to attract and retain high performers.

In the standards-based or threshold approach, anyone who passes a certain threshold of performance—even if it is 50% or more of all employees and regardless of comparison to colleagues—can enter the talent program. Providing clear criteria for inclusion signals to employees how they need to improve themselves to be included in the future. We identify three sub-approaches that will increase the size of the talent pool: (1) attributing another threshold to talent, (2) focusing on attributes other than output so that more employees make the cut, and (3) helping more employees make the cut.

Lowering the talent threshold
First of all, any threshold in a forced ranking approach is arbitrary—there is no ultimate criterion to decide whether it is better to identify 1% of employees

as talents, versus 10% or 50% (Church et al., 2015). Ho (2005) provides the example of accounting and law firms limiting the number of associates who can make partner to create a feeling of scarcity (Hirsch, 1977) as a form of artificial resource restriction. Similarly, the literature on intellectual giftedness (in schoolchildren and students) describes the arbitrary and subjective nature of thresholds for considering someone 'talented' (Gagné, Bélanger, & Motard, 1993). This implies that organizations are free to set the threshold for inclusion into their talent management programs at any level they choose (Dries, 2013). Several companies have reported drastic changes to their talent management programs in this regard, for instance by increasing the percentage of employees in their talent pool from 1 to 30% (cf. case study by Hjordrup, Minbaeva, & Jensen, 2015).

The threshold approach may strengthen the psychological contract so that more employees feel impelled to work harder and remain employed with their organizations, and improve their organization-based self-esteem (OBSE), which is defined as the value individuals perceive themselves to have in their role as organizational members and is the extent to which a person perceives him- or herself as a competent individual, or a 'person of worth' (Pierce et al., 1989). Employees with high OBSE perceive themselves as important, meaningful, capable, and worthwhile within the specific context of their employing organization. Three typical sources of OBSE include implicit signals sent by the organization (e.g., through its practices); messages from significant others (e.g., supervisors) that are received and internalized; and feelings of efficacy and competence derived from work and organizational experiences (e.g., experiences of success; Pierce & Gardner, 2004). All three of these are at play in talent programs, as they send both direct and indirect messages about the relative value of employees and how those included or considered talent are valued more than those excluded or considered non-talent (Malik & Singh, 2014; Michaels et al., 2001). The threshold approach may also enhance knowledge gain as employees can focus on being the best at their jobs rather than comparing themselves to others who may be perceived as better or superior.

Focusing on attributes other than output
A second sub-approach involves focusing on attributes other than output, which also lowers the threshold. When it comes to TM, most organizations focus solely on output—typically operationalized as past performance—in assessments of talent (Silzer & Church, 2009a). However, some argue that natural talent may be overrated, especially for sustaining organizational performance (Pfeffer & Sutton, 2006). It has been hypothesized that only 30% of a talent's performance stems from individual capabilities and 70% from resources and qualities specific to the organization including reputation, technology, leadership, training, and teamwork (Groysberg, Nanda, & Nohria,

2004). Performance also depends on teams that have experience working together (Taylor & Greve, 2006), and context matters such that people do well in certain environments but not in others (e.g., Thomas & Lazarova, 2006). Furthermore, individuals and teams gain knowledge the longer they work at the organization where their knowledge can be managed in a way that helps the organization (Vance et al., 1991).

If employees make the cut into talent programs by being valued for criteria other than output, this may again boost employees' sense of OBSE and reduce unfavorable outcomes associated with upward social comparison, including envy, a reduction in self-esteem, and hostility toward others who are better off (Fiske, 2011; Sterling, van de Ven, & Smith, 2006; Taylor & Lobel, 1989). This sub-approach may further reduce the risk of selecting the wrong people in an exclusive strategy which can backfire (Walker & LaRocco, 2002).

As opposed to the first sub-approach of increasing the percentage—which redefines the criterion for talent pool entry in quantitative terms (e.g., top 30% is 'good enough')—focusing on attributes other than output implies considering different qualitative criteria altogether for determining who is 'talented' (for instance, motivation rather than only performance, knowledge rather than only education). As such, everyone who meets a basic threshold of performance, and is also motivated, passionate, and willing, can be considered a talent.

Within this sub-approach, we also find the (often controversial) practice of affirmative action. Noon's (2010) article on this topic asks the question whether having equal standards or thresholds for all groups is fair. Noon questions whether the groups that have been historically marginalized or institutionally discriminated against require more help to reach the same threshold, or, alternatively, the standard might be lowered specifically for them. These ideas are mirrored in heated debates for instance around quotas in companies and minority-group admission criteria at elite universities. Similar to the first sub-approach, this mechanism provides employees opportunity via participation, but rejects setting a predetermined threshold that is likely subjective and perhaps enshrines a biased vision of talent (Swailes et al., 2014). This approach may reflect fairness in that everyone gets a more equitable opportunity, not only those who display desired traits and fit the mold of 'talent,' or who have benefited from advantages and opportunities throughout their lives (Gagné, 1993).

Helping employees reach the threshold
In the third and final sub-approach, employees who do not meet the threshold can be provided with coaching for improvement so that they can make the cut. This sub-approach reflects the basic notion of remediation of poor performance through training—which may appear obvious, but we know from

research that once a person is branded as a poor performer it is hard to turn that perception around (Dries, 2013). This differs from exclusive TM strategies, which exclude and separate people into in-groups and out-groups, and into categories of high and low value. Rather, this sub-approach promotes effort where feelings of efficacy and competence can be instilled through work and organizational experiences (Pierce & Gardner, 2004) and eventual knowledge attainment (Vance et al., 1991). Similar to the first approach, when an employee's talents are deemed to fall below reasonable thresholds that the organization has democratically established, the organization should help the employee to either improve, or encourage them to deploy their talents elsewhere. Fully inclusive TM only exists if this step is at least attempted when a person is branded as a poor or mediocre performer. 'Inclusive' means that employees are not given up on or left out (Swailes, 2013).

Third Approach: Defining a Broader Range of Talent Domains

A third approach to inclusive TM involves asking the *'talent for what?'* question (Nijs et al., 2022). In this approach, criteria are considered such that the idea of forced ranking is maintained—i.e., the practice of comparison employees against each other to see who is more 'talented'—but the number of relevant talent domains (exactly what one is talented *at*) is expanded. For instance, in the context of academia, a talented faculty member could be defined as someone who is in the top 10% of scientific research, *and* teaching, *and* service, *and* science outreach, which represents a conjunctive view of talent. Alternatively, a talented faculty member could be defined as someone who is in the top 10% of scientific research, *or* teaching, *or* service, *or* science outreach. This view proposes that excellence in one talent domain compensates for being moderate in other domains (and that expecting people to be excellent at everything is unrealistic), which represents a disjunctive view of talent. According to Bélanger and Gagné (2006):

Conjunctive: Talent = X and Y and Z

Disjunctive: Talent = X or Y or Z

Taking the disjunctive approach means that more employees are included in the talent pool and implies a more collective/team-based approach to talent management where not every individual employee needs to excel at everything. This list can be expanded depending on the needs and strategies of an organization—the more different types of talent domains are recognized, the more inclusive TM becomes. Different categorizations of talent domains are found in the literature, especially that on giftedness and gifted education. Sternberg (1985), for instance, distinguished between three forms of giftedness associated with the three major components of his tri-archic theory of intelligence (meta components, performance components, and knowledge-acquisition components). Tannenbaum (2000) defined four categories of talent (scarcity, surplus, quota, anomalous). Gardner (1990) distinguished seven types of intelligence, and Gagné (1983, 1985) described four different domains of giftedness (intellectual, creative, socioaffective, sensorimotor), each further subdivided into multiple subdomains.

In general, if there is a disjunctive view that talent that can take many forms (e.g., intellectual, social, artistic, athletic), the number of people who are seen as talented 'at something' will increase proportionally to the increase in the number of talent domains recognized. In addition, the higher (less selective) the cut-off value chosen (e.g., top 20 vs. top 1%), the larger the number of individuals labeled talented. Furthermore, if two talent domains are not highly correlated, those who excel in one talent domain will not necessarily simultaneously excel in another talent domain, which will further increase the total number of individuals excelling in either domain. For instance, when good researchers are also good teachers, this means that the talent domains of research and teaching are highly correlated, narrowing the potential pool of talents again. In other words, highly correlated measures tend to create a high overlap between selected subgroups, whereas uncorrelated measures create different subgroups of talented individuals. It is thus important to define and acknowledge different talent domains that are sufficiently different from each other, if one wishes to become more inclusive (Bélanger & Gagné, 2006).

In general, disjunctive versus conjunctive have opposite impacts on prev-alence estimates. For instance, Bélanger and Gagné (2006) provide the example of assuming an identical threshold of top 10% for each talent domain. Conjunctive definitions lead to low inclusion percentages as the number of talent domains increases in that most of those who survive the first cutoff score (A) will not survive the second (B), and most of the A and B survivors will fail to exceed the third threshold (C). As the number of criteria included in the definition and identification process increases, the resulting number of individuals labeled talented will soon become overwhelmingly small. In the case of disjunctive definitions, the impact is reversed; if talent can manifest itself as A or B or C, then the resulting population of persons labeled gifted or talented will increase with each new criterion added. One begins with the top 10% on criterion A, then adds all those not already chosen who excel on B, and so forth with each additional criterion. Taylor (1973) applied this reasoning in the context of his theory of multiple talents; assuming his eight talents to be uncorrelated, he estimated that 99% of the members of a population would be identified as above average (top 50%) on at least one of these eight abilities. With a much stricter 10% selection ratio, the corresponding prevalence would still be 57%. In other words, more than half of the population would be among the top 10% in at least one of his talent domains. To understand the impact of correlated criteria on prevalence values, Bélanger and Gagné calculate that when the disjunctive approach is used and includes 10 talent traits, each correlated at 0.1, with a selection ratio of 15%, then the inclusivity rate is as high as 74%.

A study by Nijs and colleagues (2022) applied the idea of talent domains—which comes from the literature on gifted education—more specifically to TM research. The authors distinguished between 14 talent domains, based on the work of Gagné (2004): linguist, scientist, analyst, technician, creative brain, critical thinker, mediator, speaker, spokesperson, planner, entertainer, leader, business(wo)man, and networker. They reported that across 44 multi-disciplinary teams, the social status of 'most talented team member' was most often granted to peers perceived as having both leadership and analytic talent with a degree in science, technology, engineering, and math (STEM) serving a dominant signaling function. Thus, they found that being seen as a talent was determined both by the type and level of talent team members were perceived to possess, pointing at a risk with this approach—that there can still be hierarchies between the different talent domains, where having a certain type of talent is still disproportionally appreciated and rewarded by one's organization (and perhaps society, as is the case for STEM; Nijs et al., 2022).

Fourth Approach: Topgrading the Entire Organization

The fourth and final approach is topgrading, which is an inclusive approach that is paradoxically *more* elitist than an exclusive approach. In essence, topgrading is an elite, ivy league approach that uses fixed contracts to eliminate the bottom performers. In this approach, an organization strictly hires only the top 10% in the labor market such that everyone in the organization is identified as a talent. Those who do not live up to the excellence threshold are replaced by those who do (Smart, 2012; Smart & Smart, 1997). What allows us to label this approach as inclusive despite its elitism is that the decision to label someone as a talent (and the interpersonal comparison that goes with it to determine who are the 'best' in the labor market) is made in the selection stage before the employee is officially hired. According to Smart (2012), topgrading is an ongoing process where development and training are provided to improve existing human capital and where lower performers are deployed into roles in which they can excel (and if that does not work, oriented out of the organization). Examples of companies priding themselves in topgrading—and claiming that everyone in their organization is a 'talent'—are McKinsey, Harvard, and Tesla.

Topgrading focuses on building a talent advantage by only hiring and promoting the most talented people available, implementing more thorough recruitment and screening techniques, and quickly removing under performers. Smart and Smart (1997) argue that the salary of an A-player is the same as that for a C-player, but the returns on investment of the former are better, so they ultimately cost less. Furthermore, it is difficult to turnover C-players, so it may be worthwhile to allow them the opportunity to become A-players, but if they fail, then they should be redeployed or counseled out of the organization. The philosophy is that everyone can be an A-player in the right role and pay, which is similar to the strengths-based approach and the sub-approach of helping more employees reach the threshold, but topgrading is more cut-throat by using fixed contracts and swiftly removing under-performers. In general, Smart and Smart (1997) argue that talent is an asset that can be controlled unlike the economy, industry, customer preferences, etc., and thus should be manipulated and controlled to the highest degree.

According to Smart and colleagues (Smart, 2012; Smart & Smart, 1997), A-players are believed to do everything better and should comprise at least 75% of employees, with almost no C-players. An example is the 1992 and 1996 Olympic men's American teams as an elite sports team where topgrading may work best, and includes other professional sports leagues such as the National Basketball Association or the National Hockey League where only athletes who display the highest levels of performance are recruited such that the whole team is truly talented (Downs & Swailes, 2013; Swaab et al., 2014). This is echoed by Swailes et al. (2014) who explain that topgrading only works in small, niche organizations or where required skills are in short supply, such as in start-up businesses. In large organizations, there will inevitably be employees with long tenure who slip to average or below average. Thus, inclusive talent management that uses topgrading would be difficult to achieve in anything but small organizations.

It is important that all managers embrace the approach and think of themselves as in the recruitment business for life (Smart, 2012; Smart & Smart, 1997). A thorough job analysis and chronological interview techniques, while considering the organizational strategy, culture, and fit help to avoid bad assessments. Multitudes of competencies are included and tailored to each job starting with the CEO. The screening process must include an extensive interview that omits easy-to-fake questions. Rather, the focus is about actual experience and includes reference checks from past supervisors. The selection process involves the hiring manager rather than only HR managers. A performance management system rewards top performers and deploys poor performers. Even after a hire, all levels of employees are interviewed for performance management including co-worker and 360° assessments with development plans implemented for each employee. With these practices, the hiring success rate should be close to 90% (Smart, 2012).

There are critics of topgrading, however, including Lewis and Heckman (2006) and Gladwell (2002), who say that that topgrading is a rebranding of strategic human resource management (SHRM) or even general HR and argue that competent performance, rather than A-level performance, may be acceptable for less strategic positions (cf. the differentiated HR architecture model; Lepak & Snell, 1999). They also contend that there are errors in raters' goals and performance appraisals and criticize past reports about topgrading that are cross-sectional, occurring during economic booms, and include no data analysis. Eichenwald (2005) points to Enron that failed miserably after taking a topgrading approach. Gladwell (2002) further criticizes topgrading for focusing on individuals rather than organizational attributes, such as team structure and physical capital.

A CONTEXTUAL NOTE: THE GREAT RESIGNATION

Referred to as the great resignation, during the COVID-19 pandemic people began to leave the workforce due to poor treatment, and/or poor pay relative to the growing distribution of world wealth, making it harder for organizations to find and retain employees especially in entry-level positions in the service industries (Hirsch, 2021).

Due to this phenomenon, employees worked longer hours on smaller staffs, in positions that require interaction with the public with little to no safety measures and no guarantee of paid sick leave where these trends quickly burned-out the lowest-paid workers (Morgan, 2021). Organizations have tackled this 'war for talent 2.0' by offering hiring bonuses and raising pay and benefits. However, 94% of retailers still cannot fill empty roles (Morgan, 2021). The inclusive forms of TM proposed in this chapter may help tackle the great resignation. For instance, the first approach of focusing on employees' strengths and potential may make employees feel valued. The second approach of increasing the size of the talent pool will be especially helpful for people who feel unfairly treated due to comparisons made between their performance and that of colleagues, and the lack of regard for performance factors other than output (such as motivation). The third approach of defining a broader range of talent domains will help clarify to organizations in which talent domains they have sufficient staff, and in which talent domains they may have a retention or attraction issue. And the fourth approach of topgrading may work in attracting and retaining the most competitive, ambitious staff as these will always flock to the organizations with the most high-status reputation.

DISCUSSION

In this chapter, we explore four different approaches to inclusive TM—a concept that is increasingly advocated for by both academics and practitioners, that has however lacked clarity and actionability. Based on the features of the four different approaches to inclusive talent management (Table 2.1), we developed a decision tree for organizations and researchers to determine which custom approach might best fit their talent philosophy. The decision tree, depicted in Figure 2.1, takes the decision-maker through four questions.

Taken together, the four approaches outlined in this chapter resonate with Swailes et al.'s (2014) ideas around 'hybrid' forms of talent management, that feature both exclusive and inclusive elements. We also believe that the nuance between the different approaches drives home the point that inclusive and exclusive TM exist on a continuum rather than as dichotomies (Adebola, Swailes, & Handley, 2015; Stahl et al., 2012).

For instance, talent management may include inclusive practices for everyone, focused on strengths and potential, with additional practices for a selected few talented employees. The most extreme pole of 'all-exclusive' TM would include a very small proportion (such as less than 5%) of the highest performing and most talented employees who are believed to contribute the most to achieving an organization's strategic goals. Alternatively, the opposite pole of 'all-inclusive' TM would include all employees and would involve the most extreme forms of any of the four approaches described in this chapter, for example, an extreme disjunctive approach that includes an infinite amount of talent domains, a high selection ratio, and uncorrelated criteria. The midpoint on the continuum may involve inclusive approaches that are not as extreme and thus do not include all employees, but perhaps 25%, 50%, or even 75% of them.

Approaching exclusive and inclusive TM as a continuum may subdue easy criticisms of the most extreme approaches to each, which may be an artificial discussion anyway (Swailes et al., 2014). For instance, those holding an exclusive philosophy have accused inclusive TM advocates of being naïve (Gill, 2002), while inclusive TM scholars say that exclusive TM promotes a neo-liberal winner-take-all ideology at the expense of more vulnerable employee groups (O'Connor & Crowley-Henry, 2019; Swailes, 2013). Indeed, fully exclusive TM can be considered elitist and exclusionary, creating unequal treatment that may harm employee morale, engagement, collaboration, trust in leadership, and productivity, where the negative effects on those left out may outweigh the possible benefits of these programs. For instance, the threshold for considering someone 'talented' is often arbitrary and subjective (Bélanger & Gagné, 2006; Ho, 2005). The opposite side of the spectrum—fully inclusive

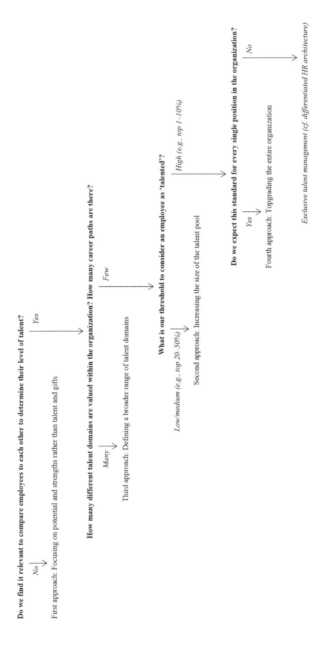

Do we find it relevant to compare employees to each other to determine their level of talent?

No → *Yes* →

First approach: Focusing on potential and strengths rather than talent and gifts

How many different talent domains are valued within the organization? How many career paths are there?

Many → *Few* →

Third approach: Defining a broader range of talent domains

What is our threshold to consider an employee as 'talented'?

Low/medium (e.g., top 20–50%) → *High (e.g., top 1–10%)* →

Second approach: Increasing the size of the talent pool

Do we expect this standard for every single position in the organization?

Yes → *No* →

Fourth approach: Topgrading the entire organization

Exclusive talent management (cf. differentiated HR architecture)

Figure 2.1   Four different approaches to inclusive talent management: a decision tree

TM—in contrast, may be a contradiction in terms, as we know that 'talent' historically and etymologically refers to human capital that is rare and difficult or impossible to imitate (Gallardo-Gallardo et al., 2013). Moreover, fully inclusive TM may be costly and not strategic by investing in all employees equally, rather than focusing investments on employees working in the most strategic roles, which will provide a higher return on investment (Collings & Mellahi, 2009; Lewis & Heckman, 2006). Most importantly, organizations may prefer to publicly make socially desirable statements such as 'everyone has talent' but lack practices to support this statement. We have even encountered cases where such organizations in fact did have secret high-potential programs behind closed doors—for only a handful of employees from a very large organizational population (Dries & De Gieter, 2014). In those cases, claiming that one's talent management is inclusive reeks of window-dressing rather than truly appreciating and developing all employees' talents in an inclusive way (Dries, 2013). For instance, in many organizations there are (explicit or implicit) hierarchies between talent domains even when they claim 'all employees are valued' (Nijs et al., 2022)—consider the relative importance (and promotability) of being excellent at research/publishing (and mediocre at teaching) versus being excellent at teaching (but mediocre at research) at most universities. Or similarly, being in a core versus support staff position at any other type of organization (Lepak & Snell, 1999). It is our impression that there are very few organizations that do not differentiate between their employees at all when it comes to the implementation of TM in practical terms. Our identification of four very different approaches may thus allow TM to be less of an all-or-nothing choice between inclusive and exclusive practices, reframing TM as a hybrid set or *bundle* of practices that best suit the needs of any individual organization (Meyers & van Woerkom, 2014).

We believe that in the above lies the solution to integrating the 'exclusive' and 'inclusive' talent management literatures—which are currently at odds with each other (Swailes et al., 2014)—into an accumulative body of knowledge. Rather than each approach arguing against the other, we believe it will be more constructive to acknowledge the different forms that talent management can take both conceptually and in organizational practice. In establishing such 'unity in diversity,' we believe talent management could finally make the transition into a more mature field of academic inquiry (Gallardo-Gallardo et al., 2015)—although clearly phenomenon-driven—characterized in equal parts by construct clarity, rigor, and relevance.

REFERENCES

Adebola, S., Swailes, S. & Handley, J. (2015). Conceptualization and evaluation of talent management: Evidence from the UK private sector. Working paper submitted to the Assessment, Measurement and Evaluation track of the 16th UFHRD Conference, University College Cork, June.

Altman, Y. (1997). The high-potential fast-flying achiever: Themes from the English language literature 1976–1995. *Career Development International*, **2**(7), 324–330.

Bélanger, J. & Gagné, F. (2006). Estimating the size of the gifted/talented population from multiple identification criteria. *Journal for the Education of the Gifted*, **30**(2), 131–163.

Blume, B.D., Rubin, R.S. & Baldwin, T.T. (2013). Who is attracted to an organisation using a forced distribution performance management system? Forced distribution systems. *Human Resource Management Journal*, **23**(4), 360–378.

Bonneton, D., Festing, M. & Muratbekova-Touron, M. (2020). Exclusive talent management: Unveiling the mechanisms of the construction of an elite community. *European Management Review*, **17**(4), 993–1013.

Briscoe, D. (2008). Talent management and the global learning organization. In Vaiman, V. & Vance, V. (eds.), *Smart Talent Management: Building Knowledge Assets for Competitive Advantage*. Cheltenham, UK and Northampton, MA, USA: Edward Elgar Publishing, pp. 195–216.

Buckingham, M. & Clifton, D.O. (2001). *Now, Discover Your Strengths*. New York: Gallup Press. 2001. https://library.macewan.ca/library-search?adv=&query= Buckingham%20Clifton&sf=au.

Church, A.H., Rotolo, C.T., Ginther, N.M. & Levine, R. (2015). How are top companies designing and managing their high-potential programs? A follow-up talent management benchmark study. *Consulting Psychology Journal: Practice and Research*, **67**(1), 17–47.

Cohen, W.M. & Levinthal, D.A. (1990). Absorptive capacity: A new perspective on learning and innovation. *Administrative Science Quarterly*, **35**(1), 128–152.

Collings, D.G. & Mellahi, K. (2009). Strategic talent management: A review and research agenda. *Human Resource Management Review*, **19**(4), 304–313.

De Boeck, G., Dries, N. & Tierens, H. (2019). The experience of untapped potential: Towards a subjective temporal understanding of work meaningfulness. *Journal of Management Studies*, **56**(3), 529–557.

Downs, Y. & Swailes, S. (2013). A capability approach to organizational talent management. *Human Resource Development International*, **16**(3), 267–281.

Dries, N. (2013). The psychology of talent management: A review and research agenda. *Human Resource Management Review*, **23**(4), 272–285.

Dries, N. (2022). What's your talent philosophy? Talent as construct vs. talent as phenomenon. In Collings, D.G., Vaiman, V., & Scullion, H. (eds.), *Talent Management: A Decade of Developments*. Bingley: Emerald Publishing, pp. 19–37.

Dries, N. & De Gieter, S. (2014). Information asymmetry in high potential programs: A potential risk for psychological contract breach. *Personnel Review*, **43**(1), 136–162.

Eichenwald, K. (2005). *Conspiracy of Fools: A True Story*. New York: Broadway Books.

Fiske, S.T. (2011). *Envy Up, Scorn Down: How Status Divides Us*. New York: Russell Sage Foundation.

Gagné, F. (1983). Douance et talent: Deux concepts à ne pas confondre. *Apprentissage et Socialisation*, **6**(3), 146–159.

Gagné, F. (1985). Giftedness and talent: Reexamining a reexamination of the definitions. *Gifted Child Quarterly*, **29**(3), 103–112.

Gagné, F. (1993). Sex-differences in the aptitudes and talents of children as judged by peers and teachers. *Gifted Child Quarterly*, **37**(2), 69–77.

Gagné, F. (2000). How many persons are gifted or talented? *Understanding Our Gifted*, **12**(2), 10–13.

Gagné, F. (2004). Transforming gifts into talents: The DMGT as a developmental theory. *High Ability Studies*, **15**(2), 119–147.

Gagné, F., Bélanger, J. & Motard, D. (1993). Popular estimates of the prevalence of giftedness and talent. *Roeper Review: A Journal on Gifted Education*, **16**(2), 96–98.

Gallardo-Gallardo, E., Dries, N. & González-Cruz, T.F. (2013). What is the meaning of "talent" in the world of work? *Human Resource Management Review*, **23**(4), 290–300.

Gallardo-Gallardo, E., Nijs, S., Dries, N. & Gallo, P. (2015). Towards an understanding of talent management as a phenomenon-driven field using bibliometric and content analysis. *Human Resource Management Review*, **25**(3), 264–279.

Gardner, H. (1990). Developing the spectrum of human intelligences. In Hedley, C.N., Houtz, J., & Baratta, A. (eds.), *Cognition, Curriculum, and Literacy*. Westport, CT: Ablex Publishing, pp. 11–19.

Gelens, J., Dries, N., Hofmans, J. & Pepermans, R. (2013). The role of perceived organizational justice in shaping the outcomes of talent management: A research agenda. *Human Resource Management Review*, **23**(4), 341–353.

Ghielen, S.T.S., Woerkom, M. van & Meyers, M.C. (2018). Promoting positive outcomes through strengths interventions: A literature review. *The Journal of Positive Psychology*, **13**(6), 573–585.

Gill, C. (2002). Two-dimensional HRM: Limitations of the soft and hard dichotomy in explaining the phenomenon of HRM. RMIT Working Paper, 4.

Gladwell, M. (2002). The talent myth: Are smart people overrated? *Market Leader*, **18**(1), 34–40.

Grant, R.M. (1996). Toward a knowledge-based theory of the firm. *Strategic Management Journal*, **17**, 109–122.

Groysberg, B., Nanda, A. & Nohria, N. (2004). The risky business of hiring stars. *Harvard Business Review*, **82**(5), 92–100.

Haesli, A. & Boxall, P. (2005). When knowledge management meets HR strategy: An exploration of personalization-retention and codification-recruitment configurations. *International Journal of Human Resource Management*, **16**(11), 1955–1975.

Hirsch, F. (1977). *Social Limits to Growth*. London: Routledge.

Hirsch, P.B. (2021). The great discontent. *Journal of Business Strategy*, **42**(6), 439–442.

Hjordrup, S.K., Minbaeva, D. & Jensen, S.H. (2015). The value of talent management: Rethinking practice, problems and possibilities. Copenhagen Business School.

Ho, V.T. (2005). Social influence on evaluations of psychological contract fulfillment. *The Academy of Management Review*, **30**(1), 113–128.

Huselid, M.A., Beatty, R.W. & Becker, B.E. (2005). A players or A positions? *Harvard Business Review*, **83**(12), 110–117.

Iles, P., Chuai, X. & Preece, D. (2010). Talent management and HRM in multinational companies in Beijing: Definitions, differences and drivers. *Journal of World Business*, **45**(2), 179–189.

Iles, P., Preece, D. & Chuai, X. (2010). Talent management as a management fashion in HRD: Towards a research agenda. *Human Resource Development International*, **13**(2), 125–145.

Leigh, A. (2009). Research topic: Talent management. *People Management*, **15**(16), 33.

Lepak, D.P. & Snell, S.A. (1999). The human resource architecture: Toward a theory of human capital allocation and development. *The Academy of Management Review*, **24**(1), 31–48.

Lepak, D.P. & Snell, S.A. (2002). Examining the human resource architecture: The relationships among human capital, employment, and human resource configurations. *Journal of Management*, **28**(4), 517–543.

Lewis, R.E. & Heckman, R.J. (2006). Talent management: A critical review. *Human Resource Management Review*, **16**(2), 139–154.

Linley, P.A. & Harrington, S. (2006). Playing to your strengths. *The Psychologist*, **19**(2), 86–89.

Lombardo, M.M. & Eichinger, R.W. (2000). High potentials as high learners. *Human Resource Management*, **39**(4), 321–329.

Malik, A.R. & Singh, P. (2014). 'High potential' programs: Let's hear it for 'B' players. *Human Resource Management Review*, **24**(4), 330–346.

Marescaux, E., De Winne, S. & Sels, L. (2013). HR practices and affective organisational commitment: (When) does HR differentiation pay off? *Human Resource Management Journal*, **23**(4), 329–345.

McCall, M. (1994). Identifying leadership potential in future international executives: Developing a concept. *Consulting Psychology Journal: Practice and Research*, **46**(1), 49–63.

Meyers, M.C. & van Woerkom, M. (2014). The influence of underlying philosophies on talent management: Theory, implications for practice, and research agenda. *Journal of World Business*, **49**(2), 192–203.

Meyers, M.C., van Woerkom, M., Paauwe, J. & Dries, N. (2020). HR managers' talent philosophies: Prevalence and relationships with perceived talent management practices. *The International Journal of Human Resource Management*, **31**(4), 562–588.

Michaels, E., Handfield-Jones, H. & Axelrod, B. (2001). *The War for Talent*. Boston: Harvard Business School Press.

Mitroff, I.I. & Denton, E.A. (1999). A study of spirituality in the workplace. *Sloan Management Review*, **40**(4), 83–92.

Morgan, K. (2021). The Great Resignation: How employers drove workers to quit. BBC. https://www.bbc.com/worklife/article/20210629-the-great-resignation-how-employ ers-drove-workers-to-quit.

Nijs, S., Dries, N., Van Vlasselaer, V. & Sels, L. (2022). Reframing talent identification as a status-organising process: Examining talent hierarchies through data mining. *Human Resource Management Journal*, **32**(1), 169–193.

Nijs, S., Gallardo-Gallardo, E., Dries, N. & Sels, L. (2014). A multidisciplinary review into the definition, operationalization, and measurement of talent. *Journal of World Business*, **49**(2), 180–191.

Noon, M. (2010). The shackled runner: Time to rethink positive discrimination? *Work, Employment and Society*, **24**(4), 728–739.

Nussbaum, M.C. (2012). *Capabilités: Comment créer les conditions d'un monde plus juste?* Paris: Climats.

O'Connor, E.P. & Crowley-Henry, M. (2019). Exploring the relationship between exclusive talent management, perceived organizational justice and employee engagement: Bridging the literature. *Journal of Business Ethics*, **156**(4), 903–917.

Pepermans, R., Vloeberghs, D. & Perkisas, B. (2003). High potential identification policies: An empirical study among Belgian companies. *Journal of Management Development*, **22**(8), 660–678.

Peters, T. (2006). Leaders as talent fanatics. *Leadership Excellence*, **23**(11), 12–13.

Pfeffer, J. & Sutton, R.I. (2006). The real brain teaser. *People Management*, **12**(8), 28–30.

Philpot, S. & Monahan, K. (2017). A data-driven approach to identifying future leaders: Rather than just relying on the subjective opinions of executives, some companies are using assessment tools to identify high-potential talent. *MIT Sloan Management Review*, **58**(4). https://library.macewan.ca/full-record/cat00565a/9120831.

Pierce, J.L. & Gardner, D.G. (2004). Self-esteem within the work and organizational context: A review of the organization-based self-esteem literature. *Journal of Management*, **30**(5), 591–622.

Pierce, J.L., Gardner, D.G., Cummings, L.L. & Dunham, R.B. (1989). Organization-based self-esteem: Construct definition, measurement, and validation. *Academy of Management Journal*, **32**(3), 622–648.

Prahalad, C.K. & Hamel, G. (1990). The core competence of the corporation. *Harvard Business Review*, **68**(3), 79–91.

Renzulli, J.S. (2005). Applying gifted education pedagogy to total talent development for all students. *Theory Into Practice*, **44**(2), 80–89.

Roberts, L.M., Dutton, J.E., Spreitzer, G.M., Heaphy, E.D. & Quinn, R.E. (2005). Composing the reflected best self-portrait: Building pathways for becoming extraordinary in work organizations. *The Academy of Management Review*, **30**(4), 712.

Roussillon, S. (2002). Perspectives from a clinical psychologist. In Derr, C.B., Roussillon, S. & Bournois, F. (eds.), *Cross-Cultural Approaches to Leadership Development*. Westport, CT: Quorum Books, pp. 261–288.

Scheffler, I. (1985). *Of Human Potential: An Essay in the Philosophy of Education*. London: Routledge & Kegan Paul.

Seligman, M.E.P. (2002). *Authentic Happiness: Using the New Positive Psychology to Realize Your Potential for Lasting Fulfillment*. New York: Free Press.

Silzer, R. & Church, A.H. (2009a). The pearls and perils of identifying potential. *Industrial and Organizational Psychology: Perspectives on Science and Practice*, **2**(4), 377–412.

Silzer, R. & Church, A.H. (2009b). The potential for potential. *Industrial and Organizational Psychology: Perspectives on Science and Practice*, **2**(4), 446–452.

Silzer, R. & Church, A.H. (2010). Identifying and assessing high potential talent: Current organizational practices. In Silzer, R. and Dowell, B.E. (eds.), *Strategy Driven Talent Management: A Leadership Imperative*. San Francisco: Jossey-Bass, pp. 213–280.

Slan-Jerusalim, R. & Hausdorf, P.A. (2007). Managers' justice perceptions of high potential identification practices. *Journal of Management Development*, **26**(10), 933–950.

Smart, B.D. (2012). *Topgrading: The Proven Hiring and Promoting Method That Turbocharges Company Performance*. New York: Portfolio/Penguin.

Smart, B.D. & Smart, G.H. (1997). Topgrading the organization. *Directors & Board*, **21**(3), 22–28.

Sparrow, P., Scullion, H. & Tarique, I. (eds.) (2014). *Strategic Talent Management: Contemporary Issues in International Context*. Cambridge: Cambridge University Press.

Spreitzer, G.M., McCall, M.W. & Mahoney, J.D. (1997). Early identification of international executive potential. *Journal of Applied Psychology*, **82**(1), 6–29.

Stahl, G., Björkman, I., Farndale, E., Morris, S.S., Paauwe, J., Stiles, P., Trevor, J. & Wright, P. (2012). Six principles of effective global talent management. *Sloan Management Review*, **53**(2), 25–42.

Sterling, C.M., van de Ven, N. & Smith, R.H. (2006). The two faces of envy: Studying benign and malicious envy in the workplace. In Smith, R.H., Merlone, U., & Duffy, M.K. (eds.), *Envy at Work and in Organizations: Research, Theory, and Applications*. Oxford: Oxford University Press, pp. 57–84.

Sternberg, R.J. (1985). *Beyond IQ: A Triarchic Theory of Human Intelligence*. New York: Cambridge University Press.

Strauss, K., Griffin, M.A. & Parker, S.K. (2012). Future work selves: How salient hoped-for identities motivate proactive career behaviors. *Journal of Applied Psychology*, **97**(3), 580–598.

Swaab, R.I., Schaerer, M., Anicich, E.M., Ronay, R. & Galinsky, A.D. (2014). The too-much-talent effect: Team interdependence determines when more talent is too much or not enough. *Psychological Science*, **25**(8), 1581–1591.

Swailes, S. (2013). Troubling some assumptions: A response to "The role of perceived organizational justice in shaping the outcomes of talent management: A research agenda." *Human Resource Management Review*, **23**(4), 354–356.

Swailes, S. & Blackburn, M. (2016). Employee reactions to talent pool membership. *Employee Relations*, **38**(1), 112–128.

Swailes, S., Downs, Y. & Orr, K. (2014). Conceptualising inclusive talent management: Potential, possibilities and practicalities. *Human Resource Development International*, **17**(5), 529–544.

Tannenbaum, A.J. (2000). Giftedness: The ultimate instrument for good and evil. In Heller, K.A., Mönks, F.J., Sternberg, R.J. & Subotnik, R. (eds.), *International Handbook of Giftedness and Talent*. Amsterdam: Elsevier, pp. 447–465.

Taylor, A. & Greve, H.R. (2006). Superman or the fantastic four? Knowledge combination and experience in innovative teams. *Academy of Management Journal*, **49**(4), 723–740.

Taylor, C.W. (1973). Developing effectively functioning people: The accountable goal of multiple talent teaching. *Education*, **94**(2), 99–110.

Taylor, S.E. & Lobel, M. (1989). Social comparison activity under threat: Downward evaluation and upward contacts. *Psychological Review*, **96**(4), 569–575.

Thomas, D.C. & Lazarova, M.B. (2006). Expatriate adjustment and performance: A critical review. In Stahl, G.K. & Björkman, I. (eds.), *Handbook of Research in International Human Resource Management*. Cheltenham, UK and Northampton, MA, USA: Edward Elgar Publishing, pp. 247–264.

Trank, C.Q., Rynes, S.L. & Bretz, R.D. (2002). Attracting applicants in the war for talent: Differences in work preferences among high achievers. *Journal of Business and Psychology*, **16**(3), 331–345.

Ulrich, D. & Smallwood, N. (2012). What is talent? *Leader to Leader*, **63**, 55–61.

Vaiman, V. & Vance, C. (eds.) (2008). *Smart Talent Management: Building Knowledge Assets for Competitive Advantage*. Cheltenham, UK and Northampton, MA, USA: Edward Elgar Publishing.

van Woerkom, M. & Meyers, M.C. (2015). My strengths count! Effects of a strengths-based psychological climate on positive affect and job performance. *Human Resource Management*, **54**(1), 81–103.

van Woerkom, M., Meyers, M.C. & Bakker, A.B. (2022). Considering strengths use in organizations as a multilevel construct. *Human Resource Management Review*, **32**(3). https://library.macewan.ca/full-record/edselp/S1053482220300401.

Vance, C.M., Boje, D.M., Mendenhall, M.E. & Kropp, H.R. (1991). A taxonomy of individual learning benefits from external knowledge-sharing meetings. *Human Resource Development Quarterly*, **2**(1), 37–52.

Walker, J.W. & LaRocco, J.M. (2002). Talent pools: The best and the rest. *Human Resource Planning*, **25**(3), 12–14.

Wood, A.M., Linley, P.A., Maltby, J., Kashdan, T.B. & Hurling, R. (2011). Using personal and psychological strengths leads to increases in well-being over time: A longitudinal study and the development of the strengths use questionnaire. *Personality and Individual Differences*, **50**(1), 15–19.

3. In the war for talent: just who is worthy of development? Talent development in organizations

Thomas Garavan, Clíodhna MacKenzie and Colette Darcy

INTRODUCTION

Major developments including globalization, digitalization, and technological disruption present major challenges and opportunities to firms when it comes to gaining and sustaining competitive advantage (Garavan et al., 2020). The development of talent has become a major strategic priority due to global skill shortages, changes in the labour market, competition for the best talent, increased global labour mobility, and greater emphasis on work-life balance present organizations with difficulties when sourcing talent (CIPD, 2021). While many organizations acknowledge the importance of developing talent, there are issues around the resources and skill sets necessary to bring this about, how to link talent development efforts to organizational strategy (Collings, 2014) and questions concerning who should be developed and when this development should take place. In addition, there is an increased acknowledgement that talent development can be used to achieve important knowledge management objectives. For example, the focus of talent development on the promotion of leadership and technical competencies involves processes of knowledge acquisition and sharing. For example, De Vos and Dries (2013) placed knowledge as pivotal to competence development in terms of (a) the process of developing competencies through coaching, on the job experience and formal training, (b) knowledge sharing as part of that development journey.

The development of talent has become a major priority for many organizations irrespective of size, sector, or geographic location (Datta et al., 2021; Johnson, Huang, & Doyle, 2019) yet the evidence of what works and what does not work is scarce in the wider talent management literature. To date, significantly more attention is given to talent management with research on talent development nascent, and significantly underdeveloped (Hedayati Mehdiabadi

& Li, 2016; Rezaei & Beyerlein, 2018). Moreover, the phenomenon of talent development is an area of major interest for practitioners, and many are struggling to deliver on talent development goals and priorities (Bleich, 2021; CIPD, 2021).

The requirement to develop talent is universal across the globe and the most pressing practice issues concern: Who should be developed? When should it take place? And how best to develop an internal talent pool that aligns with strategic goals and priorities (Chaudhuri, Park, & Johnson, 2022; Dalal & Akdere, 2018). The two dominant paradigms concerning what organizations should focus on when it comes to talent development emphasize exclusive and inclusive approaches (Garavan et al., 2020). Exclusive approaches emphasize that organizations should invest most of their development resources in a small number of highly talented individuals (Meyer & Xin, 2018; Stahl et al., 2012). This will mean that approximately 1–15% of the workforce will have access to development opportunities. The inclusive approach to talent development, on the other hand, is grounded on the assumption that *all* employees possess talent and competencies that can be productively used in the organization (Swailes, 2013). Research by CIPD (2021) reveals that about 40% of organizations implement more inclusive approaches to the development of talent and provide talent development opportunities for all employers within an organization. Many smaller and public sector organizations are increasingly prioritizing an inclusive approach to talent development largely triggered by a concern to achieve employee well-being and performance.

In this chapter we take an inclusive approach to talent development, while also acknowledging that one of the topics we review and discuss is concerned with high potential talent groups. Our broad working definition of talent development for the purposes of this chapter is as follows: *talent development is concerned with the planning, selection and implementation of development strategies that focus on the entire talent pool with the objective of ensuring that employee wellbeing is sustained, that key competencies for job and career are developed and that an organization has the supply of current and future talent to achieve organizational goals* (Garavan, Carbery, & Rock, 2012). We argue that talent development helps an organization to configure its total human resource pool to achieve organizational performance goals (Collings, Mellahi, & Cascio, 2019), but it also creates value for both employees and organizations through focusing on a strengths-based approach. This perspective on talent development is consistent with general notions of development found in the training and development literature (Garavan et al., 2020) and the increased emphasis on a strengths-based approach (Dries, 2013; Gallardo-Gallardo et al., 2015) that is concerned with preparing the workforce for the future and ensuring that they possess the knowledge, skills, and abilities to achieve career and organizational goals. We also envisage that this approach to talent development is strongly aligned with the role of talent development within a knowl-edge management paradigm. Knowledge management is conceptualized as a continuous process that includes socialization, externalization, combination, and internalization (Nonaka & Takeuchi, 1995). It gives emphasis to the acquisition of knowledge, the use of knowledge, the organizing of knowledge, the sharing of knowledge, the internalization of knowledge, and the creation of new knowledge (Naim & Lenka, 2017). We discuss the role of talent develop-ment in these processes later in this chapter.

This chapter therefore has several important aims. First, it explores the concept of talent development and where and how it sits within the broader talent management literature. Talent development represents a key component of the overall talent management process (Cappelli, 2008; Johnson et al., 2019). Second, it explores several important debates around talent develop-ment including how talent development approaches differ depending on the organizational context, the role of development in the context of the creation of talent pools, the different support strategies and interventions that make up the concept of talent development, the issue of generational difference and talent development, the contribution of talent development to knowledge management and talent development, and the notion of sustainable talent development. Third, given the many gaps in knowledge concerning talent development in organizations, this chapter considers the key research gaps and identifies important research questions. The concluding section of the chapter considers the key practice implications that arise for talent development in organizations.

DEFINING TALENT DEVELOPMENT: EXCLUSIVE AND INCLUSIVE APPROACHES

Talent development is viewed as one of the three major talent management activities found in organizations (Gallardo-Gallardo et al., 2015). The two key additional key components that are emphasized are talent acquisition and talent retention (Holland & Scullion, 2021). Following a configurational approach, talent development is linked horizontally to these and other talent management activities; however, its primary focus is the enhancement of the knowledge, skills, and abilities of the total human resource pool to ensure that the organization's human capital is characterized by high value and uniqueness in addition to enhancing the careers of employees (Lepak & Snell, 1999). The exclusive approach argues that only key talent within an organization is worthy of development whereas 'talent' considered to have low value and uniqueness will fall outside the remit or scope of talent development (De Vos & Dries, 2013). Employees that fall into this category are unlikely to receive much in the way of investment in their development (Garavan et al., 2020). Almost invariably in the context of an exclusive approach to talent development, these talent pools consist of leaders and individual contributors that possess important and high value knowledge and expertise.

Rezaei and Beyerlein (2018: 76–77) proposed a more employee centred definition that gives emphasis to the subjective experience of talent development as follows:

> a comprehensive, inclusive system that is personalized and socially constructed for and by individual employees; it is not limited to specific work-related interventions such as training, but includes career development, organizational development and individual training and learning for the benefit of employees and organizations.

This definition is notable and important for several reasons. First it places emphasis on the inclusive nature of talent development, it personalizes *development* to the needs of individual employees rather than a one size fits all approach, and utilizes a multitude of different development interventions and approaches. Second, it emphasizes the socially constructed nature of talent development and that talent development is personal, subjective, crafted by employees and may consist of formal and informal components; however, the critical issue is how the employee *experiences* them. Third, the definition advocates a mutual gains perspective, whereby talent development can achieve important outcomes for both employees and organizations. Employees will achieve enhanced competencies and human capital value while organizations will have a strong and well-developed pool of engaged employees committed to the firm and its objectives.

An exclusive approach to talent development fits less with these mutual gains, humanistic and growth focused conceptualizations of development (Garavan et al., 2020). It is also out of sync with a strengths-based notion of development that talks about individual strengths rather than talents. Individual strengths are conceptualized as trait-like individual characteristics that enable individuals to achieve their personal best and that they both perform effectively and maximize their mental well-being (Peterson & Seligman, 2004). This approach to talent development highlights that the focus should be on strengths that energize employees rather than exhaust them, and thus it is in marked contrast to the exclusive approach (Nijs et al., 2014). It is not focused on comparison, which is central to the exclusive approach.

This perhaps helps to explain that many of the definitions of talent development as proposed by scholars worked within HRD and learning and development rather than those working within HRM. The strengths-based approach is emphasized within the HRD and learning and development literatures. For example, it gives emphasis to the energizing nature of talent development, the contribution of talent development to employee well-being, and that employees are most effective when their strengths are developed (Myers & van Woerkom, 2014). The definitions of talent development proposed by Garavan et al. (2012), Rezaei and Beuerlein (2018), and Johnson et al. (2019) envisage a much more inclusive approach to talent development and the identification and development of strengths and capabilities. They propose that organizations will use development processes to develop the full pool of talent to meet current and future business needs. They conceptualize talent development as intentional and structured (Dalal & Akdere, 2018; Hedayati Mehdiabadi & Li, 2016) and that all talent has the potential to contribute to the strategic goals of the organization. They also envisage that talent development will be of benefit to the individual personally and in terms of employability.

Therefore, definitions of talent development espouse an investment principle and focus on the development of skills, knowledge, and capabilities and recognize that talent retention and attraction are important outcomes of organizational talent development activities (Crowley-Henry, O'Connor, & Al Ariss, 2018). Unsurprisingly, inclusive notions of talent development are concerned with issues of strengths, personal development, equity, and fairness and that all employees have strengths that can be developed. There is some evidence of firms implementing this type of inclusive approach. For example, the Cisco Systems 'People Deal' focuses on placing all employees at the centre of what it does, and it develops people not to solely focus on achieving results, but to also focus on the behaviours required in achieving these results (Cisco, 2022). In many respects, Cisco Systems places enormous responsibility and value in its people knowing that in developing and valuing its people, the beneficiaries are likely to be not just customers but Cisco's entire stakeholder community. Meyers and van Woerkom (2014) found that a strengths-based talent development approach was beneficial to the use of individual strengths, and to enhance employee well-being and performance impacts.

However, while concentrating on an inclusive approach to talent development in this chapter, it is important to acknowledge that MNCs implement more exclusive approaches to talent development (Garavan et al., 2020). These exclusive approaches propose that organizations should direct a significant amount of their efforts and resources to developing those employees who have the greatest potential to contribute to organizational goals. This chapter addresses this approach later in the context of high potential development programmes.

KEY RESEARCH THEMES IN TALENT DEVELOPMENT

Contextual Influences on Talent Development Approaches

There are relatively limited insights concerning talent development in different organizational contexts. There is some evidence suggesting different approaches to talent development in SMEs compared to MNCs and public sector organizations. The literature on talent development in SMEs is nascent with few studies that directly focus on formal talent development approaches. Nolan and Garavan (2016) for example, found in the context of developing leaders in SMEs that the primary drivers were the personal values of the owner-manager and the existence of a formal HR role. The HR role was important because in SMEs with more formal HR roles, greater emphasis was given to formal development processes and there was a greater willingness to invest in the development of leaders as a key talent pool. Nolan, Garavan, and Lynch (2020) found that the emphasis on development in tourism SMEs was largely informal, systemic, and organic with much development taking place as part of experimental learning and day-to-day working processes. This study found support for an evolutionary approach to the development of professionals and managers. Sheehan and Garavan (2022) found that SMEs did over time invest in development activities as part of high-performance work practices (HPWPs) and that the strategic orientation of the owner-manager towards HRM was central to that investment. Festing, Schäfer, and Scullion (2013) explored talent management in German SMEs and found various levels of intensity when it came to talent management, which included talent development: highly engaged, reactive talent management (TM) and retention-based approaches. They found that the prevalence of these approaches depended on annual sales, industry affiliations, TM networks and cooperative behaviour with respect to HR, and the long-term focus of the SME when it came to HR and TM budgets. Other research findings highlight that there is generally a strong emphasis and over reliance on informal development processes in SMEs with less attention given to career development processes and succession planning (Nolan & Garavan, 2016). These characteristics are explained by liability of firm size and the scarcity of resources (Rauch & Hatak, 2016).

The situation in public sector organizations is significantly different. These organizations tend to be more conservative when it comes to talent development and are less likely to use the label talent management (Grant, Garavan, & Mackie, 2020). They do, however, prioritize talent development processes with major emphasis given to personal and management/leader development activities. There is limited evidence that public sector organizations have adopted the strong market logics that underpin talent development in for example MNCs. They tend to avoid talent development processes that are competitive and that emphasize potential assessment, and there is a strong focus on rank when it comes to who might have access to talent development processes. Many public sector organizations implement 'soft' approaches to talent development that are driven by the strengths and career requirements of managers and professional staff.

The situation in MNCs is in stark contrast to both SMEs and public sector organizations. It is in this context that we find the most extensive array of talent development approaches with emphasis given to *career development* (Bialek & Hagen, 2021; Claussen et al., 2014; Vo, 2009), *developing future leaders* (Chami-Malaeb & Garavan, 2013), talent *pools and practices* (Jooss, Burbach, & Ruël, 2021; Kanabar & Fletcher, 2022; McDonnell et al., 2021; Sonnenberg, van Zijderveld, & Brinks, 2014), and *return on investment* (ROI) associated with TM strategies (Cooke et al., 2021; McNulty & De Cieri, 2016). MNCs make extensive use of high potential development programmes and unlike the public sector and SMEs, are more likely to implement exclusive approaches to talent development (Garavan et al., 2020; Malik & Singh, 2014). In addition, talent pools are an increasingly important strategy in MNCs (Jooss et al., 2021; McDonnell et al., 2021). However, Kwon & Jang (2021) urged caution when developing talent pools because membership of such pools does not guarantee long-term commitment of these precious and distinct resources. It is also possible that being identified as talented and having membership of talent pools can be squandered by the firm if it relies too much on the assumption that simply being a member of a talent pool results in long-term commitment to the firm—it does not.

An important and significantly under-researched aspect of context concerns the impact of cross-cultural differences on talent development processes. These include but are not limited to the impact of the factors identified by Hofstede's (1983) typology on the way that organizations approach talent development. For example in collectivist cultures it is likely that exclusive approaches will be less acceptable, whereas in individualistic cultures, they are more likely to be acceptable and effective (Froese, 2020). Many studies on talent development approaches are based on Western theories, and do not factor in differences in cultural values. In addition, the influence of institutional differences is unclear. For example, it is likely that talent development approaches will differ in market economies versus socialist market economies and different varieties of capitalism (Hartmann, Feisel, & Schober, 2010; Muyia, Wekullo, & Nafukho, 2018; Ready, Hill, & Conger, 2008). Another challenge relates to cross-cultural considerations associated with talent management more broadly, and talent development, more specifically. Liu et al. (2021) provide some insightful observations in respect of bi-cultural individuals in cross-cultural mergers and acquisitions. The authors point to the benefits of integrating an awareness of the unique insights which bi-cultural employees can render to the firm when it comes to understanding the nuances of local markets. Considering the benefits of this, one could argue that the same principles could be applied to leveraging the uniqueness of employees that straddle multiple identities as well as cultures, especially when it comes to the attraction, retention, and development of a more diverse cohort of employees.

Whilst HR as a function more broadly and HRD (talent development) more specifically is constantly reinventing and repositioning itself to remain relevant to the firm, another challenge for talent development has been the COVID-19 pandemic. The response to the impact of COVID-19 has demonstrated that HR can be a *tour de force* when it comes to innovation, creativity, and implementing leading edge solutions that will attract and retain the best and brightest (Collings et al., 2021). However, as Gorska et al. (2021) and Staniscuaski et al. (2021) note, the impact of COVID-19 on careers and development opportunities in an academic setting has been significant. Given the gendered nature of academia, and the fact that women occupy far less senior positions than their male counterparts and would have been more likely to have faced significantly more challenges achieving a work-life balance during the pandemic, means that those in most need of development opportunities were the cohort most impacted by the social distancing aspects of the pandemic. Akanji et al.'s (2022) study of Nigerian female academics illustrated this fact with issues such as mental and physical health, as well as career stagnation being commonly experienced as a direct result of the pandemic. More specifically, the authors allude to the 'profound adverse effects' of the pandemic in relation to contextual and physical resources such as 'career and health' with broader 'cultural inclinations of patriarchy' exacerbating stress levels among the cohort. As a valuable source of knowledge, skills and expertise, female academics as well as other female workers are far more likely to miss out on talent development opportunities than their male equivalents.

Talent Development and Generational Issues

Unique talent development issues arise in respect of employees from different generations. While the concept of generations is controversial in the HRM literature (Parry & Urwin, 2021) research highlights that when it comes to talent development priorities and expectations there are interesting similarities (Nelson & Duxbury, 2020) and some differences (Kodagoda & Wijeratne, 2021; Pant & Venkateswaran, 2019). For example, Nelson and Duxbury (2020) found a number of similarities between Gen X and Gen Y, namely that both generations wanted their employer to provide clear and consistent treatment of employees and demonstrate appreciation and respect irrespective of generational differences; they also valued clear and consistent communication about task and role obligations as well as succession planning and career development and progression. Additionally, both generations in the accounting firm at the centre of the study expected personal growth and development strategies, as well as access to opportunities for learning and development. However, whilst there were quite a number of similarities in respect of the generational differences, there were some dissimilarities also. Gen Y for example, expected an appropriate level of work-life balance and compensation commensurate with how talented they perceived themselves to be. Moreover, the Gen Y cohort in the study cited higher compensation opportunities as an indicator of intention to leave. Gen X on the other hand, were more likely to indicate intention to leave if they believed the firm to be unfair or unjust.

In contrast, both Kodagoda and Wijeratne (2021) and Pant and Venkateswaran (2019) found that the Gen Ys in their studies had an expectation that they were 'talented' and therefore were *entitled* to career development opportunities, accelerated career growth, as well as job and resource support. It might be worth considering what impact a Gen Y manager, who has control over resources, would have on the career development opportunities of Gen X and Gen Y employees reporting directly to him/her? This generational difference might be the critical dimension in whether TM-TD strategies fail or succeed in the firm, given the likelihood that Gen Y employees are more likely to leave the firm if their needs for career development and personal growth are not being met compared with their Gen X colleagues who are less likely to leave for that reason. When it comes to Gen-Zs the focus is on using technology to deliver talent development. They also value bite-sized development processes and continuous development opportunities. According to LinkedIn, Gen-Xs want to learn quickly and move through the career ladder with speed. They are highly motivated to grow their careers and the majority see learning and development as key to their development and progression (Perna, 2021). These studies highlight the need for organizations to think about how they customize and tailor talent development strategies and avoid the one size fits all approach when addressing generational differences.

Talent Development Supports, Approaches, and Interventions

The literature is prescriptive and normative on talent development supports, approaches and interventions. When it comes to supports for talent development, the concept of talent development climate is emphasized and is conceptualized as an ambient characteristic of organizations that signals to employees that their development is valued and prioritized. Two important dimensions of the talent development climate are supervisory support and organizational support for talent development. For example, Datta et al. (2021) proposed that the talent development climate in the firm must be considered as a distinct and independent strategy for TM to implement in order to maximize innovation and creativity within the firm. A supportive talent development climate facilitates creativity, knowledge sharing, and innovation and promotes learning, which is considered essential to 'harnessing talent' (wherever it might be) in an effort to achieve superior performance and competitive advantage.

When it comes to the types of talent development strategies, Garavan et al. (2012: 12) proposed four distinct TD programme interventions that facilitate the firm's talent management strategy: *formal programmes, relationship-based development experiences, job-based development practices*, and *informal and non-formal development opportunities*. Garavan et al.'s broad categorization reflects the importance of the TD function as a distinct and separate area of inquiry within the broader TM literature. Different content dimensions of talent development are emphasized including capabilities (Thijssen & van der Heijden, 2003), managerial skills (Claussen et al., 2014), and competencies (Lehmann, 2009; Siikaniemi, 2012). Both McLean (2006) and Rezaei and Beyerlein (2018) highlight an extensive menu of approaches that organizations deploy to achieve talent development objectives. These include:

- *Formal Training and Development*, which includes in-house seminars, expertise and talent training, individualized training, leadership and management training.
- *Individual-Level Organizational Development*, which comprises job design and job rotation, stretch assignments, job enlargement and enrichment, career development plans, and visibility by top management.
- *Team-Level Organizational Development*, which includes teamworking and development, social networks and networking events, community engagement events, and autonomy and agency focused opportunities.
- *Global-Level Organizational Development*, comprising attracting and recruiting global talent, global succession planning, international assignments/rotations, overseas training and exposure on global platform/ex-pat assignments.
- *Organization-Level Development*, which can include succession planning, knowledge sharing, benchmarking, accountability and performance-related rewards, managerial support, building and populating talent pools, development of knowledge networks and sponsorship of talent.

However, there is an absence of insights concerning the types of personalization and customization of talent development strategies aimed at addressing specific populations with one exception: that of high potential development programmes. It is estimated that 50–70% of global firms implement such programmes (Campbell & Smith, 2014; Silzer & Church, 2010). Variously described as high-flier or fast-track development programmes (Feild & Harris, 1991; Garavan & Morley, 1997), high potential programmes (Dries & De Gieter, 2014), or HIPD programmes (Malik & Singh, 2014; Swailes, 2013) they focus on the 'systematic identification, socialization, and development of cohorts of employees considered to have high potential for a top management position or advancement to a higher level of responsibility more generally (Dries & De Gieter, 2014: 137). While conventionally there has been a focus on 'A' potential, scholars and practitioners increasingly call attention to the importance of 'B' potential (Beechler & Woodward, 2009; DeLong & Vijayaraghavan, 2003). As Vaiman, Scullion, and Collings (2012: 926) point out, the focus on the implementation of high potential programmes in MNCs is driven by the strategic priority afforded to 'identifying, attracting, and retaining high value employees'. High potential development programmes vary in duration from 12 months to 2 years (Fulmer, Stumpf, & Bleak, 2009) and involve intensive and accelerated development processes. MNCs use a combination of formal and informal approaches to identify high potentials who will participate in these programmes. Formal approaches include the use of talent assessment and review processes (Mäkelä, Björkman, & Ehrnrooth, 2010) that seek to objectively identify those that are top rank (Becker, Huselid, & Beatty, 2009). Informal approaches rely on manager judgment and championing (Kravariti & Johnston, 2020). A typical programme will see the MNC expose high potentials to multiple development processes, including multi-source feedback, formal mentoring, coaching and classroom development (Yost & Chang, 2009). They also make extensive use of experience-based strategies such as challenging assignments, job rotations and stretch assignments (Finkelstein, Costanza, & Goodwin, 2019; King, 2016). Experienced-based development strategies provide a major impetus for growth (McCall, 2010) and they are frequently accompanied by intensive feedback (DeRue & Wellman, 2009). The use of these programmes is not without criticism, and they depart from the inclusive approaches to talent development highlighted in this chapter.

Talent Development and Knowledge Management

The role of talent development in the context of knowledge management is an area of increasing research and practice. For example, the development of competencies, which is a key component of talent development involves processes of knowledge sharing and acquisition. Knowledge acquisition emphasizes the organizational knowledge held, acquired, or created whereas knowledge sharing is focused on the dissemination of knowledge (Whelan & Carcary, 2011). Talent development processes can be used to facilitate the acquisition of new skills and to help new knowledge be shared between individuals and teams. For example, Hakkarainen and Paavola (2007) found that components of knowledge management may help talent development and that knowledge sharing in communities of practice helped to develop the competencies of members. Hsu (2008) found that knowledge sharing practices were valuable in enhancing both the organizational level of human capital and performance. Talent development processes may also be valuable in the context of knowledge exploitation, which focuses on the use of knowledge for creativity and innovation purposes. These practices help employees to combine knowledge in unique ways and generate important job and organizational outcomes (Sveiby, 2001). More importantly however, as Inkpen and Tsang (2005), Chang and Chuang (2011) and Yli-Renko, Autio, and Sapienza (2001) argue, the willingness to acquire and share knowledge is predicated on the degree to which the environment supports such endeavours and within the context of a more inclusive, rather than exclusive approach to talent development, this can translate to higher levels of productivity, profitability and more importantly, innovation and creativity. The need to pursue more inclusive talent development strategies is not just based on the business justification of doing so, it centres on the need to act in ways that regard talent, knowledge, and insight as the potential that all employees possess—firms just need to know how to create the right conditions to let that knowledge flourish so that it can become a unique source of competitive advantage.

Responsible Talent Development

In recent times, scholars have begun to advocate for the implementation of responsible talent management and development approaches. For example, Anlesinya and Amponsah-Tawiah (2020: 284) provide a definition of responsible talent management (RTM) as follows:

> TM practices and strategies that emphasize an organization's responsibility to identify, *develop*, and *nurture* the unique and diverse talents of *all workers* by expanding access to available talent development opportunities, by fairly managing their weaknesses and by recognizing their contributions while giving them *equal opportunities to flourish* as valued employees to ensure their commitment to the organization so as to achieve mutual sustainable outcomes for employees and their organizations.

Central to their notion of responsible talent management is the argument that organizations should implement inclusive approaches to talent development. Swailes (2020) envisages that responsible talent development will have several important characteristics including:

- Organizational actors that advocate exclusive approaches to talent development should as a matter of principle be able to articulate clear and plausible reasons as to why they think some employees have more potential than others.

- It is important that organizations produce talent descriptions that are realistic, aspirational, and non-discriminatory, and are aligned effectively with the various levels of the organization to which they relate.
- Talent development processes should be inclusive and factor into account the motivations of employees to be involved in development programmes.
- Talent actors should be able to articulate clearly how different talent development programmes are linked to organizational goals.
- Where exclusive talent development programmes are used, it is important that organizations monitor their impacts on the well-being of those who participate. In addition, it is important to understand how these programmes impact employees who are not part of them.

Responsible talent development involves questioning important assumptions that lie at the heart of exclusive talent management and development approaches. This strongly aligns with the notions of development found in the employee development and learning and development literatures.

RESEARCHING TALENT DEVELOPMENT

Talent development is ripe for research simply because the field of investigation is nascent and underdeveloped. There are a number of reasons for this. First, talent development tends to be included as part of an overall TM strategy where talent that has been identified further upstream will require some development support after the fact. Unsurprisingly, the TM literature tends to put great emphasis on identifying, attracting and recruiting talent (externally) as well as identifying the high potential and high performers within the firm as the source of human capital for various talent pools. The primary role of talent development in this scenario is to provide the formal/informal training and development of what the firm has designated talent. Second, in an effort to maximize citations and impact of TD focused research, authors may elect to submit their research to high ranking (relative to sub-discipline focused) journals and tailor the focus of TD so that it aligns with the dominant TM literature that views TD as supporting rather than driving TM strategies. Finally, it is conceivable that the reason TD appears less often in the literature as a distinct research focus is because it is included within HRD and Career Development focused research, which is predominantly found in lower ranked (although not necessarily less impactful) sub-discipline journals.

A number of priority research areas are highlighted here:

- The talent development-performance link is widely assumed in the literature, yet there is an absence of research that has investigated this link. This research needs to be undertaken in a longitudinal way and with a view to equifinality (Garavan et al., 2021) whereby the relative effectiveness of inclusive and exclusive approaches can be investigated. In addition, there is a need to be careful when it comes to measurement and isolation of the impact of talent development programmes as distinct for learning and development processes (Swailes, 2020). Researchers investigating the link between talent development and performance need to carefully specify both the measures and the levels of analysis. What are the priority individual and organizational level measures that are considered important?
- The concept of talent development climate is a recent addition in the literature; however, we know relatively little about its makeup and how it is developed. So, for example will it differ in terms of elements depending on the organizational context? And will its impacts be more potent and impactful in SMEs versus MNCs for example? What are the most important factors or situational contingencies that will elevate or diminish the effects of the talent development climate and what are its impacts on outcomes?
- There is a notable absence of theoretical frameworks that can be used to conceptualize and explain the impacts of talent development (Rezaei & Beyerlein, 2018). Scholars therefore can utilize motivation and resource theories (Eisenhardt & Martin, 2000; Helfat & Peteraf, 2003; Ryan & Deci, 2000; Weiner, 1985) to understand the individual impacts of talent development. There is significant scope to invoke open systems theory to address important organizational level impacts including congruence, adaptation, internal interdependence, equifinality and capacity for feedback (Garavan et al., 2021). Systems theory can help researchers understand the impact of external factors such as institutional differences, national culture and environmental uncertainty on the types of talent development approaches adopted by organizations. It can also shed light on how internal factors such as HR strategies, firm strategy and leadership impact on talent development processes. The concept of the feedback loop helps researchers to understand how feedback on the effectiveness of talent development impacts future talent development efforts. Finally there is also scope to understand how different combinations of antecedents and talent development interventions lead to different individual and organizational outcomes.
- The prevalence and types of talent development approaches that are used in different organizations contexts need further investigation. For example,

we have relatively few insights on what SMEs and public sector organizations do. What do they do that is the same or different? How do they make choices about talent development processes? What role do owner/managers in the case of SMEs and cultural heritage and public sector motivation in the case of public sector organizations have on how they approach talent development? How do different institutional logics of organizations influence talent development?

- The extensive area of talent development strategies needs much more investigation (Garavan et al., 2012). For example, what impacts do self versus organizationally initiated talent development approaches have on the motivation and effectiveness of employees? What are the impacts of continuous and just-in time talent development approaches on outcomes of talent development initiatives? How are these approaches perceived by employees? What types of talent climate features sustain these talent development approaches? What is the most effective way of measuring their effectiveness? How sustainable are these approaches?
- Another research area is the role of talent development and its reciprocal links with knowledge management. For example, what are the impacts of talent development processes on knowledge acquisition, sharing and utilization components of knowledge management? How do knowledge management processes contribute to the development of talent? Which knowledge management processes are most valuable? How best can organizations leverage both talent management and knowledge management so that they are synergistically integrated?

IMPLICATIONS FOR PRACTICE

The implementation of talent development approaches has important practice implications, some of which we address here. It would appear sensible that organizations should strive to focus on creating a talent development climate that is conducive to growth and development. Therefore, in order to create a conducive organization level talent development climate, HR and talent management practitioners should focus on the implementation of organization-wide policies, practices and processes that support talent development. At the operational or macro level it is important to develop managers and supervisors so that they can support the implementation of talent development interventions.

The discussion of inclusive versus exclusive approaches raises a number of important practical questions for managers and HR practitioners. These include the following: What is the organization's definition of talent? What are the criteria for inclusion in talent development processes? What is the relative focus on generic competencies versus technical competencies? What talent development needs take priority, and how will that be decided? Should the organization's talent be accelerated or should a more progressive approach to talent development be adopted by firms? What should be the blend of talent development strategies? How will the effectiveness of talent development be evaluated and when? It is also important that organizations should consider the issues of personalization and customization of talent development approaches to address individual needs and expectations. In addition, there is value in a generational approach that considers the unique requirements of each generational category in addition to needs that they share.

Finally, an important practice issue concerns how talent development is linked to the other components of talent management including attraction and retention and knowledge management processes. Talent development can be used as an important talent attractor as well as a strategy to retain talented employees within an organization. It is also an important strategy to develop a strong internal supply of talent. In addition, talent development can make an important contribution to organizational knowledge management processes and vice versa, so organizations should consider how aligned these sets of processes are and their potential to generate important benefits for individuals and the organization.

REFERENCES

Akanji, B., Mordi, C., Ajonbadi, H. & Adekoya, O. (2022). The impact of COVID-19 on the work-life balance of working mothers: Evidence from Nigerian academics. *Personnel Review*. doi:10.1108/pr-08-2020-0636.

Anlesinya, A. & Amponsah-Tawiah, K. (2020). Towards a responsible talent management model. *European Journal of Training and Development*, **44**(2/3), 279–303.

Becker, B.E., Huselid, M.A. & Beatty, R.W. (2009). *The Differentiated Workforce: Transforming Talent into Strategic Impact*. Boston, MA: Harvard Business School Publishing.

Beechler, S. & Woodward, I.C. (2009). The global "war for talent". *Journal of International Management*, **15**(3), 273–285.

Bialek, T.K. & Hagen, M.S. (2021). Cohort-based leadership development for high-potential employees: A model for programmatic design. *Human Resource Development Quarterly*. https://doi-org.ucc.idm.oclc.org/10.1002/hrdq.21459.

Bleich, C. (2021). How to recruit, train and retain employees during the Great Resignation. https://www.edgepointlearning.com/blog/recruit-train-retain -employees-great-resignation/.

Campbell, M. & Smith, R. (2014). High-potential talent: A view from inside the leadership pipeline. online. https://www.ccl.org/wp-content/uploads/2016/09/high -potential-talent-center-for-creative-leadership.pdf.

Cappelli, P. (2008). Talent management for the twenty-first century. *Harvard Business Review*, **86**(3), 74–81.

Chami-Malaeb, R. & Garavan, T. (2013). Talent and leadership development practices as drivers of intention to stay in Lebanese organisations: The mediating role of affective commitment. *The International Journal of Human Resource Management*, **24**(21), 4046–4062.

Chang, H.H. & Chuang, S.S. (2011). Social capital and individual motivations on knowledge sharing: Participant involvement as a moderator. *Information & Management*, **48**(1), 9–18.

Chaudhuri, S., Park, S. & Johnson, K.R. (2022). Engagement, inclusion, knowledge sharing, and talent development: Is reverse mentoring a panacea to all? Findings from literature review. *European Journal of Training and Development*, **46**(5–6), 468–483.

CIPD (2021). *Learning and Development Strategy and Policy*. CIPD. https://www.cipd .co.uk/knowledge/strategy/development/factsheet#gref.

Cisco (2022). *Our People Deal*. https://blogs.cisco.com/tag/our-people-deal.

Claussen, J., Grohsjean, T., Luger, J. & Probst, G. (2014). Talent management and career development: What it takes to get promoted. *Journal of World Business*, **49**(2), 236–244.

Collings, D.G. (2014). Toward mature talent management: Beyond shareholder value. *Human Resource Development Quarterly*, **25**(3), 301–319.

Collings, D.G., McMackin, J., Nyberg, A.J. & Wright, P.M. (2021). Strategic human resource management and COVID-19: Emerging challenges and research opportunities. *Journal of Management Studies*, **58**(5), 1378–1382.

Collings, D.G., Mellahi, K. & Cascio, W.F. (2019). Global talent management and performance in multinational enterprises: A multilevel perspective. *Journal of Management*, **45**(2), 540–566.

Cooke, G.B., Chowhan, J., Mac Donald, K. & Mann, S. (2021). Talent management: Four "buying versus making" talent development approaches. *Personnel Review*. doi:10.1108/PR-08-2020-0621.

Crowley-Henry, M., O'Connor, E. & Al Ariss, A. (2018). Portrayal of skilled migrants' careers in business and management studies: A review of the literature and future research agenda. *European Management Review*, **15**(3), 375–394.

Dalal, R. & Akdere, M. (2018). Talent development: Status quo and future directions. *Industrial and Commercial Training*, **50**(6), 342–355.

Datta, S., Budhwar, P., Agarwal, U.A. & Bhargava, S. (2021). Impact of HRM practices on innovative behaviour: Mediating role of talent development climate in Indian firms. *The International Journal of Human Resource Management*. doi:10.1 080/09585192.2021.1973063.

DeLong, T.J. & Vijayaraghavan, V. (2003). Let's hear it for B players. *Harvard Business Review*, **81**(6), 96–102.

DeRue, D.S. & Wellman, N. (2009). Developing leaders via experience: The role of developmental challenge, learning orientation, and feedback. *Journal of Applied Psychology*, **94**(4), 859–875.

De Vos, A. & Dries, N. (2013). Applying a talent management lens to career management: The role of human capital composition and continuity. *The International Journal of Human Resource Management*, **24**(9), 1816–1831.

Dries, N. (2013). The psychology of talent management: A review and research agenda. *Human Resource Management Review*, **23**(4), 272–285.

Dries, N. & De Gieter, S. (2014). Information asymmetry in high potential programs: A potential risk for psychological contract breach. *Personnel Review*, **43**(1), 136–162.

Eisenhardt, K.M. & Martin, J.A. (2000). Dynamic capabilities: What are they? *Strategic Management Journal*, **21**(10–11), 1105–1121.

Feild, H.S. & Harris, S.G. (1991). Participants' frustrations in fast-track development programmes. *Leadership & Organization Development Journal*, **12**(4), 3–8.

Festing, M., Schäfer, L. & Scullion, H. (2013). Talent management in medium-sized German companies: An explorative study and agenda for future research. *The International Journal of Human Resource Management*, **24**(9), 1872–1893.

Finkelstein, L.M., Costanza, D.P. & Goodwin, G.F. (2019). Do your high potentials have potential? The impact of individual differences and designation on leader success. *Personnel Psychology*, **71**(1), 3–22.

Froese, F.J. (2020). Ready for global success? Strengths and weaknesses of Korean HRM. *Asian Business & Management*, **19**(2), 179–183.

Fulmer, R.M., Stumpf, S.A. & Bleak, J. (2009). The strategic development of high potential leaders. *Strategy & Leadership*, **37**(3), 17–22.

Gallardo-Gallardo, E., Nijs, S., Dries, N. & Gallo, P. (2015). Towards an understanding of talent management as a phenomenon-driven field using bibliometric and content analysis. *Human Resource Management Review*, **25**(3), 264–279.

Garavan, T.N., Carbery, R. & Rock, A. (2012). Mapping talent development: definition, scope and architecture. *European Journal of Training and Development*, **36**(1), 5–24.

Garavan, T.N., McCarthy, A., Lai, Y., Clarke, N., Carbery, R., Gubbins, C., ... Saunders, M.N.K. (2021). Putting the system back into training and firm performance research: A review and research agenda. *Human Resource Management Journal*, **31**(4), 870–903.

Garavan, T.N. & Morley, M. (1997). The socialization of high-potential graduates into the organization. *Journal of Managerial Psychology*, **12**(2), 118–137.

Garavan, T.N., Morley, M., Cross, C., Carbery, R. & Darcy, C. (2020). Tension in talent: A micro practice perspective on the implementation of high potential talent development programs in multinational corporations. *Human Resource Management*, **60**(2), 273–293.

Gorska, A.M., Kulicka, K., Staniszewska, Z. & Dobija, D. (2021). Deepening inequalities: What did COVID-19 reveal about the gendered nature of academic work? *Gender Work and Organization*, **28**(4), 1546–1561.

Grant, K., Garavan, T. & Mackie, R. (2020). Coaction interrupted: Logic contestations in the implementation of inter-organizational collaboration around talent management in the public sector in Scotland. *European Management Review*, **17**(4), 915–930.

Hakkarainen, K. & Paavola, S. (2007). From monological and dialogical to trialogical approaches to learning. Paper presented at the international workshop on Guided Construction of Knowledge in Classrooms.

Hartmann, E., Feisel, E. & Schober, H. (2010). Talent management of western MNCs in China: Balancing global integration and local responsiveness. *Journal of World Business*, **45**(2), 169–178.

Hedayati Mehdiabadi, A. & Li, J. (2016). Understanding talent development and implications for human resource development: An integrative literature review. *Human Resource Development Review*, **15**(3), 263–294.

Helfat, C.E. & Peteraf, M.A. (2003). The dynamic resource-based view: Capability lifecycles. *Strategic Management Journal*, **24**(10), 997–1010.

Hofstede, G. (1983). The cultural relativity of organizational practices and theories. *Journal of International Business Studies*, **14**(2), 75–89.

Holland, D. & Scullion, H. (2021). Towards a talent retention model: Mapping the building blocks of the psychological contract to the three stages of the acquisition process. *International Journal of Human Resource Management*, **32**(13), 2683–2728.

Hsu, I.C. (2008). Knowledge sharing practices as a facilitating factor for improving organizational performance through human capital: A preliminary test. *Expert Systems with Applications*, **35**(3), 1316–1326.

Inkpen, A.C. & Tsang, E.W.K. (2005). Social capital, networks, and knowledge transfer. *Academy of Management Review*, **30**(1), 146–165.

Johnson, K.R., Huang, T. & Doyle, A. (2019). Mapping talent development in tourism and hospitality: A literature review. *European Journal of Training and Development*, **43**(9), 821–841.

Jooss, S., Burbach, R. & Ruël, H. (2021). Examining talent pools as a core talent management practice in multinational corporations. *The International Journal of Human Resource Management*, **32**(11), 2321–2352.

Kanabar, J. & Fletcher, L. (2022). When does being in a talent pool reap benefits? The moderating role of narcissism. *Human Resource Development International*, **25**(4), 415–432.

King, K.A. (2016). The talent deal and journey. *Employee Relations*, **38**(1), 94–111.

Kodagoda, T. & Wijeratne, D. (2021). Talent development of Generation Y: Evidence from Sri Lanka. *Millennial Asia*. doi:10.1177/09763996211052402.

Kravariti, F. & Johnston, K. (2020). Talent management: A critical literature review and research agenda for public sector human resource management. *Public Management Review*, **22**(1), 75–95.

Kwon, K. & Jang, S. (2021). There is no good war for talent: A critical review of the literature on talent management. *Employee Relations: The International Journal*. doi:10.1108/ER-08-2020-0374.

Lehmann, S. (2009). Motivating talents in Thai and Malaysian service firms. *Human Resource Development International*, **12**(2), 155–169.

Lepak, D.P. & Snell, S.A. (1999). The human resource architecture: Toward a theory of human capital allocation and development. *The Academy of Management Review*, **24**(1), 31–48.

Liu, Y.P., Vrontis, D., Visser, M., Stokes, P., Smith, S., Moore, N., … Ashta, A. (2021). Talent management and the HR function in cross-cultural mergers and acquisitions: The role and impact of bi-cultural identity. *Human Resource Management Review*, **31**(3). doi:10.1016/j.hrmr.2020.100744.

Mäkelä, K., Björkman, I. & Ehrnrooth, M. (2010). How do MNCs establish their talent pools? Influences on individuals' likelihood of being labeled as talent. *Journal of World Business*, **45**(2), 134–142.

Malik, A.R. & Singh, P. (2014). 'High potential' programs: Let's hear it for 'B' players. *Human Resource Management Review*, **24**(4), 330–346.

McCall, M.W. (2010). Recasting leadership development. *Industrial and Organizational Psychology*, **3**(1), 3–19.

McDonnell, A., Skuza, A., Jooss, S. & Scullion, H. (2021). Tensions in talent identification: A multi-stakeholder perspective. *The International Journal of Human Resource Management*. doi:10.1080/09585192.2021.1976245.

McLean, G. (2006). *Organizational Development: Principles, Processes, Performance*. San Francisco: Berrett-Koehler.

McNulty, Y. & De Cieri, H. (2016). Linking global mobility and global talent management: The role of ROI. *Employee Relations*, **38**(1), 8–30.

Meyer, K.E. & Xin, K.R. (2018). Managing talent in emerging economy multinationals: Integrating strategic management and human resource management. *The International Journal of Human Resource Management*, **29**(11), 1827–1855.

Meyers, M.C. & van Woerkom, M. (2014). The influence of underlying philosophies on talent management: Theory, implications for practice, and research agenda. *Journal of World Business*, **49**(2), 192–203.

Muyia, M.H., Wekullo, C.S. & Nafukho, F.M. (2018). Talent development in emerging economies through learning and development capacity building. *Advances in Developing Human Resources*, **20**(4), 498–516.

Naim, M.F. & Lenka, U. (2017). Linking knowledge sharing, competency development, and affective commitment: Evidence from Indian Gen Y employees. *Journal of Knowledge Management*, **21**(4), 885–906.

Nelson, S. & Duxbury, L. (2020). Breaking the mold: Retention strategies for generations X and Y in a prototypical accounting firm. *Human Resource Development Quarterly*, **32**(2). https://doi-org.ucc.idm.oclc.org/10.1002/hrdq.21414.

Nijs, S., Gallardo-Gallardo, E., Dries, N. & Sels, L. (2014). A multidisciplinary review into the definition, operationalization, and measurement of talent. *Journal of World Business*, **49**(2), 180–191.

Nolan, C.T. & Garavan, T.N. (2016). Human resource development in SMEs: A systematic review of the literature. *International Journal of Management Reviews*, **18**(1), 85–107.

Nolan, C.T., Garavan, T.N. & Lynch, P. (2020). Multidimensionality of HRD in small tourism firms: A case study of the Republic of Ireland. *Tourism Management*, **79**, 104029. https://doi.org/10.1016/j.tourman.2019.104029.

Nonaka, I. & Takeuchi, H. (1995). *The Knowledge-Creating Company: How Japanese Companies Create the Dynamics of Innovation*. New York: Oxford University Press.

Pant, J.J. & Venkateswaran, V. (2019). Exploring millennial psychological contract expectations across talent segments. *Employee Relations: The International Journal*, **41**(4), 773–792.

Parry, E. & Urwin, P. (2021). Generational categories: A broken basis for human resource management research and practice. *Human Resource Management Journal*, **31**(4), 857–869.

Perna, M.C. (2021). Why millennials have a chance to create a more generation-agnostic workplace. *Forbes*. https://www.forbes.com/sites/markcperna/2021/07/20/why-millennials-have-a-chance-to-create-a-more-generation-agnostic-workplace/?sh=4bec7a2434a1.

Peterson, C. & Seligman, M.E.P. (2004). *Character Strengths and Virtues: A Handbook and Classification*. New York: Oxford University Press.

Rauch, A. & Hatak, I. (2016). A meta-analysis of different HR-enhancing practices and performance of small and medium sized firms. *Journal of Business Venturing*, **31**(5), 485–504.

Ready, D.A., Hill, L.A. & Conger, J.A. (2008). Winning the race for talent in emerging markets. *Harvard Business Review*, **86**(11), 63.

Rezaei, F. & Beyerlein, M. (2018). Talent development: A systematic literature review of empirical studies. *European Journal of Training and Development*, **42**(1/2), 75–90.

Ryan, R. M. & Deci, E. L. (2000). Self-determination theory and the facilitation of intrinsic motivation, social development, and well-being. *American Psychologist*, **55**(1), 68–78.

Sheehan, M. & Garavan, T.N. (2022). High-performance work practices and labour productivity: A six wave longitudinal study of UK manufacturing and service SMEs. *The International Journal of Human Resource Management*, **33**(16), 3353–3386.

Siikaniemi, L. (2012). Information pathways for the competence foresight mechanism in talent management framework. *European Journal of Training and Development*, **36**(1), 46–65.

Silzer, R. & Church, A.H. (2010). Identifying and assessing high potential talent: Current organizational practices. In Silzer, R. and Dowell, B.E. (eds.), *Strategy Driven Talent Management: A Leadership Imperative*. San Francisco: Jossey-Bass, pp. 213–280.

Sonnenberg, M., van Zijderveld, V. & Brinks, M. (2014). The role of talent-perception incongruence in effective talent management. *Journal of World Business*, **49**(2), 272–280.

Stahl, G., Björkman, I., Farndale, E., Morris, S.S., Paauwe, J., Stiles, P., Trevor, J. & Wright, P. (2012). Six principles of effective global talent management. *Sloan Management Review*, **53**(2), 25–42.

Staniscuaski, F., Kmetzsch, L., Zandona, E., Reichert, F., Soletti, R.C., Ludwig, Z.M.C., … de Oliveira, L. (2021). Gender, race and parenthood impact academic productivity during the COVID-19 pandemic: From survey to action. *Frontiers in Psychology*, **12**. doi:10.3389/fpsyg.2021.663252.

Sveiby, K.E. (2001). A knowledge-based theory of the firm to guide in strategy formulation. *Journal of Intellectual Capital*, **2**(4), 344–358.

Swailes, S. (2013). The ethics of talent management. *Business Ethics: A European Review*, **22**(1), 32–46.

Swailes, S. (2020). Responsible talent management: Towards guiding principles. *Journal of Organizational Effectiveness: People and Performance*, **7**(2), 221–236.

Thijssen, J.G.L. & van der Heijden, B.D. (2003). Evaporated talent? Problems with talent development during the career. *International Journal of Human Resources Development and Management*, **3**(2), 154–170.

Vaiman, V., Scullion, H. & Collings, D. (2012). Talent management decision making. *Management Decision*, **50**(5), 925–941.

Vo, A.N. (2009). Career development for host country nationals: A case of American and Japanese multinational companies in Vietnam. *The International Journal of Human Resource Management*, **20**(6), 1402–1420.

Weiner, B. (1985). An attributional theory of achievement-motivation and emotion. *Psychological Review*, **92**(4), 548–573.

Whelan, E. & Carcary, M. (2011). Integrating talent and knowledge management: Where are the benefits? *Journal of Knowledge Management*, **15**(4), 675–687.

Yli-Renko, H., Autio, E. & Sapienza, H.J. (2001). Social capital, knowledge acquisition, and knowledge exploitation in young technology-based firms. *Strategic Management Journal*, **22**(6–7), 587–613.

Yost, P.R. & Chang, G. (2009). Everyone is equal, but some are more equal than others. *Industrial and Organizational Psychology*, **2**(4), 442–445.

4. Accelerated development of organizational talent and executive coaching: a knowledge management perspective

Konstantin Korotov

ACCELERATED TALENT DEVELOPMENT IN ORGANIZATIONS

This chapter considers talent in line with the ideas of Vance and Vaiman (2008: 3), calling for attention to 'value, rarity, and inimitability' that employees and managers deploy in achieving their organization's competitive advantage. Managing talent means creating conditions for productive utilization of the current value that an employee can bring to the organization, and spotting and developing future potential in the interest of the organization and the human being. An important outcome of talent management efforts is the acquisition by the employee of the implicit and tacit knowledge in the organization that they want to use discretionarily in the interest of the organization (Vance & Vaiman, 2008). In the past two decades organizations in many parts of the world have been experimenting with ways to speed up the development of their management and employee talent in order to respond to current and anticipated pressures of markets and societies (e.g., Kets de Vries & Korotov, 2007; Korotov, 2008a, 2008b). They have been aiming at equipping organizational members with the skills, knowledge, attitudes, and behavioral patterns necessary for success in defined or potential future roles and tasks. Those future roles and tasks have been perceived to be more challenging and important than the ones currently held by the targeted organizational members. At the same time, preparation for the next steps in one's career has been combined with the expectation of ongoing success in one's current position (Abel, 2005). Stepping up to the next level was contingent upon doing extremely well in the current role, (over-)achieving the targets set, and demonstrating readiness for the next challenge. Accelerated development has also been a part of the organization's succession management efforts or a part of quick development in business as a response to the newly opening opportunities in a new geography (e.g. Korotov, 2008a, Khapova & Korotov, 2007). As a consequence of an expected promotion of an executive, knowledge needed to be transferred to their potential replacement, and the latter needed support in preparation for the new job.

Accelerated development means, contrary to the usual, more traditional developmental path, bypassing traditionally expected career steps, stretched over a longer period of time learning opportunities, and/or age-related developmental progression (Korotov, Khapova, & Arthur, 2010). Accelerated development is a necessity for organizations facing unprecedented growth, lack of qualified individuals in the internal or external labor markets, and significant pressures from other organizations that are ready to 'poach' talented executives and employees and offer them even higher levels of responsibility and remuneration. Organizations also respond with accelerated development initiatives to the individuals engaged in career entrepreneurship, i.e., those who make alternative career investments in order to enjoy quicker returns in terms of career growth and progression (Korotov et al., 2010).

While most of the above reasons for accelerated development of organizational talent are still relevant, the motives for quicker support for people's ability to embrace new and larger responsibilities have become broader. For example, the content of the job or role may change drastically without an advancement along a career ladder, or the person brought into the organization may be expected to get up to speed with their role much quicker than before. The organization may, for example, think about ways of helping an employee or manager returning from child-caring leave (e.g. Fitzenberger, Steffes, & Strittmatter, 2016) to get up to speed with the latest changes in the company and acquire knowledge needed for success in the environment that may have changed from the time before the leave. Another example may be an organizational restructuring, as a consequence of which a manager becomes responsible for a significantly large unit composed of several previously independent departments each with their own head. With the developments occurring at the time of writing this chapter, such as the COVID-19 pandemic, increase in demand for societal fairness, intolerance towards 'woke-washing' (Dowell & Jackson, 2020), additional challenges of being more compassionate and meeting the emotional needs of the employees (e.g. Kauffman, 2020), and growing expectations to lead organizations towards a better world for all stakeholders, organizations face the need to support executives with the new competencies. Those skills, behaviors and attitudes may not have been part of the previously developed management competencies portfolios, but they become crucial for legitimate claiming and executing of leadership roles under the new expectations of organizations and societies. New developmental dimensions go beyond the cognitive functioning of an executive and involve their affective responses to external events and stimuli (e.g. Vance & Vaiman, 2008).

With another development taking place at the time of writing this chapter, the so called 'great resignation,' or mass departure of employees from their organizations in the wake of the COVID-19 pandemic (e.g. Cook, 2021), the topic of accelerated talent development has become even more acute. Resignation of mid-career employees and managers is associated with organizational fear of losing critical organizational knowledge (e.g. Woods, 2021). Massive movement to hybrid (onsite and online) or fully remote ways of working has raised questions of the type of leadership required to make the most of the talents and knowledge of organizational members (e.g. Hopkins & Figaro, 2021), forcing companies to seek ways to help managers adjust quickly to the new demands. Organizational socialization (often referred to as on-boarding by HR professionals), a transformative process of helping a newcomer quickly gain tacit and implicit knowledge and become fully efficient in their functioning in the new organization (Katz & Kahn, 1978; Bradt, 2010; Gruman & Saks, 2011, Caldwell & Peters, 2018) has become further complicated by the decreased or totally non-existent opportunities for face-to-face contact, leading organizations to rethink the way they handle it, including knowledge acquisition by the incoming workforce (Blöndal, 2021, Korotov, 2021a). Executives without previous experience of starting in a new organization without physical contact with their subordinates may need to obtain knowledge about their organizations and people in a manner different from what they have been accustomed to before.

With the variety of individual needs of managers for whom development must take place at an accelerated pace, and due to increased pressure to make people effective in their changing roles quickly, many of the traditionally used methods (e.g. training program, executive courses at business schools, rotational assignments, expatriation to smaller markets for obtaining needed knowledge and experience, shadowing and acting in the shoes of a higher level manager, and even simple observation) are not deemed any longer suitable. Hence the turn to personalized, just-in-time, developmental support in the form of executive coaching.

EXECUTIVE COACHING

Executive coaching is a professional intervention aiming to help executives to formulate and specify their goals, explore ways of achieving them and overcome hurdles in the process of realizing them (Kilburg, 2000; Korotov et al., 2012). Professional coaching has its talent management origins in remedial activities for those who did not meet organizational expectations. Nowadays, it is seldom viewed as a remedial tool, but rather as a developmental instrument

(Kets de Vries et al., 2016), although it can still be offered as a corrective measure or a consolation package for managers facing an organizational impasse (e.g. Reynolds, 2012). The purpose of coaching as a developmental tool is not only about helping an executive be more successful, but also often to support the latter in their ability to mobilize efforts for change or to implement already agreed upon and approved change efforts (Korotov, 2010).

Coaching has been growing in popularity as a stand-alone intervention or as an amplifier of other developmental efforts (Frankovelgia & Riddle, 2010). It caters to the specific needs of a particular executive, most often in the context of a particular organization (Ely et al., 2010). The exceptions to the context of the specific organization are coaching sessions offered as part of educational programs, such as MBAs, outplacements activities, or sessions initiated privately by a coachee looking for support not related to their current job.

From the perspective of knowledge management, coaching can be seen as a tool for guiding the individual executive's efforts in obtaining tacit knowledge, turning implicit organizational knowledge into explicit knowledge for the executive concerned, and gaining insights into the reasons for things happening in the organization. In addition, coaching helps executives obtain knowledge about themselves. Day, Harrison, and Halpin (2009) and Day et al. (2014), for example, claim that leadership development can be examined as an unfolding progressive process that starts with an early age influence of critical caretakers and continues with acquisition of leadership skills. Building on this position, Korotov (2017) suggests that executive coaching can be a suitable intervention for discovery, processing, and making sense of the data about a manager's key developmental moments (for example, in the childhood or youth of the executive). Kets de Vries and Korotov (2016) recommend to executives and coaches working with them to obtain an understanding of how their past can impact today's behaviors, and to what extent corrections in perceptions, attitudes or response patterns may be needed.

Coaching literature often views the coaching process as a quasi-research activity in which the role of the coach is to help the coachee engage in a discovery process (e.g. De Haan, 2019; Korotov, 2021b). Coaching sessions and work associated with tasks completed by managers based on those sessions generate data. These data are further processed by the executive to form their view of the current situation, available options, specific action and their consequences. In addition to guiding the coachee to gather and analyze information and search for organizational data helpful for the manager in their work, coaching is about creating an environment for the executive to gain insights. Insights are moments of understanding by the coachee of what they are searching for or answering the questions they have. The literature considers coachee insights to be a successful coaching outcome (Lightfoot, 2019).

Research on what is really happening behind the closed doors of a coaching session often relies on reported coaching cases or coaching notes. The latter serve as an access to what is normally considered an extremely difficult domain for research—the inner issues and challenges of senior executives (Hambrick, 2007; Kets de Vries et al., 2016). Coaches are encouraged to keep coaching notes for maintaining continuity between the sessions and for use in a de-identified form in supervision—reflections on their practice with another coach (Moyes, 2009; Korotov, 2021b). Through such notes and cases—written accounts of coaching experience—we can understand how coaching, among other things, guides knowledge acquisition and sensemaking as part of accelerated development (Korotov et al., 2012; De Haan, 2019; Louis & Diochon, 2019; Korotov, Bernhardt, & Radeke, 2021, Korotov, 2021b). The section below is based on the coaching notes taken by the author in his role as a coach for a senior executive in a large organization.

An Example of an Executive Coaching Engagement for Accelerated Development of a Senior Manager

This coaching assignment was initiated by the HR department of a large financial institution based on the specific request of Alexander, a senior executive with the aim of supporting a recently hired top manager, Victor. The latter had been in the organization for a few months already, and the formal onboarding process was over. However, the hiring executive still thought that Victor was not yet fully integrated in the company and thus not fully realizing his talents.

Alexander brought in Victor from a competing organization with a strikingly different corporate culture. However, he had worked with Victor earlier, and thus personally trusted him. The hiring executive was genuinely interested in supporting the new hire in finding his way in the company.

Alexander had worked with an executive coach previously, and had found the experience to be beneficial for his own developmental needs. He thus recommended to Victor an engagement with an executive coach with the purpose of getting external support in finding his way and establishing himself in the organization. Alexander had also expressed his willingness to provide further support from his part mentoring Victor, while simultaneously acting as his direct boss. Victor did not object to the proposed intervention, and HR got involved to organize the process.

Victor had neither worked with an executive coach nor used help of professional psychologist or counsel before. The HR department briefed him about coaching as a professional service and explained the process of establishing the coaching relationship. Victor, the coachee, was offered an opportunity to have so called 'chemistry' meetings with three potential coaches picked up by HR from their lists of external coaches. The purpose of a 'chemistry' session is to let the would-be partners (coachee and coach) assess mutual perception of compatibility for the purposes of development. While the organization maintained a pool of internal HR professionals with coaching qualifications, it was decided that for the purposes of this assignment an external person, someone familiar with but independent from the organization should be chosen. The reason for going for an external coach was that the coachee would feel more comfortable in exploring his sensitive issues with someone who is not embedded in internal organizational processes or politics. After 'chemistry' sessions, Victor expressed his preferences, and the preferred coach confirmed his willingness to work with the coachee. A formal contract for coaching services was signed between the organization and the coach. The contract stipulated six face-to-face coaching sessions of 60 minutes each for the next four months (roughly, one coaching session every three weeks).

Session 1
The first session was dedicated to the refinement of the contract, although not the legal one, between the organization (acting as a client) and the coach (acting as the service provider), but rather the working contract between Victor (the coachee, or service recipient), and the coach (service provider). During this first session, the coachee tried to formulate his coaching request. Given that the engagement had been initiated by his boss, it was important for the coach to work with Victor on identifying how the latter saw his own agenda when working with the coach. Although Victor had been briefed about what executive coaching is by HR and had discussed coaching as a developmental service for executives in the 'chemistry' sessions, he went again through an exploration of what the service could offer him, the role expectations, as well as confidentiality principles and ways of assessing progress. It should be noted that in this particular engagement it was agreed that no feedback would be provided by the coach to the organization, while the coachee was free to discuss his coaching experience with whoever he wanted to.

Developmental approaches may not be familiar to executives invited to or forced to use them, therefore it is important to help the manager in question understand the rules of the engagement and their role in the process. In the case presented here, the boss who initiated the intervention had been familiar with the process based on his own experience. Victor, the coachee, although accepting the opinion of his superior and HR, still needed to obtain his own comfort with and trust in the process.

The session clarified that Victor was responsible for the choices ahead of him, that he would need to find out what he may not know, and that he would need to stage experiments as he went through his developmental journey. The broad goals of the coaching engagement were defined as being accepted by the organization as a legitimate and trustworthy leader (as seen by the subordinates), and as being accepted by the top leadership circle in the organization (as seen by his superior and, broadly, the rest of the top executives).

During the session it was also agreed upon that a certain portion of each session would be dedicated to the analysis of what was going on in the professional life of the coachee at the moment. The coachee has also asked the coach for recommended resources (e.g. readings, videos, or podcasts) on topics of relationships, people management, and leadership. The coachee agreed to carry out an 'audit' of his understanding of the organization for the next session. He would take note of the developments in the organization or behaviors of the people that would make him ask 'What is going on here?' The coach also asked Victor to take notice of his emotional reactions to instances making him ask this question.

Session 2

In the second session, the coach asked Victor to compare visible differences between the organizational culture of his new employer and his previous organization. Special attention was paid to the differences that felt most irritating. The coach then invited Victor to go deeper into the underlying reasons for artifacts and observable behaviors, to encourage exploration of values and assumptions of the company. A list of such values and assumptions was produced. Victor went through the latter, identifying points that he had enough validation for, and the ones where he would need additional information or observation in order to confirm them.

With the help of the coach, he looked at some of the internal approval practices and juxtaposed them with the formal organizational structure—the explicit formal division, grouping and coordination of activities in the organization. Discrepancies or inconsistencies between observed processes and the formal structure opened the door to analysis of organizational power and politics. Victor worked with the coach on the question of dependencies that existed between him and his stakeholders. Hypotheses were developed for further verification by Victor. Methods for such verification were explored (e.g. observing behaviors at formal meetings and social events, addressing long-term members of the organization with 'naïve' questions, and directly asking his boss, using the assignment from the coach as a potential excuse). Victor was encouraged by the coach to develop a version of his own power map in the organization, indicating his connections and dependencies (roughly following Clark, 2012).

Victor also discussed with the coach the visible aspects of organizational culture that caused discomfort for him. The coach probed into Victor's understanding of his role in adjusting to and maintaining the current organizational culture, or explicit or implicit expectations of him to bring changes to the company and its culture. The topic of further exploration of the expectations held by the key stakeholders of Victor was left as part of the homework for him. The latter would involve looking into employee sentiment (as expressed through various climate assessments), and a mentoring conversation with his boss.

Session 3
Victor reported a better understanding of some of the previously surprising behaviors and relationships in the organization based on the exploratory work done after the previous session. He explained his assumptions in verification work and its findings, and he reported on clarification of expectations. Some of the findings related to established process and procedures revealed ingrained reasons that no longer made sense and allowed Victor to change them directly or involve the stakeholders who could change them. At the same time, he found out that some of the processes involved power struggles beyond his direct influence. In a particular case he received a clear signal to stay away from the issue of interest due to a long-standing feud between powerful organizational players.

The question of political sensitivity of organizational issues has naturally led to the exploration of individual preferences of the coachee. With the help of the Big 5 model (McCrae & Costa, 1997), and based on the self-assessment completed by Victor as part of the preparation for the session, the coachee and the coach discussed the influence of personality preference of Victor on his interpretation of the organizational events and his interactions with key stakeholders. The discussion led to Victor's interpretation of some findings from the employee survey results. For example, his high level of Agreeableness, a Big Five personality dimension showing propensity to cooperate with and possibly defer to others, could be interpreted as not standing for the interests of the units reporting to him vis-à-vis aggressive colleagues from the other parts of the organization. The expectation of the people to be protected by their boss seemed to be frustrated. Victor, who believed that he was a good fighter for his people, decided to pay attention to the question of perception by his people.

Session 4
During this session the question of relationships with senior members of the organization was raised. Victor wanted to explore what he needed to know and do in order to feel trusted and accepted by the top leadership circle. The coach offered an academic model of trust (e.g. Colquitt, Scott, & LePine, 2007) to start exploration of the topic. The discussion looked at the trustworthiness of Victor based on his perceived competence, personal integrity and benevolence (supportive behaviors towards others), and then it quickly went to the exploration of the propensity to trust (Schoorman, Mayer, & Davis, 2007) by the critical members of the top leadership circle.

Building on his previous exploration of his own personality and its influence on the relationships with others, Victor developed hypotheses related
to possible personality traits of key members of the top leadership circle and
agreed to test them further. The coach reminded the coachee about the powerful resource in his possession, namely, the mentoring relationships with his
boss, Alexander, and the expressed interest of the latter to support Victor in his
development within the organization.

The session continued with a discussion of making the best use of mentoring
relationships and opportunities. The coach probed into possible reservations
about the relationships between Victor and his boss and mentor. Some of the
reservations were scrutinized for their rationality. The coachee has expressed
his willingness to explicitly discuss with Alexander hypotheses stemming
from the discussion in this session.

Session 5

Victor was very enthusiastic about the mentoring discussion he had had with
Alexander. Apparently, Alexander was happy to see that Victor had understood
the importance of building productive relationships with the key leaders, and
that he had identified potential barriers on the way to develop those relationships. Alexander had spent a considerable amount of time explaining to Victor
some of the not-so-obvious aspects of relationships between top managers,
including existing tensions and disagreements. From time to time he referred
to moments in organizational history that had not been known to Victor.

As Victor became aware of some of those aspects, he developed new
insights into the comments received in the employee surveys, including the
frustration about not protecting people under his management explored with
the coach in Session 3. Victor had executed some personnel decisions made
above him without having gone deeply into the events behind them, as they
had taken place before his arrival in the organization. While rational and
not too difficult for him, those events and subsequent consequences had had
a much stronger emotional impact on the employees.

The coachee decided to use the session with the coach to process again the
discussion with his boss and identify actionable steps. In particular, Victor
raised the options of establishing informal contacts (e.g. by joining his boss
for lunch with a critical top manager), asking for a formal discussion (e.g. on
the interaction between different parts of the organization), or using HR in
initiating a structured 360-degree review assessment involving the top leaders
as respondents.

The coach invited Victor to reassess his power map and try to draw power
maps of the key stakeholders, trying to assess their dependencies and needs.
The coach also recommended trying to assess how Victor could support the
people into whose inner circle he wanted to be accepted in achieving their

organizational goals. One of Victor's spontaneous reactions was reference to the type of work and specific competencies that the people under his management possessed. As his homework, he wanted to look at how he could better leverage the competencies and work of his subordinates to influence the critical top leaders. Victor realized that he may not have yet developed a full picture about the people below him.

Session 6
This was the final session in the contracted intervention. The coachee reported on his latest progress, his attempts to understand better the employees, including some of the key players further down the hierarchy. He also mentioned spontaneous emotionally-charged feedback he had recently received from his boss after a couple of critical incidents involving him. Victor mentioned that he reacted to the feedback in a more resilient manner than he probably would have reacted without the coaching sessions behind his back. He said that his understanding of the organizational history, current political trends, and personality traits of people involved had allowed him to take the useful elements of the feedback while not wasting his energy on the not-so-professional packaging.

With this reference to the usefulness of engagement in coaching, the coach asked Victor to summarize the outcomes of the coaching process. The coach suggested that the results of this exercise could be used by Victor in reporting back to the organization and his direct boss on the coaching engagement. The coach reminded about the broader goals of the coaching engagement agreed upon at the start of the process: acceptance by the subordinates and by senior leaders in the organization. Looking back at the work done during the coaching sessions, Victor identified the following topics that guided his work on finding his place in the company:

- Understanding the organization, its culture, and its politics.
- Understanding self and the influence of personal idiosyncrasies on relationship with others.
- Understanding the talents, limitations, and needs of subordinates.
- Understanding the talents, limitations, and needs of superiors.
- Understanding interactions between self and other stakeholders and assessing tactics for establishing relationships.

The session concluded with the coachee's taking stock of his progress with the subordinates and with the people above him, as well as work in progress and specific areas where further efforts were necessary. The coachee also mentioned a few further items on the developmental agenda.

COACHING AS A KNOWLEDGE MANAGEMENT TOOL

From the discussion above and the example of a coaching engagement provided we can see potential areas where the coach can help a manager or employee in need of accelerated development to specifically seek data, analyze patterns, and possibly develop insights.

Coaching can guide the coachee to seek implicit knowledge and turn it into explicit knowledge for themselves (e.g. Percy & Dow, 2021). Some of the areas for coaching as knowledge management are listed below.

Understanding the Expectations

One of the areas of discovery can be a better understanding of the coachee's role expectations as held by their superiors and subordinates. The coach can suggest a variety of tactics for getting knowledge about such expectations. For example, the coachee can approach the critical stakeholders directly for a discussion or try to interpret the results of a 360-degree survey or another employee's attitudes research. The coach can engage the coachee in the stakeholder analysis with an attempt to become clear on what others need from them. Alternatively, the coach may suggest a visioning exercise in which the coachee works out their own view of the role. The coach then encourages the coachee to check out the perceptions of such expectations by the stakeholders involved. Another method used by advanced coaches in high-level engagements is live 360-degree feedback. Authorized by the coachee and supported by the HR function of the organization, the coach conducts one-to-one personal meetings with the key stakeholders of the coachee in order to gather first-hand impressions about the functioning of a particular executive.

The results are then presented to the coachee and discussed with them so that the latter can decide if any actions from their side is needed.

Understanding the Stakeholder Landscape

The coach encourages the coachee to explore the needs, pressures, and limitations of the key stakeholders. The coachee understands better the power dynamics in the organization, and develops sensitivity to the specific needs of particular individuals in their surroundings. In rare cases of working with an internal coach, someone who is also an employee of the organization (e.g. Korotov, 2010), the coach may provide direct information about the political situation in the company. With external coaches, the coachee usually gets an impulse to go and explore the relationships among key players. The coach may, for example, encourage the employee to identify the sources for the required knowledge, for example, a mentor. Understanding stakeholders involves looking in all directions around the coachee—bosses, peers, and subordinates. With the latter, for example, the coach could suggest conducting an audit of current skills and attitudes of the employees.

Knowledge about Organizational Culture

The coach encourages the coachee to observe cultural artifacts and to inquire into the reasons behind their existence. If the role expectations of the manager include changes in the culture, the coach may specifically work with them on assessing the strength of culture, identifying subcultures, and looking into the barriers for change. The findings about the differences between the previously experienced organizational culture and the current ones can help the coachee identify what they may be taking for granted based on their past experience that is no longer relevant. As a specific case, national culture context can be the area in which the executive concerned needs to obtain additional knowledge in order to choose appropriate behaviors in a cultural setting different from their country of origin or previous expatriate experiences.

Knowledge about Self and Aspects of One's Identity

A critical issue in the process of accelerated development is often not just a set of skills or knowledge that an employee or manager has to master, but rather the development of a new identity, a new sense of self that is claimed by the manager, and that is supported by the organization and people around the individual. Taking on a new role (e.g. Hill, 1992) has been shown to require a significant change in one's professional identity. When working on a new identity, as suggested by Ibarra (2003, 2004), individuals need to start doing new things, start developing new networks, and start telling a new story about themselves. The role of the coach is to support the executive in their knowledge of the current state and the expected future state of how they answer to the 'Who am I?' question in the context of their changing professional role. The starting points for developing knowledge about self can be examination of one's personality preferences, comparisons of role expectations, excursions into the person's past, or perceptions held by others.

Technical Knowledge

While a coach may be less helpful in supporting the coachee with gaining the critical technical knowledge, they still may help the coachee identify areas where they may need to get up to speed. The coach may help the coachee prioritize between the areas where they need to brush up or obtain from scratch what they know about technology, customers, products, etc. The role of the coach is to support the coachee in deciding how much they can rely on others in providing technical advice or decisions. While the coach may not be able to tell the coachee whether to trust a senior engineer on their recommendation of solutions, they can still discuss what constitutes trust for the coachee, and what the latter should do in order to evaluate the trustworthiness of the existing expert. In some areas, however, the coach can take the consultant approach (Carey, Philippon, & Cummings, 2011), particularly when supporting the coachee with models and tools associated with leadership behaviors, such as running team-meetings, responding to employee uncertainty-driven anxieties, bringing bad news, etc. (Korotov, 2017). The coach can also provide the coachee with resources, such as readings or videos.

Knowledge about the Group and Its Functioning

As a special case we can consider knowledge about the group, its members, and its functioning. This is a special case of coaching, often referred to as group or team coaching. The latter, as argued by Kets de Vries (2005) and DeRue and Myers (2014) can support leadership groups and teams in reflecting on their collaboration. With the help of a coach, the group can explore the implicit assumptions or expectations from its members. By making the assumptions explicit, the group can proceed to discussion of possible action points for increasing its effectiveness.

CONCLUSION

Meyers and van Woerkom (2014) identified four possible talent management philosophies that stem from categorizing talent along two dimensions: exclusivity (rareness)–inclusivity (universalism) and stability–developability. The coaching program described in this chapter was certainly embedded in looking at talent as something that can be enhanced and advanced based on obtaining tacit knowledge about the organization, its members, and self. From the organizational perspective, offering coaching to the executive mentioned in the chapter was seen as a special case of supporting someone who is otherwise exceptionally valuable for the organization with the exclusive (and often resource-intense) offering of a developmental intervention. Coaching provides opportunities for personalized accelerated development of talent. By guiding the coachee towards asking questions and developing hypotheses, obtaining data, and analyzing them, coaching offers an executive an opportunity to generate and assess options for achieving their goals. In particular, coaching helps the executive gain knowledge about the expectations of them in the role, the needs and circumstances of the stakeholders, and peculiarities of the organizational culture. Furthermore, coaching helps the executive obtain or accentuate knowledge about self and juxtapose it to the requirements of the situation. The executive gets an understanding of what they need to keep doing, stop doing, or continue doing and evaluate the costs of such identity transformation. Coaching can also help an executive assess what kind of technical knowledge they may need to obtain in order to become quickly proficient or at least comfortable in their new role. While not discussed in detail in this chapter, group coaching can help a leadership group know how it functions and what may need to be changed in the collective and individual behaviors of its members.

Given the resource-intensity of using coaching as a developmental tool, it may be tempting to consider that this type of talent management intervention is reserved for the special cases of employees who are considered particularly valuable for the organization and who already stand out from the rest of the organizational talent. This view would be leaning towards the exclusivity end of the rareness–universalism dimension in accordance with the classification of Meyers and van Woerkom (2014). Nevertheless, coaching principles have been recently expanded beyond use in executive coaching, for example, to peer coaching (Parker, Hall, & Kram, 2008), in-house employee coaching (Von der Heydt, 2021), or coaching as a leadership style (Hicks & McCracken, 2013). Such an expansion provides opportunities for helping employees gain tacit organizational knowledge and develop their cognitive and affective responses at various organizational levels. For managers or employees acting in a coaching capacity, it provides an opportunity to play an important role in accelerating talent development through being a partner in knowledge creation and dissemination.

REFERENCES

Abel, D. (2005). Leadership education as a moving target. *International Journal of Leadership Education*, **1**(1), 9–21.

Blöndal, S.V. (2021). Becoming an insider in a virtual environment: Key elements of successful remote onboarding. Master's thesis, University of Jyväskylä, Finland. https://jyx.jyu.fi/handle/123456789/76281.

Bradt, G. (2010). Onboarding: An act of transformational leadership. *People & Strategy*, **33**(2), 4–6.

Caldwell, C. & Peters, R. (2018). New employee onboarding: Psychological contracts and ethical perspectives. *Journal of Management Development*, **37**(1), 27–39.

Carey, W., Philippon, D.J. & Cummings, G.G. (2011). Coaching models for leadership development: An integrative review. *Journal of Leadership Studies*, **5**(1), 51–69.

Clark, D. (2012). A campaign strategy for your career. *Harvard Business Review*, **90**(11), 131–134.

Colquitt, J.A., Scott, B.A. & LePine, J.A. (2007). Trust, trustworthiness, and trust propensity: A meta-analytic test of their unique relationships with risk taking and job performance. *Journal of Applied Psychology*, **92**(4), 909–927.

Cook, I. (2021). Who is driving the great resignation? *HBR Online*, September 15. https://hbr.org/2021/09/who-is-driving-the-great-resignation.

Day, D.V., Fleenor, J.V., Atwater, L.E., Sturm, R.E. & McKee, R.A. (2014). Advances in leader and leadership development: A review of 25 years of research and theory. *The Leadership Quarterly*, **25**(1), 63–82.

Day, D.V., Harrison, M.M. & Halpin, S.M. (2009). *An Integrative Theory of Leadership Development: Connecting Adult Development, Identity, and Expertise*. New York: Psychology Press.

De Haan, E. (2019). *Critical Moments in Executive Coaching*. New York: Routledge.

DeRue, D.S. & Myers, C.G. (2014). Leadership development: A review and agenda for future research. In Day, D. (ed.), *The Oxford Handbook of Leadership and Organizations*. New York: Oxford University Press, pp. 832–855.

Dowell, E. & Jackson, M. (2020). 'Woke-washing' your company won't cut it. *HBR Online*. https://hbr.org/2020/07/woke-washing-your-company-wont-cut-it.

Ely, K., Boyce, L.A., Nelson, J.K., Zaccaro, S.J., Hernez-Broome, G. & Whyman, W. (2010). Evaluating leadership coaching: A review and integrated framework. *The Leadership Quarterly*, **21**(4), 585–599.

Fitzenberger, B., Steffes, S. & Strittmatter, A. (2016). Return-to-job during and after parental leave. *The International Journal of Human Resource Management*, **27**(8), 803–831.

Frankovelgia, C.C. & Riddle, D.D. (2010). Leadership coaching. In Van Velson, E., McCauley, C.D., & Ruderman, M. (eds.), *The Center for Creative Leadership Handbook of Leadership Development*, 3rd edition. San Francisco: Jossey-Bass, pp. 125–146.

Gruman, J. A. & Saks, A. M. (2011). Socialization preferences and intentions: Does one size fit all? *Journal of Vocational Behavior*, **79**(2), 419–427.

Hambrick, D.C. (2007). Upper echelons theory: An update. *Academy of Management Review*, **32**(2), 334–343.

Hicks, R. & McCracken, J. (2013). *Coaching as a Leadership Style*. Abingdon: Routledge.

Hill, L. (1992). *Becoming a Manager*. Boston, MA: Harvard Business School Press.

Hopkins, J.C. & Figaro, K.A. (2021). The great resignation: An argument for hybrid leadership. *International Journal of Business and Management Research*, **9**(4), 393–400.

Ibarra, H. (2003). *Working Identity: Unconventional Strategies for Reinventing Your Career*. Boston, MA: Harvard Business School Press.

Ibarra, H. (2004). *Identity Transitions, Possible Selves, Liminality, and the Dynamic of Career Change*. INSEAD Working Paper 2004/98/OB.

Katz, D. & Kahn, R.L. (1978). *The Social Psychology of Organizations*. New York: Wiley.

Kauffman, C. (2020). Without compassion resilient leaders will fall short. *HBR Online*. https://hbr.org/2020/08/without-compassion-resilient-leaders-will-fall-short.

Kets de Vries, M. (2005). Leadership group coaching in action: The Zen of creating high performance teams. *The Academy of Management Executive*, **19**(1), 61–76.

Kets de Vries, M. & Korotov, K. (2007). Creating transformational executive education programs. *Academy of Management Learning & Education*, **6**(3), 375–387.

Kets de Vries, M. & Korotov, K. (2016). The clinical paradigm: A primer for personal change. In Kets de Vries, M.F.R., Korotov, K., Florent-Treacy, E. & Rook, C. (eds.), *Coach and Couch: The Psychology of Making Better Leaders*, 2nd edition. Basingstoke: Palgrave Macmillan, pp. 19–28.

Kets de Vries, M.F.R., Korotov, K., Florent-Treacy, E. & Rook, C. (eds.) (2016). *Coach and Couch: The Psychology of Making Better Leaders*, 2nd edition. Basingstoke: Palgrave Macmillan.

Khapova, S.N. & Korotov, K. (2007). Dynamics of Western career attributes in the Russian context. *Career Development International*, **12**(1), 68–85.

Kilburg, R.R. (2000). *Executive Coaching: Developing Managerial Wisdom in a World of Chaos*. Washington, DC: American Psychological Association.

Korotov, K. (2008a). Citius, altius, fortius: Challenges of accelerated development of leadership talent in the Russian context. *Organizational Dynamics*, **37**(3), 277–287.

Korotov, K. (2008b). Accelerated development of organizational talent. In Vaiman, V. & Vance, C.M. (eds.), *Smart Talent Management: Building Knowledge Assets for Competitive Advantage*. Cheltenham, UK and Northampton, MA, USA: Edward Elgar Publishing, pp. 139–157.

Korotov, K. (2010). Executive coaches in organizations: Insiders from outside. In Vaiman, V. (ed.), *Talent Management of Knowledge Workers: Embracing the Non-Traditional Workforce*. Basingstoke: Palgrave Macmillan, pp. 180–196.

Korotov, K. (2017). Coaching for leadership development. In Bachkirova, T., Spence, G., & Drake, D. (eds.), *The Sage Handbook of Coaching*. Los Angeles: Sage, pp. 139–158.

Korotov, K. (2021a). Bringing company culture to the home office. *Forbes*, March 29. https://www.forbes.com/sites/esmtberlin/2021/03/29/bringing-company-culture-to -the-home-office/.

Korotov, K. (2021b). Executives and career shocks: Observations from coaching practice. *Career Development International*, **26**(4), 582–595.

Korotov, K., Bernhardt, A. & Radeke, J. (eds.) (2021). *Cases in Executive Coaching: From the Annals of the ESMT Coaching Colloquia*, 2nd edition. Berlin: ESMT.

Korotov, K., Kets de Vries, M.F.R., Florent-Treacy, E. & Bernhardt, A. (eds.) (2012). *Tricky Coaching: Difficult Cases in Leadership Coaching*. Basingstoke: Palgrave Macmillan.

Korotov, K., Khapova, S. & Arthur, M. (2010). Career entrepreneurship. *Organizational Dynamics*, **40**(2), 127–135.

Lightfoot, I. (2019). Insight events in coaching sessions. *International Journal of Evidence-Based Coaching and Mentoring*, **S13**, 94–101.

Louis, D. & Diochon, P.F. (eds.) (2019). *Complex Situations in Coaching: A Critical Case-Based Approach*. Abingdon: Routledge.

McCrae, R.R. & Costa, P.T., Jr. (1997). Personality trait structure as a human universal. *American Psychologist*, **52**(5), 509–516.

Meyers, M.C. & van Woerkom, M. (2014). The influence of underlying philosophies on talent management: Theory, implications for practice, and research agenda. *Journal of World Business*, **49**(2), 192–203.

Moyes, B. (2009). Literature review of coaching supervision. *International Coaching Psychology Review*, 4(2), 162–173.

Parker, P., Hall, D.T. & Kram, K.E. (2008). Peer coaching: A relational process for accelerating career learning. *Academy of Management Learning and Education*, **7**, 487–503.

Percy, W. & Dow, K. (2021). The coaching dance: Beyond Nonaka – knowledge management in post-Tayloristic Confucian China. In Hooke, A., Vachharadjani, H., Kaur, H. & Dow, K. (eds.), *Emerging Business and Trade Opportunities in Oceania and China*. Hershey, PA: IGI Global, pp. 199–228.

Reynolds, M. (2012). Can you coach around a dead end? In Korotov, K., Kets de Vries, M.F.R., Florent-Treacy, E. & Bernhardt, A. (eds.) (2012). *Tricky Coaching: Difficult Cases in Leadership Coaching*. Basingstoke: Palgrave Macmillan, pp. 139–145.

Schoorman, F.D., Mayer, R.C. & Davis, J.H. (2007). An integrative model of organizational trust: Past, present, and future. *Academy of Management Review*, **32**(2), 344–354.

Vance, C.M. & Vaiman, V. (2008). Smart talent management: On the powerful amalgamation of talent management and knowledge management. In Vaiman, V. & Vance, C.M. (eds.), *Smart Talent Management: Building Knowledge Assets for Competitive Advantage*. Cheltenham, UK and Northampton, MA, USA: Edward Elgar Publishing, pp. 1–15.

Von der Heydt, A. (2021). An in-house coaching model & implementation plan to onboard and integrate new employees more successfully with managers as coaches. Doctoral dissertation, Northeastern University.

Woods, A. (2021). The great resignation doesn't have to threaten your DE&I efforts. *HBR Online*, September 1. https://hbr.org/2021/09/the-great-resignation-doesnt -have-to-threaten-your-dei-efforts.

5. Employee learning and development from the perspective of strategic HRM

Saba Colakoglu, Yunhyung Chung and Ying Hong

The capability to acquire, capture, unleash, and mobilize knowledge is one of the most important strategic and dynamic capabilities that can help organizations to gain and sustain a competitive advantage (Barley, Treem, & Kuhn, 2018; Buckley & Carter, 2004; Kogut & Zander, 1993; Takeuchi & Nonaka, 2002). Indeed, a recent survey conducted by Deloitte reported that business leaders recognize knowledge management as one of the top three factors that influence company success and performance (Behme & Becker, 2021). In today's rapidly changing global environment, exploring and exploiting knowledge assets and increasing knowledge flows and stocks within an organization have become a business imperative for all organizational leaders (Zahra & George, 2002). However, effective knowledge management—acquisition and generation of new ideas and knowledge, mobilization and promotion of those ideas and knowledge within the organization, and ultimate commercialization of ideas through innovation—does not materialize spontaneously. It requires intentionality with systematic planning and strategy pertaining to managing talent. Because organizational knowledge mostly resides in the minds of its talent pool and the social relationships that exist among its members (Subramaniam & Youndt, 2005), intentionally managing an organization's knowledge assets also means effectively managing its talent processes to maximize employee learning, development, and knowledge creation.

Among the many definitions of talent management as an academic discipline (Sparrow, 2019), Collings, Mellahi, and Cascio (2019) define talent management comprehensively, as the systematic identification of pivotal positions that contribute to an organization's competitive advantage, development of a talent pool of high-potential and high-performing individuals to fill these mission-critical positions, and implementation of a differentiated human resource architecture to fill these positions with the best available talent. In this chapter, we adopt a talent management perspective that is more inclusive and that captures all employees of an organization as talent or potential talent (Dries, 2013; Meyers & Von Woerkom, 2014), since effective knowledge management requires unleashing the knowledge and potential of essentially everyone at all levels and positions. As such, we define talent management as the systematic attraction, identification, development, engagement/retention, and differential deployment of all individuals who—through their potential and knowledge assets—have a positive immediate or long-term impact on organizational effectiveness (Sparrow, 2019; CIPD, 2008).

Such a tall order and organizational imperative requires an integrated set of processes and procedures at the organizational level to attract, onboard, retain, develop, differentiate, move, and exit talent in order to achieve strategic objectives (Avendon & Scholes, 2010). And such an integrated and systematic process requires the talent management field to answer the underlying and ultimate question of how organizations can derive value from their human and social capital (Boudreau & Ramstad, 2006, 2007). We believe the answer to this ultimate talent management question lies partially within the strategic human resource management field and its fundamental theoretical principles (e.g., Glaister et al., 2018). In a similar vein, the theoretical premise of strategic human resource management can also provide insight into what the organization can do to enhance and facilitate learning and development within its talent pool and consequently, unleash and fully mobilize its knowledge assets to develop its organizational absorptive capacity (Zahra & George, 2002).

In this chapter and in connection with the knowledge management premise of this volume, we specifically focus on employee learning and development (ELD) that is facilitated by strategic human resource management (HRM) systems. We take a broad view of ELD to capture both employees' learning and their knowledge creation. The dictionary definition of learning is 'the activity or process of gaining knowledge or skill by studying, practicing, being taught, or experiencing something' (Merriam-Webster). According to Weiss (1990: 172), learning is 'a relatively permanent change in knowledge or skill produced by experience.' Such definitions of individual-level learning take an information-processing perspective and are consistent with concepts of learning derived from research in cognitive sciences (e.g., Piaget & Cook, 1952)—incorporating both explicit and tacit forms of new knowledge acquired. Our definition of learning goes beyond such definitions to further capture new insights and ideas that employees generate, promote, and realize as part of their learning, development, and growth in an organization at large. Hence, our definition of ELD encompasses both the acquisition and the generation of new knowledge (tacit and explicit) in organizations and represents all knowledge assets residing in the minds of its entire talent pool. Thus, we define HR systems for promoting ELD as a bundle of HR practices that are designed to acquire, maintain, and promote organizational knowledge through employee learning and development (ELD) processes.

Investigating ELD from the perspective of HRM systems is critical for both knowledge and talent management since a large body of research indicates that specific configurations of HRM practices operate in concert to influence employee outcomes, and ELD is no exception. Researchers also argue that HR systems work outward and upward to influence firm-level outcomes—primarily through their immediate effects on mission-critical employee attitudes and behaviors (Dyer & Reeves, 1995). As such, researchers have been paying closer attention to more proximal employee outcomes such as job satisfaction, affective commitment, and organizational citizenship behaviors to further understand the critical meso-level mediating mechanisms through which HRM systems impact firm-level outcomes (Gong et al., 2009; Kehoe & Wright, 2013; Liao et al., 2009; Takeuchi et al., 2007). Thus, HR systems designed for ELD are likely to improve employee behaviors and attitudes regarding learning and development (i.e., ELD), which is a more immediate outcome of HR systems than firm-level outcomes such as organizational innovation or performance. We note that consistent with most of the research on strategic human resource management highlighting internal fit (e.g., HR practices that are mutually supporting of each other), we view the exclusive perspective of talent management for pivotal jobs and high-performing individuals as a critical dimension of ELD-centered HR systems and contend that the effectiveness of talent management is warranted when it is aligned with all other HR practices in place. In line with this line of logic and in what follows, we develop a series of propositions that connect HRM systems with ELD, based on the main tenets of strategic HRM research. We also discuss how ELD-centered HRM systems influence employee behavior and attitudes regarding learning and development through creating and stimulating several organizational work climates. Our conceptual framework is summarized in Figure 5.1.

Based on the overarching premise of this edited volume, we first provide a summary of the existing state of talent management literature that informs the practical recommendations we develop in this chapter to maximize ELD in organizations.

TALENT MANAGEMENT AND STRATEGIC HUMAN RESOURCE MANAGEMENT

Discourse on talent management first started appearing in the world of HR practitioners in the late 1990s with *The War for Talent* as its major impetus (Michaels, Handfield-Jones, & Axelrod, 2001). The practitioner-oriented term encompasses a wide range of key HR practices such as internal and external staffing, succession planning, employee development, and career management, to name a few (Cappelli & Keller, 2014). Academic discourse

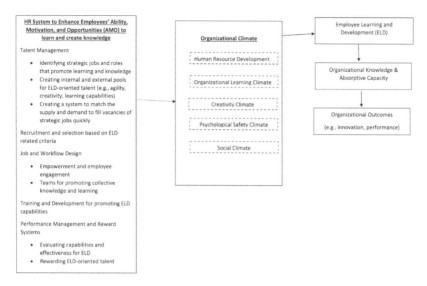

Figure 5.1   A conceptual framework of HR systems for employee learning and development (ELD)

soon followed and escalated rapidly, along with multiple definitions and the-oretical frameworks to define this area (Collings, Scullion, & Vaiman, 2011; McDonnell, Collings, & Burgess, 2012; Scullion, Collings, & Caligiuri, 2010; Vaiman & Collings, 2013). Most recently, multiple special issues analyzing and integrating current theories and suggesting future research directions were published (Al Ariss, Cascio, & Paauwe, 2014, Collings, Scullion, & Vaiman, 2015; Scullion, Vaiman, & Collings, 2016; Vaiman, Collings, & Scullion, 2017), firmly establishing talent management as a specific area of scholarly interest among a community of scholars. Despite the academic progress and vast amount of writing on talent management during the past two decades, however, some scholars criticize the field and argue that the body of knowl-edge in the talent management field remains fragmented, and definitions of talent and talent management remain imprecise (e.g., Collings & Mellahi, 2009; Sparrow, 2019).

Along with the academic evolution and growth of the field and despite criticisms, organizational leaders have continued to pay increasing attention to talent management processes to maximize the value that employees can gener-ate for organizations. In a research report by McKinsey & Company published in 2018, it was reported that companies with very effective talent management processes outperformed six times those with very ineffective talent manage-ment processes. Related, in line with the increasing importance and relevance of talent management for organizational effectiveness, the percentage of new board members with HR backgrounds has doubled for the last three years, according to research from the National Association of Corporate Directors (Fortune, 2021). Indeed, identifying, attracting, attaining, and developing top talent, and winning the so-called *war for talent*, remains a pivotal issue for contemporary organizations (Khilji, Tarique, & Shuler, 2015; Meyers & Van Woerkom, 2014).

From an academic perspective, Dries (2013), in a summary of the talent management literature, identifies five critical tensions that permeate this body of work to this day. The first tension is what (or who) constitutes *talent*. Subjective perspectives on talent suggest the focus should be on identifying and developing talented people, while objective perspectives emphasize identifying and developing 'characteristics' of talented people. Second, scholars have two distinct perspectives on the target employees for talent management. An inclusive perspective suggests that all employees are subjects of talent management regardless of performance and potential, which is consistent with most strategic HRM research (Collings & Mellahi, 2009) and the position we take in this chapter. An exclusive perspective argues that organizations should identify gifted and talented people and focus on relative resource allocations (e.g., training budgets, incentives, and promotion opportunities) based on levels of talent identified using a differentiated HR architecture (Collings et al., 2019). Third, there are input and output perspectives on talent management. Input perspectives suggest that talent assessment should be processed using individual inputs such as efforts, motivation, career orientation, etc., while output perspectives highlight assessments of outputs such as performance, achievements, and results. The fourth tension is related to debates on the extent to which talent can be learned. Innate perspectives focus on identifying, assessing, and selecting talent because talent is an innate characteristic by nature. However, acquired perspectives on talent center on education, training, and learning because it is believed talent can be taught and developed. The last tension is related to environmental contingencies. Transferable perspectives on talent assume that talented people will perform well regardless of their environment, while context-dependent perspectives assume that the influence of talent on performance hinges on the nature of contexts.

Amid these tensions, research on talent management has been burgeoning for the last decade. Nevertheless, many scholars have long pointed out that it is often hard to differentiate it from human resource management, which makes talent management merely a rebranding of traditional human resource management (Bolander, Werr, & Asplund, 2017; Cappelli & Keller, 2014; Collings & Mellahi, 2009; Narayanan, Rajithakumar & Menon, 2019). To reduce the ambiguity of the talent management concept and make a clear distinction from human resource management, talent management researchers have elucidated the concept of talent management. Most of the research on talent management defines talent management as processes and activities through which organizations identify pivotal jobs that are strategically important to gain and sustain a sustainable competitive advantage and locating, developing, and maintaining talent who currently have or may in future have the potential to fill such pivotal jobs (Cappelli & Keller, 2014; Collings & Mellahi, 2009). Shifting away from inclusive perspectives that suggest 'all people are talented in different ways' (Dries, 2013: 279), talent management includes a series of HR practices that help identify core jobs that are strategically critical in organizations, examine and develop internal and external pools of specific talented people, and match talent and those core jobs (Cappelli & Keller, 2014; Collings & Mellahi, 2009; Narayanan et al., 2019; Vaiman, Haslberger, & Vance, 2015). Emphasizing high value-added, strategic jobs and top-notch talent in workforce management is consistent with key principles of strategic human resource management (Huselid & Becker, 2011). In addition, to manage talent, it is important to have other supporting HR practices (e.g., reward systems, performance management, training and development programs) for optimal employee outcomes. Therefore, we view talent management as a critical part of HR systems to identify, retain, mobilize, motivate, and develop talent who perform (or potentially perform) strategically key roles and to motivate and manage talent to work effectively together. Our holistic view on talent management ensures consistency with the concept of internal fit, suggesting that an isolated group of talent management practices is not as effective as a bundle of comprehensive HR practices, including such talent management practices.

In sum, while there are diverse perspectives on what talent management is focused on, how talent is defined, and how talent management is different from traditional HRM, for the purpose of this chapter, we take an all-encompassing, holistic perspective of talent management since it has greater connections with strategic HRM theory and research we adopt to develop our theoretical propositions (Collings & Mellahi, 2009). It is also more in line with the imperatives of knowledge management, where unleashing and mobilizing every ounce of human potential and knowledge can be critical for competitive advantage. The practical recommendations that follow our propositions have implications for talent management in practice.

STRATEGIC HUMAN RESOURCE MANAGEMENT

The research field of strategic human resource management (SHRM) is defined as 'the pattern of planned human resource deployments and activities intended to enable an organization achieve its goals' (Wright & McMahan, 1992: 298) and 'organizational systems designed to achieve competitive advantage through people' (Snell, Youndt, & Wright, 1996: 62). SHRM research has enjoyed a great deal of managerial and scholarly attention over the last decades as companies tried to identify inimitable and valuable resources to create a sustained source of competitive advantage (Colakoglu, Hong, & Lepak, 2010). The outcome variable of scholarly interest in traditional SHRM research is typically some aspect of a firm's performance such as shareholder value, labor productivity, or return on assets—with direct bottom-line relevance and significance for managers (Colakoglu, Lepak, & Hong, 2006). For example, in a meta-analysis of 92 studies examining links between HRM and firm performance, Combs et al. (2006) found that an increase of one standard deviation in the use of high-performance work systems—work practices that are focused on enhancing employee ability and motivation and providing opportunities to utilize their competencies—is associated with a 4.6% increase in return on assets. That is, based on roughly three decades of accumulated research findings, the relationship between systems of HR practices and organizational performance and success is an irrefutable empirical fact. Yet, theoretical questions linger as to how and why such effects are observed, posed unanimously under the SHRM lingo as 'the black box' (Lepak et al., 2006).

While there are numerous theoretical frameworks shedding light on the black box ranging from the resource-based view of the firm (Barney, 1991) to complexity theory (Colbert, 2004), in this chapter, we focus on those theoretical explanations and key underlying assumptions that we believe provide the greatest actionable implications for maximizing ELD in organizations. First, we argue that HR systems that are synergistically oriented to enhance employees' ability, motivation, and opportunities to learn and create knowledge can maximize ELD. Second, we propose organizational climate for learning as the mediating mechanism that exists between HR systems and ELD.

Synergistic Orientation of HRM

In highlighting the systems-orientation of SHRM research, Delery (1998: 281) states that 'The basic assumption is that the effectiveness of any practice depends on the other practices in place. If all the practices fit into a coherent system, the effect of that system on performance should be greater than the sum of the individual effects from each practice alone.' Accordingly, a synergistic perspective with an emphasis on mutually reinforcing HRM practices has become the theoretical norm to conceptualize HRM systems (Lepak et al., 2006; Wright & McMahan, 1992). That is, one unique characteristic of SHRM theory is its systems-orientation, rather than only examining individual HRM practices as the primary driver of organizational and individual outcomes, such as ELD (Colakoglu et al., 2010; Lepak et al., 2006). The practical logic underlying this argument is that employees are exposed to multiple HR practices simultaneously in their organizational lives. In organizations and in practice, HRM practices are never used in isolation from one another. Similarly, employees are not likely to respond to single HRM practices irrespective of the nature and content of other HRM practices that exist in the workplace (Delery, 1998). Based on this synergistic logic, mutually reinforcing HRM practices implemented in concert would also be instrumental in facilitating and maximizing ELD in organizations.

> **Proposition 1:** HR systems targeting ELD are more effective in maximizing ELD for knowledge management than single HR practices, such as focusing only on training and development.

Types of HR Systems

Despite agreement on conceptualizing HR practices as a synergistic bundle, however, there has been a lack of consensus in identifying which specific HR practices would constitute a meaningful and internally consistent system, with researchers using different titles for various configurations of HR practices such as high-commitment (Arthur, 1994; Lepak & Snell, 2002), high-involvement (MacDuffie, 1995; Osterman, 1994), and high-performance HR systems (Huselid, 1995). Amid such differences, a common thread across conceptualizations, as stated in the preceding section, is a focus on work practices that promote and enhance employees' ability, motivation, and opportunities to perform and behave in ways consistent with organizational goals (Appelbaum et al., 2000; Boxall & Purcell, 2011).

In addition to these configurations of HR practices that have been shown to improve various aspects of firm effectiveness and performance, researchers also developed theoretical configurations of HR systems aimed at specific strategic objectives such as human capital enhancement (Youndt et al., 1996), network-building (Collins & Clark, 2003), customer service (Chuang & Liao, 2010), knowledge-intensive teamwork (Chuang, Jackson, & Jiang, 2016; Jackson et al., 2006), and HR flexibility (Chang et al., 2013). Strategically-anchored HR systems have been found to be associated with the specific outcomes they are designed to achieve, presumably because they guide and elicit employee behaviors and contributions in line with the strategic objectives they are designed to serve (Schuler & Jackson, 1987). For example, HR systems targeting customer service enhance service climate and customer satisfaction (Chuang & Liao, 2010), HR systems supporting knowledge-intensive teamwork are associated with greater team knowledge acquisition and team knowledge-sharing (Chuang et al., 2016), HR systems emphasizing flexibility improve absorptive capacity and innovation in organizations (Chang et al., 2013), and HR systems anchored around occupational safety create a climate of safety and improve employees' safety orientation and reduce reported work injuries (Zacharatos et al., 2005). Accordingly, and based on this logic and previous empirical findings, in order to maximize ELD in organizations, it is critical to strategically anchor the content of different HR practices to ELD-oriented attitudes, behaviors, and outcomes.

> **Proposition 2:** HR practices targeting employees' ability, motivation, and opportunities to learn and create knowledge lead to improved ELD.

Ability-Motivation-Opportunity for ELD

Researchers have relied on the ability-motivation-opportunity (AMO) paradigm of HRM to identify three essential pillars of HRM systems that create synergistic impacts on important employee outcomes. Empirical evidence also suggests that HRM practices designed and implemented to target employees' ability, motivation, and opportunities to perform and display desired attitudes and behaviors are what create synergies across mutually reinforcing HRM practices. Extending this logic, HRM systems designed to maximize ELD can be viewed as a composition of three dimensions intended to enhance employee skills, motivation, and opportunity to learn, develop, and create knowledge (Boxall & Purcell, 2011; Delery & Shaw, 2001; Gerhart, 2007; Katz, Kochan, & Weber, 1985; Lepak et al., 2006). The practical issue concerned with the AMO paradigm of relevance to this chapter is the identification of the nature and content of HRM practices that can be categorized as enhancing the skills, motivation, and opportunities for ELD.

Extending on the AMO paradigm, Lepak and colleagues (2006) conceptualize HRM practices as falling into one of three primary categories: skill-enhancing HRM practices, motivation-enhancing HR practices, and opportunity-enhancing HR practices. Skill-enhancing HR practices are designed to ensure employees have the right and required skillsets, competencies, and expertise. They include comprehensive recruitment, rigorous selection, and extensive training focused on ensuring appropriately skilled employees are on board.

To facilitate and maximize ELD, skill-enhancing HR practices, in particular recruitment and selection, should target personal qualities such as London's (1983: 623) development orientation—'desire to expand one's skill or knowledge'; Kozlowski and Farr's (1988) 'updating orientation,' consisting of willingness to participate in professional activities (conventions, meetings, etc.), continuing education, developmental work assignments sought, and technical interest and curiosity; Noe's (1986) 'motivation to learn'; and Senge's (1990) 'personal mastery' or the pursuit of continuous personal growth and learning within the 'learning organization'; as Senge stated: 'people with a high level of personal mastery live in a continual learning mode' (1990: 142). Finally,

Cherrington (1991) discussed 'growth-need' and described it as an intrinsic need that concerns yearnings for self-development, mastery, and challenge, and Maurer, Le Grand, and Mondloch (2002) developed a comprehensive model of learning and development orientation that integrates cognitive, affective, and behavioral constructs which together describe a tendency toward involvement in continuous learning. This orientation is posited to be a motivational state that depends on the degree to which learning and development are relevant to the self.

As a result of screening and selecting talent that possesses such qualities, extensive training to further enhance job-related knowledge and skills can lead to better learning outcomes such as reactions to training activities (Hughes et al., 2016), affective-, cognitive-, and skill-based learning (Kraiger, Ford, and Salas; 1993; Weiss, 1990), transfer of learning to actual behavior and performance, and generation of novel and innovative ideas as a result of increased know-how in one's domain of expertise (Amabile, 1988).

Motivation-enhancing HR practices are implemented to enhance employee motivation—the intrinsic psychological state that determines one's direction of effort and its intensity and persistence (Vroom, 1964). HR practices targeting employee motivation might include developmental performance management processes, competitive compensation, incentives and rewards tied to achievement of desired employee goals and objectives, extensive benefits, promotion and career development, and job security. For maximizing ELD, the most critical motivation-enhancing HR practices are likely to be those that both motivate and reward learning and development. These might include performance goals related to participation in learning and development activities such as workshops, skill-building seminars, or accepting stretch job assignments (Rouiller & Goldstein, 1993). Performance management systems that provide developmental feedback for assessing both growth and future developmental needs can motivate employees to better reflect and act upon their personal and professional growth. Skills-based compensation elements such as bonuses, awards, or increase of base salary tied to ELD would reward upskilling of employees and can further motivate employees to achieve their ELD goals. Finally, opportunities for promotion and career development based on learning and growth can motivate them to take ownership and responsibility for their professional growth (Greenhaus, 1988; London, 1983, 1991).

Finally, opportunity-enhancing HR practices are designed to empower employees to use their skills and motivation to achieve organizational objectives. Practices such as flexible job design, work teams, employee involvement, and information sharing are generally used to offer these opportunities. In the context of ELD, opportunities for employees to put their new skills, abilities, and knowledge to use in their jobs and work teams, tolerance for risk and failure in job design and work team context as employees navigate their learning curves, as well as active involvement in decisions where their knowledge assets can be fully tapped into, can be considered as HR practices enhancing opportunities for furthering ELD.

Talent management recommendation 1: Companies should holistically evaluate their HR practices to make sure they all focus on and target the necessary knowledge, skills, and abilities of employees that are related to ELD.

Internal Fit and ELD

Based on the theoretical and practical logic developed so far, then, achieving *internal fit* among different HR practices is critical for realizing desired outcomes in employee behaviors and attitudes. In practice, eliciting, rewarding, and reinforcing desired behaviors and attitudes would require selection, onboarding, training, performance management, and reward systems to be aligned with one another, mutually supporting and reinforcing each other's impact. Existing research empirically validates this assumption and confirms the potential of *internally aligned* HR systems in facilitating organizational effectiveness (e.g., Becker & Gerhart, 1996; Delery & Doty, 1996; Ichniowski, Shaw, & Prennushi, 1997) and thus provides an actionable principle for facilitating ELD. Accordingly, organizations that are trying to improve ELD and unleash the collective talents of their employees should not only assess the skills and abilities required for learning and knowledge creation as a focus in its selection and screening processes but also should design and implement all other HR practices including training, performance management and evaluation, job design, career development, and rewards mechanisms around this same focus.

According to Bowen and Ostroff (2004), when internally aligned HRM systems create strong situations for employees, individuals share a common interpretation of what behaviors are important, expected, and rewarded by the organizations and modify their behaviors accordingly. A weak situation, in contrast, is one in which HR practices that either contradict or do not complement one another send ambiguous or conflicting signals to employees, reducing the relative power of HR practices in controlling and changing employee behavior. In sum and in practice, therefore, achieving internal fit among HR practices becomes critical when maximizing ELD. Otherwise, employees are likely to receive and perceive conflicting or ambiguous signals from the organization, which they are less likely to respond to by displaying learning-related behaviors and attitudes.

Proposition 3: Internally aligned HR systems targeting learning-related behaviors and attitudes will create strong situations for employees and maximize ELD for knowledge management.

ORGANIZATIONAL CLIMATE FOR ELD

We have previously discussed the role of HR systems in facilitating ELD. However, HR systems also require a conducive climate for them to achieve their intended goals. In this final segment, we explore possibilities of organizational climate constructs that might be related to ELD. Reichers and Schneider (1990: 22) defined organizational climate as employees' 'shared perceptions of organizational policies, practices, and procedures, both formal and informal.' Organizational climate is distinguished from organizational culture, which pertains to deeply-rooted and unconscious values, beliefs, and assumptions of employees (Rousseau, 1990). In other words, organizational climate is a conscious process involving the perception and interpretation of organizational policies, practices, and procedures to understand the expected and desirable behaviors and attitudes at the organization. Through the shared perceptions of the HRM policies, practices, and procedures (e.g., formal and informal training, career development, performance management, incentives and rewards, and coaching and mentoring), employees infer the types of behaviors and attitudes (e.g., human resource development, learning, creativity, and trust) that are expected, encouraged, and rewarded in the organization. As such, organizational climate is often considered an intermediate mechanism that translates the organizational policies, practices, and procedures into employee perceptions and exhibitions of desirable behaviors and attitudes (Bowen & Ostroff, 2004). Besides the HR system, organizational climate also reflects leaders' values and implementation of organizational policies, practices, and procedures (Schein, 1993). Employees deduce the priority of the organization based on leaders' role modeling, teaching, and mentoring, as well as the actual criteria that leaders use to recruit, select, appraise, reward, promote, and publish employees.

Several types of organizational climate are relevant to ELD. *Human resource development climate* concerns employees' perceptions of the organization such as 'importance given to human resources, openness of communication, encouragement given to risk-taking and experimentation, feedback given to employees to make them aware of their strengths and weaknesses, a general climate of trust, faith in employee's capabilities, employees' tendency to assist and collaborate with each other, team spirit, tendency to discourage stereotypes and favoritism, and supportive personal policies and practices' (Benjamin & David, 2012: 92). Human resource development climate is central in facilitating the effective implementation of the HR system to ensure the abilities, motivation, and opportunities of ELD. Employees' perception of human resource development climate is often shaped by HR practices such as career system (workforce planning, potential appraisal and promotion, and career planning and development), work planning (role analysis, contextual analysis, and performance appraisal system), development system (learning and training opportunities, performance guidance and development, and other mechanisms of development), self-renewal system (role efficacy, organizational development, and action-oriented research), and HRD system (organizational values, reward and recognition, information, and empowerment) (Hassan, Hashim, & Ismail, 2006: 6). Human resource development climate, in turn, was positively related to employee attitudes such as work engagement (Chaudhary, Rangnekar, & Barua, 2011), affective commitment, continuance commitment, and normative commitment (Benjamin & David, 2012), which are essential for ELD.

Organizational learning climate relates to employees' perception of the extent to which the organization encourages the acquisition and development of new knowledge and skills, continuous performance improvement, and experimentation, creativity, and innovation (Bates & Khasawneh, 2005). Employees develop their shared perception of organizational learning climate through HR practices such as recruitment and selection of individuals with a learning orientation, appraisal and reward of continuous learning and development, offering training and development opportunities, ensuring autonomy, responsibility and accountability, and guidelines to carry out activities (Carrim & Basson, 2013), encouraging employee inquiry, dialogues, suggestions, and participation in decision making (Jamali, Khoury, & Sahyoun, 2006), internal social network building, collaboration, and information sharing across functions (Swift & Hwang, 2008). Learning climate has been shown to be associated with employee intention to explore (Maruping & Magni, 2012).

Creativity climate refers to an organizational climate that enhances the creativity and innovation of the organization by allowing the expression of different viewpoints (Amabile et al., 1996). Elements of creativity climate include employee perceptions of the challenge of one's work, freedom to try different things, support for expressing ideas, trust and openness in exchanging ideas, dynamism and liveliness of the organization, playfulness and humor at work, debates on ideas and approaches, constructive conflicts, encouragement of risk-taking, and value of idea time (Ekvall, 1996). HR practices such as recruitment and selection of creative individuals, as well as formal and informal training and development of a creative mindset, help acquire and develop the abilities of employees to be creative. HR practices such as incorporating creativity into performance appraisal, incentives, and rewards, as well as encouragement and support for creativity, operate to stimulate employee motivation to be creative. Further, allowing sufficient autonomy and freedom, designing challenging tasks, effective information sharing, encouraging voice and dialogues, and removing obstacles such as time and workload pressure create optimal opportunities for employees to be creative. In addition, organizational learning mechanisms including cognitive mechanisms (e.g., shared understanding of the value of creativity, common language, and dialogues and learning), structural mechanisms (e.g., a platform for collaboration and dialogues, communication channels, and cross-functional projects), and procedural mechanisms (e.g., collaborative routines, feedback and recognition, and review and briefing procedures) were shown to contribute to creativity climate (Cirella et al., 2016). Creative climate, in turn, will encourage employees to venture into unfamiliar territories and absorb and combine new knowledge to be creative. Some researchers consider creative climate as an enabling factor of high-performance work systems on developing employee competencies (van Esch, Wei, & Chiang, 2016).

Psychological safety climate refers to employees' shared perception of safety, or lack of interpersonal threat resulting from mistakes and failures, in the collective environment (Edmondson, 1999, 2003). Psychological safety climate is important for ELD because ELD often involves reflecting and analyzing failures that can cause harm to one's social image. HR system cultivates psychological safety climate by allowing autonomy and trial-and-error, encouraging voice and suggestions, providing sufficient support such as resources and development opportunities, and removing contingency attached to failures or poor results. Psychological safety climate has been shown to be related to employees' reduced fear of failure and increased voice and learning (Deng et al., 2019), and being alive and creative (Kark & Carmeli, 2009). Nonetheless, Deng et al. (2019) also demonstrated that psychological safety climate could be a double-edged sword in that its supportive and forgiving nature impairs social evaluation and monitoring, which can also reduce employee work motivation.

Social climate is defined as 'the collective set of norms, values, and beliefs that expresses employees' views of how they interact with one another while carrying out tasks for the firm' (Prieto & Pilar Pérez Santana, 2012: 193). It depicts the cognitive (shared understanding and language), affective (trust), and structural (collaborative network) social capital that employees experience in the organization (Nahapiet & Ghoshal, 1998; Prieto & Pilar Pérez Santana, 2012). HR systems can influence social climate through their ability-, motivating-, and opportunity-enhancing practices (Prieto & Pilar Pérez Santana, 2012). For example, hiring practices help ensure that employees share similar values; training can emphasize cooperation and relationship building. Incentive programs that tie rewards to group and organizational results help build trust and collaboration among employees (Kang, Morris, & Snell, 2007). The use of teamwork and flexible job design allows employees to collaborate and develop trust; participative decision-making helps to build shared knowledge and perception of fairness. Social climate will facilitate employee ambidextrous (exploratory and exploitative) learning by enabling employees to access, share, interpret, and expand knowledge (Prieto & Pilar Pérez Santana, 2012). Based on these arguments, we propose:

> **Proposition 4:** HR systems will be related to ELD via the mediation of organizational climate for knowledge management (e.g., human resource development climate, organizational learning climate, creativity climate, psychological safety climate, and social climate).

> **Talent management recommendation 2:** Organizations should periodically assess their climate for learning and knowledge management and take corrective action to strengthen social climates conducive to ELD and managing knowledge.

CONCLUSION

Theoretical Implications and Future Research Directions

In this chapter, we developed a series of propositions connecting foundational principles of strategic human resource management to improved learning and development outcomes in organizations. We argued that for effective knowledge management and to release all knowledge assets residing in the minds of an organization's talent pool, talent management and HR practices should intentionally and specifically target learning-related skills, behaviors, and attributes. In our definition and treatment of talent and talent management, we moved away from an exclusive approach of only concentrating on a small percentage of high-performance, high-potential individuals in pivotal jobs, and adopted an inclusive approach to cover all employees in all positions (Dries, 2013). We did this for two main reasons. First, with the assumption that an effectively designed and implemented strategic HR system—including but not limited to a differentiated HR architecture for different groups of employees and positions (Lepak & Snell, 1999)—leads to a capable, engaged, and motivated talent force across the organization. Second, effective knowledge management requires tapping into all forms and levels of knowledge assets no matter where knowledge in the organization resides. In summary, we argued that through implementing ELD-oriented talent and HR processes across the board, critical knowledge management outcomes such as knowledge acquisition, mobilization, and utilization can be facilitated and individual and collective organizational absorptive capacity expanded (Zahra & George, 2002).

Although talent management research has burgeoned over the last two decades, many scholars tried to identify the concrete boundary for talent management which makes it distinct from traditional or strategic human resource management (Sparrow, 2019). The most common point of departure is to solely focus on mission-critical jobs and managing high-potential individuals differentially to fill those jobs (e.g., Collings et al., 2019). However, there is a dearth of theoretical and empirical research on how such an exclusive perspective of talent management should be understood within broader HR systems, except for a few notable studies (e.g., Collings & Mellahi, 2009). Therefore, we theorized the exclusive talent management approach to be part of a broader strategic HR system and call for future research to investigate how and what kinds of talent management processes work with other elements of a broader HR system (e.g., compensation, performance management); the extent to which the congruence between talent management and other HR practices has a synergistic effect on employee behaviors, attitudes and organizational outcomes; and how talent management in the form of identifying pivotal jobs and staffing those jobs with high-performing individuals contributes to the effectiveness of an overall HR system.

Drawing on strategic human resource management literature, we proposed that HR systems strategically designed to motivate employees to learn and develop knowledge and skills are likely to improve ELD through creating social climates effective for learning and knowledge creation. ELD-oriented HR systems are important because HR practices with such specific purposes and goals improve employee understanding of the importance of ELD and guide employees to put more effort into displaying ELD-related behaviors and attitudes (e.g., expanding social networks for seeking knowledge). Given that knowledge management is recognized to be essential for acquiring a sustainable competitive advantage by academics, practitioners, and business leaders alike, examining ELD-centered HR systems and talent management is vital. However, while there are studies that focus on how other existing HR systems such as commitment HR systems, knowledge-based HR systems, and high-performance HR systems influence ELD-related behaviors such as employee innovation, knowledge sharing, and social capital (Colakoglu et al., 2019; Colakoglu, Chung, & Ceylan, 2022; Jyoti & Rani, 2017; Singh et al., 2021), to our knowledge, there is no research on ELD-centered HR systems. In addition, there is limited research on talent management that is strategically anchored at any domain, including ELD even if there are a few recent studies emphasizing the importance of a talent management architecture (Bolander et al, 2017; Glaister et al., 2018). Therefore, we call for research that theoretically develops ELD-centered talent management and HR systems and quantitatively and qualitatively examines how they influence ELD, social work climates, and other forms of knowledge management outcomes such as acquisition, assimilation, transformation and exploitation of knowledge with the organization.

Practical Implications

Organizations that aim to gain and sustain their competitive advantage need to ensure the continuous acquisition and development of knowledge through

ELD. This starts from a top-down philosophy of talent management which values employee agility, creativity, and learning capabilities. Managers can orchestrate a holistic HR system that is oriented towards ELD by implementing a set of ELD ability-, motivation- and ability-enhancing HR practices. For example, organizations can systematically screen for applicants with curiosity and a growth-mindset, deploy ELD-oriented pay, bonuses, favorable appraisals, and advancement, and provide employees with the autonomy, encouragement, and career assurance to enable ELD. Such a synergistic HR system conveys a consistent message to employees that ELD is highly encouraged and expected in the organization, thereby cultivating a strong climate for learning and development. Managers can also periodically assess the climates for learning and development to diagnose whether the top ELD-oriented philosophy is effectively translated into employee perceptions of ELD-enabling policies and practices. In summary, for effective knowledge management, intentional design and implementation of talent and HR management processes is critical for facilitating innovation and performance.

REFERENCES

Al Ariss, A., Cascio, W.F. & Paauwe, J. (2014). Talent management: Current theories and future research directions. *Journal of World Business*, **49**(2): 173–179.

Amabile, T.M. (1988). A model of creativity and innovation in organizations. *Research in Organizational Behavior*, **10**(1): 123–167.

Amabile, T.M., Conti, R., Coon, H., Lazenby, J. & Herron, M. (1996). Assessing the work environment for creativity. *Academy of Management Journal*, **39**(5): 1154–1184.

Appelbaum, E., Bailey, T., Berg, P., Kalleberg, A.L. & Bailey, T.A. (2000). *Manufacturing Advantage: Why High-performance Work Systems Pay Off*. Ithaca, NY: Cornell University Press.

Arthur, J.B. (1994). Effects of human resource systems on manufacturing performance and turnover. *Academy of Management Journal*, **37**(3): 670–687.

Avendon, M.J. & Scholes, G. (2010). Building competitive advantage through integrated talent management. In Silzer, R. & Dowell, B.E. (eds.), *Strategy-Driven Talent Management: A Leadership Imperative*. San Francisco, CA: Jossey-Bass, pp. 73–122.

Barley, W.C., Treem, J.W. & Kuhn, T. (2018). Valuing multiple trajectories of knowledge: A critical review and agenda for knowledge management research. *Academy of Management Annals*, **12**(1): 278–317.

Barney, J. (1991). Firm resources and sustained competitive advantage. *Journal of Management*, **17**(1): 99–120.

Bates, R. & Khasawneh, S. (2005). Organizational learning culture, learning transfer climate and perceived innovation in Jordanian organizations. *International Journal of Training and Development*, **9**(2): 96–109.

Becker, B. & Gerhart, B. (1996). The impact of human resource management on organizational performance: Progress and prospects. *Academy of Management Journal*, **39**(4): 779–801.

Behme, F. & Becker, S. (2021). The new knowledge management: Mining the collective intelligence. *Deloitte Insights*. https://www2.deloitte.com/us/en/insights/focus/technology-and-the-future-of-work/organizational-knowledge-management.html.

Benjamin, A. & David, I. (2012). Human resource development climate and employee commitment in recapitalized Nigerian banks. *International Journal of Business and Management*, **7**(5): 91.

Bolander, P., Werr, A. & Asplund, K. (2017). The practice of talent management: A framework and typology. *Personnel Review*, **46**(8): 1523–1551.

Boudreau, J.W. & Ramstad, P.M. (2006). Talentship and HR measurement and analysis: From ROI to strategic, human resource planning. *Human Resource Planning*, **29**(1): 25–33.

Boudreau, J.W. & Ramstad, P.M. (2007). *Beyond HR: The New Science of Human Capital*. Boston, MA: Harvard Business School Press.

Bowen, D.E. & Ostroff, C. (2004). Understanding HRM–firm performance linkages: The role of the 'strength' of the HRM system. *Academy of Management Review*, **29**(2): 203–221.

Boxall, P. & Purcell, J. (2011). *Strategy and Human Resource Management*. New York: Palgrave Macmillan.

Buckley, P.J. & Carter, M.J. (2004). A formal analysis of knowledge combination in multinational enterprises. *Journal of International Business Studies*, **35**(5): 371–384.

Cappelli, P. & Keller, J.R. (2014). Talent management: Conceptual approaches and practical challenges. *Annual Review of Organizational Psychology Organizational Behavior*, **1**(1): 305–331.

Carrim, N.M.H. & Basson, J.S. (2013). Creating a learning climate: A South African study. *The Learning Organization*, **20**(1): 6–19.

Chang, S., Gong, Y., Way, S.A. & Jia, L. (2013). Flexibility-oriented HRM systems, absorptive capacity, and market responsiveness and firm innovativeness. *Journal of Management*, **39**(7): 1924–1951.

Chaudhary, R., Rangnekar, S. & Barua, M. (2011). Relation between human resource development climate and employee engagement: Results from India. *Europe's Journal of Psychology*, **7**(4): 664–685.

Cherrington, D. (1991). Need theories of motivation. In Steers, R. & and Porter, L. (eds.), *Motivation and Work Behavior*. New York: McGraw-Hill, pp. 31–43.

Chuang, C.H., Jackson, S.E. & Jiang, Y. (2016). Can knowledge-intensive teamwork be managed? Examining the roles of HRM systems, leadership, and tacit knowledge. *Journal of Management*, **42**(2): 524–554.

Chuang, C.H. & Liao, H. (2010). Strategic human resource management in service context: Taking care of business by taking care of employees and customers. *Personnel Psychology*, **63**(1): 153–196.

CIPD (2008). *Talent Management: Design, Implementation and Evaluation*. CIPD Online Practical Tool. London: CIPD.

Cirella, S., Canterino, F., Guerci, M. & Shani, A.B. (2016). Organizational learning mechanisms and creative climate: Insights from an Italian fashion design company. *Creativity and Innovation Management*, **25**(2): 211–222.

Colakoglu, S., Chung, Y. & Ceylan, C. (2022). Collaboration-based HR systems and innovative work behaviors: The role of information exchange and HR system strength. *European Management Journal*, **40**(4): 518–531.

Colakoglu, S.S., Erhardt, N., Pougnet-Rozan, S. & Martin-Rios, C. (2019). Reviewing creativity and innovation research through the strategic HRM lens. In Buckley, M.R.,

Wheeler, A.R., Baur, J.E. & Halbesleben, J.R.B. (eds.), *Research in Personnel and Human Resources Management*, vol. 37. Bingley: Emerald Publishing, pp. 227–271.

Colakoglu, S., Hong, Y. & Lepak, D.P. (2010). Models of strategic human resource management. In Wilkinson, A., Redman, T., Snell, S., & Bacon, N. (eds.), *The SAGE Handbook of Human Resource Management*. Thousand Oaks, CA: Sage, pp. 31–50.

Colakoglu, S., Lepak, D.P. & Hong, Y. (2006). Measuring HRM effectiveness: Considering multiple stakeholders in a global context. *Human Resource Management Review*, **16**(2): 209–218.

Colbert, B.A. (2004). The complex resource-based view: Implications for theory and practice in strategic human resource management. *Academy of Management Review*, **29**(3): 341–358.

Collings, D.G. & Mellahi, K. (2009). Strategic talent management: A review and research agenda. *Human Resource Management Review*, **19**(4): 304–313.

Collings, D.G., Mellahi, K. & Cascio, W.F. (2019). Global talent management and performance in multinational enterprises: A multilevel perspective. *Journal of Management*, **45**(2): 540–566.

Collings, D.G., Scullion, H. & Vaiman, V. (2011). European perspectives on talent management. *European Journal of International Management*, **5**(5): 453–462.

Collings, D.G., Scullion, H. & Vaiman, V. (2015). Talent management: Progress and prospects. *Human Resource Management Review*, **25**(3): 233–235.

Collins, C.J. & Clark, K.D. (2003). Strategic human resource practices, top management team social networks, and firm performance: The role of human resource practices in creating organizational competitive advantage. *Academy of Management Journal*, **46**(6): 740–751.

Combs, J., Liu, Y., Hall, A. & Ketchen, D. (2006). How much do high-performance work practices matter? A meta-analysis of their effects on organizational performance. *Personnel Psychology*, **59**(3): 501–528.

Delery, J.E. (1998). Issues of fit in strategic human resource management: Implications for research. *Human Resource Management Review*, **8**(3): 289–309.

Delery, J.E. & Doty, D.H. (1996). Modes of theorizing in strategic human resource management: Tests of universalistic, contingency, and configurational performance predictions. *Academy of Management Journal*, **39**(4): 802–835.

Delery, J.E. & Shaw, J.D. (2001). The strategic management of people in work organizations: Review, synthesis, and extension. *Research in Personnel and Human Resources Management*, **20**: 165–197.

Deng, H., Leung, K., Lam, C.K. & Huang, X. (2019). Slacking off in comfort: A dual-pathway model for psychological safety climate. *Journal of Management*, **45**(3): 1114–1144.

Dries, N. (2013). The psychology of talent management: A review and research agenda. *Human Resource Management Review*, **23**(4): 272–285.

Dyer, L. & Reeves, T. (1995). Human resource strategies and firm performance: What do we know and where do we need to go? *International Journal of Human Resource Management*, **6**(3): 656–670.

Edmondson, A. (1999). Psychological safety and learning behavior in work teams. *Administrative Science Quarterly*, **44**(2): 350–383.

Edmondson, A.C. (2003). Speaking up in the operating room: How team leaders promote learning in interdisciplinary action teams. *Journal of Management Studies*, **40**(6): 1419–1452.

Ekvall, G. (1996). Organizational climate for creativity and innovation. *European Journal of Work and Organizational Psychology*, **5**(1): 105–123.

Fortune (2021). The value of HR expertise on a board of directors. *Fortune*, October 8. https://fortune.com/2021/10/08/who-should-be-on-a-board-of-directors-hr-professional/.

Gerhart, B. (2007). Horizontal and vertical fit in human resource systems. In Ostroff, C. & Judge, T.A. (eds.), *Perspectives on Organizational Fit*. New York: Psychology Press, pp. 317–348.

Glaister, A.J., Karacay, G., Demirbag, M. & Tatoglu, E. (2018). HRM and performance: The role of talent management as a transmission mechanism in an emerging market context. *Human Resource Management Journal*, **28**(1): 148–166.

Gong, Y., Law, K.S., Chang, S. & Xin, K.R. (2009). Human resources management and firm performance: The differential role of managerial affective and continuance commitment. *Journal of Applied Psychology*, **94**(1): 263–275.

Greenhaus, J. (1988). Career exploration. In London, M. & Mone, E. (eds.), *Career Growth and Human Resource Strategies*. New York: Quorum, pp. 17–30.

Hassan, A., Hashim, J. & Ismail, A.Z.H. (2006). Human resource development practices as determinant of HRD climate and quality orientation. *Journal of European Industrial Training*, **30**(1): 4–18.

Hughes, A.M., Gregory, M.E., Joseph, D.L., Sonesh, S.C., Marlow, S.L., Lacerenza, C.N. & Salas, E. (2016). Saving lives: A meta-analysis of team training in healthcare. *Journal of Applied Psychology*, **101**(9): 1266–1304.

Huselid, M.A. (1995). The impact of human resource management practices on turnover, productivity, and corporate financial performance. *Academy of Management Journal*, **38**(3): 635–672.

Huselid, M.A. & Becker, B.E. (2011). Bridging micro and macro domains: Workforce differentiation and strategic human resource management. *Journal of Management*, **37**(2): 421–428.

Ichniowski, C., Shaw, K. & Prennushi, G. (1997). The effects of human resource practices on manufacturing performance: A study of steel finishing lines. *American Economic Review*, **87**(3): 291–313.

Jackson, S.E., Chuang, C.H., Harden, E.E. & Jiang, Y. (2006). Toward developing human resource management systems for knowledge-intensive teamwork. In Martocchio, J.J. (ed.), *Research in Personnel and Human Resources Management*, vol. 25. Bingley: Emerald Group Publishing, pp. 27–70.

Jamali, D., Khoury, G. & Sahyoun, H. (2006). From bureaucratic organizations to learning organizations: An evolutionary roadmap. *The Learning Organization*, 13(4): 337–352.

Jyoti, J. & Rani, A. (2017). High performance work system and organizational performance: Role of knowledge management. *Personnel Review*, **46**(8): 1770–1795.

Kang, S.C., Morris, S.S. & Snell, S.A. (2007). Relational archetypes, organizational learning, and value creation: Extending the human resource architecture. *Academy of Management Review*, **32**(1): 236–256.

Kark, R. & Carmeli, A. (2009). Alive and creating: The mediating role of vitality and aliveness in the relationship between psychological safety and creative work involvement. *Journal of Organizational Behavior*, **30**(6): 785–804.

Katz, H.C., Kochan, T.A. & Weber, M.R. (1985). Assessing the effects of industrial relations systems and efforts to improve the quality of working life on organizational effectiveness. *Academy of Management Journal*, **28**(3): 509–526.

Kehoe, R.R. & Wright, P.M. (2013). The impact of high-performance human resource practices on employees' attitudes and behaviors. *Journal of Management*, **39**(2): 366–391.

Khilji, S.E., Tarique, I. & Schuler, R.S. (2015). Incorporating the macro view in global talent management. *Human Resource Management Review*, **25**(3): 236–248.

Kogut, B. & Zander, U. (1993). Knowledge of the firm and the evolutionary theory of the multinational corporation. *Journal of International Business Studies*, **24**(4): 625–645.

Kozlowski, S. & Farr, J. (1988). An integrative model of updating and performance. *Human Performance*, **1**: 5–29.

Kraiger, K., Ford, J.K. & Salas, E. (1993). Application of cognitive, skill-based, and affective theories of learning outcomes to new methods of training evaluation. *Journal of Applied Psychology*, **78**(2): 311–328.

Lepak, D.P. & Snell, S.A. (1999). The human resource architecture: Toward a theory of human capital allocation and development. *Academy of Management Review*, **24**(1): 31–48.

Lepak, D.P. & Snell, S.A. (2002). Examining the human resource architecture: The relationships among human capital, employment, and human resource configurations. *Journal of Management*, **28**(4): 517–543.

Lepak, D.P., Takeuchi, R., Erhardt, N.L. & Colakoglu, S. (2006). Emerging perspectives on the relationship between HRM and performance. In Burke, R.J. & Cooper, C.L. (eds.), *The Human Resource Revolution: Why Putting People First Matters*. Oxford: Elsevier, pp. 31–54.

Liao, H., Toya, K., Lepak, D.P. & Hong, Y. (2009). Do they see eye to eye? Management and employee perspectives of high-performance work systems and influence processes on service quality. *Journal of Applied Psychology*, **94**(2): 371–391.

London, M. (1983). Toward a theory of career motivation. *Academy of Management Review*, **8**(4): 620–630.

London, M. (1991). Career development. In Wexley, K. and Hinrichs, J. (eds.), *Developing Human Resources*. Washington, DC: Bureau of National Affairs, pp. 152–184.

MacDuffie, J.P. (1995). Human resource bundles and manufacturing performance: Organizational logic and flexible production systems in the world auto industry. *Industrial and Labor Relations Review*, **48**(2): 197–221.

Maruping, L.M. & Magni, M. (2012). What's the weather like? The effect of team learning climate, empowerment climate, and gender on individuals' technology exploration and use. *Journal of Management Information Systems*, **29**(1): 79–114.

Maurer, D., Le Grand, R. & Mondloch, C.J. (2002). The many faces of configural processing. *Trends in Cognitive Sciences*, **6**(6): 255–260.

McDonnell, A., Collings, D.G. & Burgess, J. (2012). Asia Pacific perspectives on talent management. *Asia Pacific Journal of Human Resources*, **50**(4): 391–398.

McKinsey (2018). Winning with your talent-management strategy. McKinsey and Co., August 7. https://www.mckinsey.com/business-functions/people-and-organizational -performance/our-insights/winning-with-your-talent-management-strategy.

Meyers, M.C. & van Woerkom, M. (2014). The influence of underlying philosophies on talent management: Theory, implications for practice, and research agenda. *Journal of World Business*, **49**(2): 192–203.

Michaels, E., Handfield-Jones, H. & Axelrod, B. (2001). *The War for Talent*. Boston, MA: Harvard Business School Press.

Nahapiet, J. & Ghoshal, S. (1998). Social capital, intellectual capital, and the organizational advantage. *Academy of Management Review*, **23**(2): 242–266.

Narayanan, A., Rajithakumar, S. & Menon, M. (2019). Talent management and employee retention: An integrative research framework. *Human Resource Development Review*, **18**(2): 228–247.

Noe, R. (1986). Trainee's attributes and attitudes: Neglected influences on training effectiveness. *Academy of Management Review*, **11**(4): 736–749.

Osterman, P. (1994). How common is workplace transformation and who adopts it? *Industrial and Labor Relations Review*, **47**(2): 173–188.

Piaget, J. & Cook, M.T. (1952). *The Origins of Intelligence in Children*. New York: W.W. Norton.

Prieto, I.M. & Pilar Pérez Santana, M. (2012). Building ambidexterity: The role of human resource practices in the performance of firms from Spain. *Human Resource Management*, **51**(2): 189–211.

Reichers, A.E. & Schneider, B. (1990). Climate and culture: An evolution of constructs. *Organizational Climate and Culture*, **1**: 5–39.

Rouiller, J.Z. & Goldstein, I.L. (1993). The relationship between organizational transfer climate and positive transfer of training. *Human Resource Development Quarterly*, **4**(4): 377–390.

Rousseau, D.M. (1990). Normative beliefs in fund-raising organizations: Linking culture to organizational performance and individual responses. *Group and Organization Studies*, **15**(4): 448–460.

Schein, E.H. (1993). How can organizations learn faster? The problem of entering the Green Room. *Sloan Management Review*, **34**: 85–92.

Schuler, R.S. & Jackson, S.E. (1987). Linking competitive strategies with human resource management practices. *Academy of Management Perspectives*, **1**(3): 207–219.

Scullion, H., Collings, D.G. & Caligiuri, P. (2010). Global talent management. *Journal of World Business*, **45**(2): 105–108.

Scullion, H., Vaiman, V. & Collings, D.G. (2016). Strategic talent management. *Employee Relations*, **38**(1): 1–7.

Senge, P.M. (1990). *The Fifth Discipline*. New York: Doubleday.

Singh, S.K., Mazzucchelli, A., Vessal, S.R. & Solidoro, A. (2021). Knowledge-based HRM practices and innovation performance: Role of social capital and knowledge sharing. *Journal of International Management*, **27**(1): 100830.

Snell, S.A., Youndt, M.A. & Wright, P.M. (1996). Establishing a framework for research in strategic human resource management: Merging resource theory and organizational learning. *Research in Personnel and Human Resources Management*, **14**: 61–90.

Sparrow, P. (2019). A historical analysis of critiques in the talent management debate. *Business Research Quarterly*, **22**(3): 160–170.

Subramaniam, M. & Youndt, M.A. (2005). The influence of intellectual capital on the types of innovative capabilities. *Academy of Management Journal*, **48**(3): 450–463.

Swift, P.E. & Hwang, A. (2008). Learning, dynamic capabilities and operating routines: A consumer package goods company. *The Learning Organization*, **15**(1): 75–95.

Takeuchi, R., Lepak, D.P., Wang, H. & Takeuchi, K. (2007). An empirical examination of the mechanisms mediating between high-performance work systems and the performance of Japanese organizations. *Journal of Applied Psychology*, **92**(4): 1069–1083.

Takeuchi, H. & Nonaka, I. (2002). Reflection on knowledge management from Japan. In D. Morey, M. Maybury, & B. Thuraisingham (eds.), *Knowledge Management: Classic and Contemporary Works*. Cambridge, MA: MIT Press, pp. 183–187.

Vaiman, V. & Collings, D.G. (2013). Talent management: Advancing the field. *International Journal of Human Resource Management*, **24**(9): 1737–1743.

Vaiman, V., Collings, D.G. & Scullion, H. (2017). Contextualizing talent management. *Journal of Organizational Effectiveness: People and Performance*, **4**(4): 294–297.

Vaiman, V., Haslberger, A. & Vance, C.M. (2015). Recognizing the important role of self-initiated expatriates in effective global talent management. *Human Resource Management Review*, **25**(3): 280–286.

Van Esch, E., Wei, L.Q. & Chiang, F.F. (2016). High-performance human resource practices and firm performance: The mediating role of employees' competencies and the moderating role of climate for creativity. *The International Journal of Human Resource Management*, **29**(10): 1683–1708.

Vroom, V.H. (1964). *Work and Motivation*. New York: Wiley.

Weiss, H.M. (1990). Learning theory and industrial and organizational psychology. In Dunnette, M.D. & Hough, L.M. (eds.), *Handbook of Industrial and Organizational Psychology*. Palo Alto, CA: Consulting Psychologists Press, pp. 171–221.

Wright, P.M. & McMahan, G.C. (1992). Theoretical perspectives for strategic human resource management. *Journal of Management*, **18**(2): 295–320.

Youndt, M.A., Snell, S.A., Dean, J.W. & Lepak, D.P. (1996). Human resource management, manufacturing strategy, and firm performance. *Academy of Management Journal*, **39**(4): 836–866.

Zacharatos, A., Barling, J. & Iverson, R.D. (2005). High-performance work systems and occupational safety. *Journal of Applied Psychology*, **90**(1): 77–93.

Zahra, S.A. & George, G. (2002). Absorptive capacity: A review, reconceptualization, and extension. *Academy of Management Review*, **27**(2): 185–203.

6. Talent staffing systems for effective knowledge management

Mark L. Lengnick-Hall and Andrea R. Neely

Few people would disagree that knowledge is becoming an increasingly important factor in firm success (Grant, 1996; Liebeskind, 1996; McFadyen & Cannella, 2004; Teece, 1998). It takes the support of HRM practices, such as staffing and training/development, to transform knowledge into 'know-how' and utilize it to achieve organizational objectives. Globalization and growing connectedness have quickened the pace for competition and placed a premium on knowing what the next trend is and rapidly mobilizing resources to develop a product or provide a service that takes advantage of opportunities—before rivals enter the fray. Though not all firms compete in a hypercompetitive market (D'Aveni, 1994), all firms need to reduce costs and increase efficiency; this emphasizes the importance of knowledge and learning as key ingredients to their success. While traditional approaches to HRM served organizations well in the twentieth century, new and innovative approaches are needed for the twenty-first century and the knowledge economy (Lengnick-Hall & Lengnick-Hall, 2003). A key component of this new approach to HRM is its emphasis on developing staffing systems that provide the necessary talent for effective knowledge management.

In a knowledge economy, organizations need a stock (supply) and flow (movement) of talent to survive and compete. Hiring people for specific jobs is insufficient; organizations need the knowledge that individuals possess to formulate innovative solutions (Anand et al., 2007; Leonard-Barton, 1995). Organizations need individuals who possess knowledge, can acquire it, and can disseminate to others. Thus, managing both people and knowledge are necessary to be competitive.

The purpose of this chapter is to integrate talent staffing systems with knowledge management. Combining traditional HRM policies, programs, and practices along with some new perspectives and approaches can help organizations develop staffing systems that effectively manage people and knowledge. The chapter is organized as follows. First, we define talent management. Second, we define key concepts in knowledge management; we need to establish a common frame of reference before proceeding. Third, we describe staffing systems as a means for managing employee stocks and flows. We take a broader perspective on managing the movements of employees into, within, and out of the organization beyond recruitment and retention. Fourth, we integrate the management of employee stocks and flows (talent staffing systems) with knowledge stocks and flows (knowledge management systems). Fifth, we discuss artificial intelligence as an emerging trend for talent management. Last, we incorporate an example (Mayo Clinic) to help solidify the role of knowledge management in talent management systems. The objectives of a knowledge management system have implications for how talent staffing systems can best be designed to achieve desired outcomes. Finally, we offer some suggestions for research and practical implications.

TALENT MANAGEMENT

According to Scullion and Collings (2011), talent management includes all HR-related activities (including attraction, selection, development, and retention) applied to talented individuals, which are those individuals who are the best employees in the most strategic roles. Though they define *global* talent management in this fashion, we have modified this definition as it is not the scope of this book chapter. We contend that talent management is a sub-process or subset of HR management; that is, HR management concerns all players and positions—A (critical), B (supporting), and C (surplus)—and talent management concerns only A players and positions. Staffing an organization with all A players is not resourceful (e.g., labor costs) as all positions are not strategically critical (Huselid, Beatty, & Becker, 2005). Further, the job of talent management is three-fold: (a) identify individuals who are the 'best' workers (A players), (b) identify the positions that are strategically critical (A positions), and (c) design an HR architecture that moves those 'best' workers to the 'best' places (Collings, Mellahi, & Cascio, 2019).

KEY CONCEPTS FROM THE KNOWLEDGE MANAGEMENT LITERATURE

Knowledge is a multidimensional construct and has been examined from several different perspectives (Spender, 1996). Many authors distinguish between information and knowledge (see, for example, Newell et al., 2002). Leonard and Sensiper (1998: 112) define knowledge as 'information that is relevant, actionable, and at least partially based on experience.' Knowledge is information that is linked to potential actions because an individual can use it, whereas data are any signals that can be sent by an originator to a recipient, and information is simply data that are intelligible to the recipient (Davenport & Prusak, 2000; Lengnick-Hall & Lengnick-Hall, 2003). For example, the outside temperature of 120 degrees would be considered data. The fact that people get exhausted at that temperature is information—data in context. And, recognizing that it is more productive to work outside early in the morning or later in the day when it is cooler is knowledge—information linked to actions.

Knowledge is frequently categorized as taking two forms: explicit and tacit. *Explicit knowledge* can be formalized, codified, and communicated, and is often gained through formal education, training programs, and experience on the job (DeNisi, Hitt, & Jackson, 2003) such as blueprints created by an architect to communicate her design to the builders. Thus, explicit knowledge can be communicated through such means as written documents, formal presentations, books, manuals, formulas, specifications, lectures, diagrams, and so on. On the other hand, *tacit knowledge* is that which people know but cannot explain (Polanyi, 1966). It is not teachable, not articulated, and not observable in use, but instead is rich, complex, and undocumented (Davenport & Prusak, 2000). It is grounded in experience and difficult to express through mere verbal instruction—individuals know it but cannot articulate and explain it (DeNisi et al., 2003). An example of tacit knowledge is a salesperson knowing the exact moment and specific content to persuade a customer to buy a product or service.

Both explicit and tacit knowledge can be directed to accomplish organizational objectives through a combination of knowledge management and human resource management. For example, pyramid builders in ancient Egypt were encouraged to share what they learned about moving stone blocks with other crews. One work crew might learn from an accident that water spilled on the ground in front of the stones helped them slide the stones more easily. Other crews in the same proximity observing this phenomenon would then incorporate it into their own behaviors. This knowledge would then be transferred to other crews throughout the construction site. More formally, *knowledge transfer* is the process through which an individual, team, department, or division is affected by the experience of another (Argote et al., 2000) and it represents one of the most important means by which organizations can gain competitive advantage through knowledge. In the pyramid example, knowledge transfer both sped up the construction process, and probably saved lives as well.

In addition to the explicit/tacit knowledge distinction, knowledge can also be categorized as general versus specific (Becker, 1964). This is particularly useful for designing talent staffing systems for knowledge management since its focus is on the individual level of analysis. *General knowledge*, or public knowledge, resides in the public domain and it is applicable across firms in a variety of industries (Matusik & Hill, 1998). For example, knowledge of basic math, reading, and writing resides in the public domain, and someone who possesses that knowledge can apply it across virtually all businesses. On the other hand, *specific knowledge* is narrower in focus with application in only some situations (Lepak & Snell, 2003). *Firm-specific knowledge* is that which can only be applied in a particular organization, such as knowledge of an organization's filing system or internal administrative procedures. *Occupation-specific knowledge* is that which is relatively codified throughout a broader professional or institutionalized group (e.g., HRM knowledge is codified and even certified through the Society for Human Resource Management). *Industry-specific knowledge* is that which, though in the public domain, is applicable only to a particular industry. For example, financial literacy and understanding of financial institutions (such as banks, investment companies, insurance companies, and real estate firms) is specific to the finance industry. Employees bring all four forms of knowledge to the organization in varying amounts (Lepak & Snell, 2003). Through knowledge management and HRM, the talents of employees can be directed to accomplish desired organizational objectives.

Knowledge management is an encompassing term that usually covers three broad capabilities: (a) knowledge acquisition and creation, (b) knowledge capture and storage, and (c) knowledge diffusion and transfer (Sparrow, 2006). *Knowledge acquisition and creation* refers to the generation of new knowledge fundamental to the long-term viability of the enterprise. *Knowledge capture and storage* refers to the creation (and maintenance in usable form so that it remains valuable) of an inventory of knowledge so the people in the organization know what it possesses and where it resides. *Knowledge diffusion and transfer* refers to the subsequent mobilization and flow of knowledge within the organization that creates knowledge-based value. Together, these three processes form the basis of gaining a competitive advantage through knowledge. However, without application of knowledge, it will do little for a firm's competitive position (Lengnick-Hall & Lengnick-Hall, 2003). Furthermore, for an organization to learn, it must create *absorptive capacity*, or the ability to identify, assimilate, and use additional knowledge (Cohen & Levinthal, 1990).

Since, typically, individuals or groups cannot take in additional knowledge that is too different from their current knowledge base, organizations engage in practices that increase their absorptive capacities over time. A well-managed talent staffing system and knowledge management system can thus contribute to increasing an organization's absorptive capacity.

In summary, firms configure knowledge-based resources to create value through knowledge stocks and flows (Morris, Snell, & Lepak, 2005) (see Figure 6.1). *Knowledge stocks* include competencies, dynamic capabilities, routines, new ideas, and innovation and they can help organizations create competitive advantage through the effective use, manipulation, and transformation of various organizational resources required to perform a task. *Knowledge flows* include the movement of knowledge within and across firms that is essential for innovation and continuous adaptation. As Lepak and Snell (2003) note, it is the configuration of knowledge stocks that produces a competitive advantage, whereas the renewal and recombination of those stocks sustain that advantage. Therefore, the integration of effective talent staffing systems and knowledge management is critical for creating knowledge stocks and flows necessary for gaining and sustaining competitive advantage.

MANAGING EMPLOYEE FLOWS THROUGH TALENT STAFFING SYSTEMS

Employees join organizations, get promoted, get demoted, transfer laterally to different jobs, retire, leave voluntarily, leave involuntarily, come back after being rehired, and even die on the job. They don't stay put; they move, sometimes for their own benefit, sometimes for the benefit of the organization, and sometimes for both. These movements of employees into, within, and out of organizations—or *employee flows*—some planned and some unexpected, make staffing organizations a continual challenge. As employees flow into, within, and out of the organization, managers or organizations must determine how to acquire, retain, and transfer valuable knowledge. When viewed from an employee flows perspective, staffing systems encompass decisions about employee movements (see Figure 6.1).

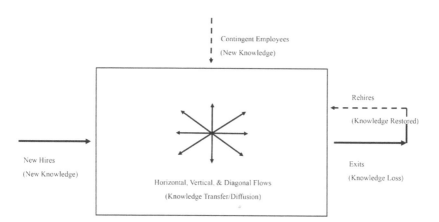

Figure 6.1   Employee flows

There are several employee flows that can occur in organizations. First, employees can be obtained externally (i.e., move from outside to inside) in three primary ways: (1) applicants can be recruited, selected, and hired from the outside, (2) former employees can be rehired (e.g., laid-off employees can be rehired), or (3) employees can be 'rented' (e.g., contingent workers, including part-time workers, independent contractors, and retirees). Second, once inside the organization, applicants (who are now employees) can move vertically, horizontally, or diagonally. Vertical movements include promotions (upward) and demotions (downward). Horizontal movement includes lateral transfers, such as those between equivalent jobs in the same department (division, unit, etc.) or to equivalent jobs in different departments. Diagonal movement includes changing job families or occupations, such as moving from an HR professional job to a line manager job in manufacturing. Third, employees can leave the organization either voluntarily (e.g., for a job at another company or to retire from work altogether), or involuntarily (e.g., terminated for job performance, laid off due to budget issues, or in some cases due to death).

Taking a big-picture perspective of employee flows and developing staffing systems—with an emphasis on systems (i.e., interacting component parts)—allows organizations to manage employee movements proactively to achieve desired objectives. As previous research has shown, for example, some turnover (employee flows out of the organization) is functional and healthy for an organization's survival (e.g., Dalton, 1997), and sometimes it even makes sense to hire (employee flows into the organization) in poor economic times (i.e., countercyclical hiring) to gain competitive advantage over rivals when economic times improve (Greer, 1984). A staffing system perspective of managing employee flows is thus more likely than a focus on individual staffing decisions to result in a steady source of human capital that is constantly renewed and adaptable to changes in the environment. From an employee flows perspective, individual staffing decisions, such as whom to promote or whom to transfer are viewed in the larger context of how they affect the overall stock and flow of talent in the organization.

Neither talent staffing systems nor knowledge management systems in isolation are adequate for effectively creating competitive advantage through knowledge assets in a firm. Each is a subsystem of the larger organizational system, and optimizing subsystems (i.e., doing each part well separately) does not result in maximum organizational system performance (von Bertalanffy, 1974). Consequently, what is needed is the integration of the two subsystems—working together—to accomplish desired organizational goals.

INTEGRATING TALENT STAFFING AND KNOWLEDGE MANAGEMENT SYSTEMS

Talent staffing systems and knowledge management systems are inextricably intertwined (see Figure 6.1). Organizations can acquire new knowledge through (1) new hires, (2) contingent employees, and (3) rehires. New employees bring new knowledge, explicit and tacit, general, occupation-specific, and industry-specific, into the organization—what they know, who they know, and what they have experienced. Once assimilated into the organization, they have the potential to move around, learn from others, apply knowledge, teach others, and diffuse knowledge. This makes it possible for employees to increase their own absorptive capacity (and their own knowledge stocks) and leverage their own value both internally and externally. This also makes it possible for the organization to increase its absorptive capacity (and knowledge stocks) and leverage knowledge for competitive advantage.

Organizations may also acquire new knowledge by using contingent employees. Contractors and other forms of temporary workers can bring new knowledge into an organization at lower financial costs but higher potential for loss of proprietary knowledge once they leave. Consequently, from a talent staffing perspective, organizations need to determine the appropriate balance between permanent and contingent staff that maximizes performance and minimizes costs. From a knowledge management perspective, organizations need to determine how best to maximize knowledge acquisition while minimizing knowledge loss (e.g., protecting especially proprietary knowledge) from these temporary workers.

Organizations may also restore lost knowledge and potentially acquire new knowledge by rehiring former employees. Rehiring former employees has advantages—these employees have firm-specific knowledge from their previous association with the organization that may have been acquired over a long period of time. Additionally, they may have acquired new knowledge while working for other employers in the interim. They can move back into old roles both faster and with fewer complications than what is involved in developing new employees and bringing them 'up to speed'. If the rehire is a retiree, the organization has another shot at capturing lost knowledge. Retirees may also be temporary workers, providing a particularly appealing staffing strategy— using their talents and 'picking their brains'—that both minimizes labor costs while filling pressing needs.

The design of talent staffing systems can play a significant role in facilitating knowledge management; designing organization structures and HR processes that promote knowledge acquisition, capture, and transfer. Developing timelines for employee transfers that capitalize on familiarity and group cohesion and recognize the benefits of broad social ties and diversity of experience can facilitate knowledge.

Returning to our pyramid example, imagine two scenarios for the staffing of stone moving crews. In the first scenario, crews are formed and reformed daily with little opportunity for creating cohesion within the group. Due to limited communication (perhaps for fear of an uprising), the capacity to transfer knowledge throughout the construction site is hindered. In the second scenario, stone moving crews are kept intact over time so crew members remain stable (except for losses due to death and injury), and the groups are able to become cohesive. This creates an opportunity for team learning. Unlike the first scenario, these crews can share what they learn, and create best practices. In the next sections, we examine ways to integrate staffing and knowledge management to create competitive advantage.

Objectives of a Talent Staffing System for Effective Knowledge Management

Though explicit practices for staffing and knowledge management will vary, there are some general guidelines for all organizations.

First, organizations need to hire individuals who have knowledge and expertise (explicit and tacit; oftentimes specialized) to contribute to innovative solutions. This is more important in knowledge-intensive firms (Anand et al., 2007; Horwitz, Heng, & Quazi, 2003) and for knowledge worker jobs (Newell et al., 2002) than in other firms and jobs, but even in less knowledge-intensive firms and in jobs requiring less knowledge, it is still a desirable goal to attain. For key knowledge workers, organizations need to hire for knowledge, not the specific job (Lepak & Snell, 2003) (e.g., law firms seeking someone knowledgeable in labor law). Thus, hiring for knowledge gaps is frequently more important than hiring for job gaps (Brelade & Harman, 2000).

Second, while hiring for human capital (or knowledge), hiring for social capital may be equally important (Newell et al., 2002; Swart & Kinnie, 2003). *Social capital* refers to 'the goodwill that is engendered by the fabric of social relations and that can be mobilized to facilitate action' (Adler & Kwon, 2002, p. 17). From this perspective, the networks of friends, colleagues, and associates that an individual brings to an organization expand the opportunities for importing knowledge into the organization from external sources. In addition, the social capital that an individual develops while within an organization is equally important for expanding its knowledge assets.

Third, organizations need to hire individuals who can teach and effectively communicate what they know to others. It is necessary, but insufficient to hire individuals with needed knowledge and expertise. Organizations also need employees who can transfer their knowledge to individuals and groups.

Fourth, for key knowledge workers, organizations should consider adapting the job, location, work, and tasks to attract, motivate, and retain them (Horwitz et al., 2003; Ronen, Friedman, & Ben-Asher, 2007). Key knowledge workers are more likely to be scarce in the labor market and demand more flexible work arrangements, as well as more likely to make valued contributions to the organization when their needs are met.

Fifth, employers should capture the knowledge of employees (e.g., technology, social systems) both while they are still in the organization and before they leave—either voluntarily or involuntarily. This applies to both full-time permanent employees and part-time contingent employees.

Sixth, some employees are more important because they can learn continuously and contribute over a longer timeframe. Firms should invest in them (e.g., training opportunities, funding outside education, job transfers, etc.) and try to retain them. On the other hand, some employees do not have the ability to learn continuously (or do not exert the effort), and consequently are less valuable over a longer time; in this case, turnover may be desirable.

Seventh, organizations need to create a climate and culture that nurtures and supports knowledge acquisition, capture, and diffusion. To attract talented workers and provide motivation and opportunity to apply their knowledge, this kind of environment is necessary. This prevents *knowledge hoarding*, or employees' reluctance to share knowledge for fear of becoming expendable.

Eighth, organizations need strategies for minimizing knowledge loss and spillover. When employees who are deeply embedded in social networks within an organization leave, the effect of their departures can often be greater than the loss of a single employee (e.g., negatively affect knowledge flows) (Fisher & White, 2000). Additionally, when employees who have proprietary knowledge leave the organization, knowledge spillovers to competitors are a serious concern. Similarly, contingent workers who may acquire firm-specific knowledge while working for the organization and then later share that knowledge with competitors.

Together, these overarching objectives provide a basis for designing talent staffing systems that support effective knowledge management within organizations and prevent undesirable, and often unintended, knowledge leakage to other organizations.

Talent Staffing System Components to Promote Knowledge Capture and Storage

Organizations need some means for capturing and storing knowledge so it can be more easily shared across people and groups, and so when individuals leave the organization, some of what they know remains behind. *Organizational memory* is how organizations store knowledge for future use and it is contingent on dispersed knowledge (e.g., held by people and documents) (Olivera, 2000). *Organizational memory systems* are sets of knowledge retention devices (e.g., people and documents) that collect, store, and provide access to the organization's experience.

Hansen, Nohria, and Tierney (1999) identified two primary ways that organizations capture and store knowledge; each has different implications for talent staffing systems. With a *codification* strategy, an organization attempts to capture knowledge—especially explicit knowledge—by having employees document what they do and what they know. Hansen et al. describe this as a 'people-to-documents' approach and the objective is to get employees to write, document, and make explicit what they know or have learned in a manner that allows other employees to learn from them. Rather than reinvent the wheel each time a similar problem or opportunity is confronted, a codification strategy enables an organization to reuse knowledge in productive ways. Hansen et al. describe how the Anderson Consulting company used codified knowledge to service clients faster and better than their competitors. By taking off-the-shelf templates, Anderson consultants could, with some modifications, adapt previously used solutions to new customers. A codification strategy can be particularly effective when implemented with information system technology, whereby employees can contribute to, have access to, and use knowledge through various communication devices. However, this strategy does not require sophisticated technology to be implemented.

For organizations pursuing primarily a codification strategy, there are some important implications for talent staffing systems. First, organizations will want to hire employees who have, among other knowledge, skills, abilities and other characteristic (KSAOs), the ability to reuse knowledge and implement solutions. For example, individuals who can identify problems, articulate those problems to yield possible solutions through an internet search, and then solve the problem would be valuable. Second, it would be desirable to hire people who can articulate what they know and contribute to a knowledge database. Equally important is hiring people who enjoy teaching others what they know rather than hoarding knowledge as a source of personal power.

With a *personalization* strategy, an organization attempts to capture knowledge—especially tacit knowledge—by having employees share what they know and have learned with others through person-to-person contact. Hansen et al. (1999) describe this as a person-to-person approach and the objective is to develop social networks that connect people with needed knowledge to one another.

With this approach, tacit knowledge is conveyed from one person to another with the expectation that it will be applied to a particular situation. Since this type of knowledge cannot be easily captured in documents and other codified forms, it is embedded in people and their networks instead. Hansen et al. describe how the consulting company Bain invests less in codified systems of knowledge capture and more in developing and retaining employees who have specialized knowledge and capabilities that can be accessed by their colleagues. A personalization strategy relies less on information technology for capturing knowledge but may use it for identifying who knows what (expert locators) and how to access people with needed knowledge.

For organizations pursuing a personalization strategy, there are some important implications for talent staffing systems. First, organizations will want to hire employees who have, among other KSAOs, critical and analytical skills and the ability to share knowledge with others through personal interaction. For example, individuals who are capable of problem solving, tolerating ambiguity, and capable of mentoring others would be valuable. With this approach, every employee is a teacher and a student. Second, organizations will want to increase the awareness of who knows what and who is working on what within the company (e.g., *transactive memory* which is an understanding of 'where' knowledge resides; Wegner, 1987). This can be accomplished using skill profiling systems and corporate yellow pages. Additionally, communities of practice, thematic help desks manned by knowledge area specialists, and knowledge fairs may be used to capture knowledge and make it more accessible (Cross, Parker, & Borgatti, 2002).

Talent Staffing System Components to Promote Knowledge Transfer and Diffusion

It is inadequate to acquire, create, capture, and store knowledge. It must also be diffused and transferred (1) individual to individual (usually expert to novice), (2) individual to group (either to broaden availability of specific knowledge or to preserve knowledge until a successor is named), (3) group to individual (transferring knowledge to a new member), and (4) group to group (preserving one group's knowledge over time, or broadening access to specific knowledge, such as best practices; DeLong, 2004). Practices for transferring knowledge can be characterized as either direct or indirect (DeLong, 2004). *Direct knowledge transfer* involves personal interaction between the sender and receiver, and includes such practices as face-to-face meetings, after-action reviews, mentoring programs, communities of practice, and storytelling. *Indirect knowledge transfer* involves little or no personal interaction between sender and receiver, and includes such practices as interviews, documentation (such as written reports or lessons-learned databases), and training. Both direct and indirect knowledge transfer practices have implications for talent staffing systems. Next, we discuss those practices where talent staffing systems are most likely to have a more direct impact on knowledge transfer.

Knowledge transfer can be facilitated through the management of employee flows: horizontally, vertically, and diagonally (see Figure 6.1). Employees both acquire and disseminate knowledge as they move through organizations. Three employee flow strategies that promote knowledge transfer will be discussed next: job rotation, expatriate assignments, and teams.

Job rotations are lateral transfers of employees between jobs in an organization (Campion, Cheraskin, & Stevens, 1994). They are typically used as a staffing strategy for employees early in their careers more so than for those in late career. Job rotation may serve as one means for employees to increase both their knowledge stocks as well as networks of contacts (social capital). Additionally, job rotation may facilitate the transfer of company culture (a form of firm-specific knowledge). At Air Products and Chemicals, new hires with engineering and information technology degrees, as well as MBAs and PhDs, participate in three job rotations averaging ten months each (DeLong, 2004). The company arranges the first assignment, but then the employees must find their second and third assignments themselves. The company also encourages these employees to take assignments in areas that they might not otherwise consider, to enhance their knowledge bases.

Expatriate assignment is a talent staffing strategy involving a job transfer (either lateral or vertical) that takes an employee to work outside the country in which he or she is a citizen (Mendenhall, 2005). From a knowledge transfer perspective, expatriates know how the parent company operates and can pass on this firm-specific knowledge to the local employees. Expatriates represent one type of boundary-spanner that may be important for developing social capital (Kostova & Roth, 2003). Network ties with peer expatriates, local working partners, and local friends may serve as channels for social resources, such as informational, emotional, instrumental, and appraisal support (Sparrow, 2006). While much has been written about selecting employees for foreign assignments, most has been concerned with cross-cultural and family adjustments.

From a knowledge management perspective, staffing concerns should additionally focus on abilities of expatriates to transfer knowledge and develop social capital abroad (Sparrow, 2006). Equally important as selecting and staffing expatriates for international assignments is the process of repatriation. *Repatriation* refers to the process of returning expatriates home from international assignments (Gregersen, 2005). While repatriation focuses on assisting expatriates and their families to the adjustment of moving back home, effective talent staffing systems must also reorient, capture, and transfer the knowledge of the expatriate. Expatriates may face challenges upon re-entry; there may be changes in the organization's rules or procedures (firm-specific knowledge) that occurred while the expatriate was abroad, requiring them to unlearn old ways of operating before new learning and knowledge transfer can occur.

The use of various types of *work teams* is a commonly used talent staffing strategy, especially in knowledge-intensive firms. For example, knowledge teams are groups of employees who perform interdependent knowledge work and who are collectively responsible for a product or service (Mohrman, 2005). They are often composed of members with several different highly advanced disciplines, each with knowledge bases that only partially overlap. Other types of knowledge teams include (Mohrman, 2005): (1) *work teams* that deliver a service or product, (2) *integrating teams* that coordinate across various parts of the organization, (3) *management teams* that integrate various parts of the organization and (4) *process improvement teams* that examine and make changes to the work processes of the organization.

In staffing teams for effective knowledge management, it is important to realize that employees may participate as members of several teams—on one as a team leader, on another as an expert adviser, on one project team that requires frequent meetings and close working relationships, and on another project team that requires working more alone with infrequent meetings of the larger team (Jackson, DeNisi, & Hitt, 2003). For example, NASA instituted a policy requiring technical experts use 20% of their time on other projects outside their primary project (DeLong, 2004).

Some work environments may be very dynamic, causing new teams to be formed, old teams to be reconfigured, and some old teams to be disbanded. The fluid nature of team formation and dissolution serves both adaptation and knowledge transfer processes well, especially in rapidly changing environments, but it makes staffing more complex. A premium is placed on hiring individuals who have needed expertise, the ability to function on different types of teams, adaptability, and high tolerance for change. Since team structures may change, individuals with high levels of organizational fit may be better equipped to serve on teams with different configurations of employees.

THE IMPACT OF ARTIFICIAL INTELLIGENCE ON TALENT STAFFING AND KNOWLEDGE MANAGEMENT SYSTEMS

Artificial intelligence and machine learning are changing the nature of work (Brougham & Haar, 2018). This will create continuing challenges for organizations in both staffing the talent and managing the knowledge for competitive advantage.

Two things are happening simultaneously. One, artificial intelligence is gaining greater use and acceptance in HRM (Vrontis et al., 2022). In particular, the use of large data sets, many types and sources of data, and algorithms that can discover meaningful relationships brings both new tools as well as new problems to the management of talent staffing systems. And two, employees can now 'collaborate' with those intelligent machines that can both 'learn' and make autonomous decisions. This, too, has implications for both talent staffing and knowledge management systems.

The use of artificial intelligence in talent staffing systems has the potential to improve how organizations recruit and select new employees. The ability to scan the internet looking for individuals with knowledge, skills, and abilities means organizations can have the most expansive labor pool imaginable—far greater than in the past. Talent staffing systems also have the ability to use multiple sources of information (social media, text, email, video, etc.) and combine different types of data to explore the largest labor pools and identify the right person for a job. Furthermore, the collaboration between humans and 'intelligent machines' may change the nature of KSAOs necessary for effective performance. Tang et al. (2021) in a recent series of studies, have demonstrated that using conscientiousness as a primary selection factor may be less important when employees are working with machines powered by artificial intelligence as machines may compensate for human deficiencies of this trait. However, these new artificial intelligence-enabled tools also come with drawbacks. Tippins, Oswald, and McPhail (2021) have identified major areas of concern (e.g., scarcity of evidence, data transparency) and offered a roadmap for future research and practice.

Fteimi and Hopf (2021) argue that artificial intelligence will require organizations to rethink codification and personalization strategies for capturing and using knowledge. They propose an adaptive strategy that combines elements of both. Artificial intelligence is no longer simply supportive in the fulfillment of tasks but also works as an independent and autonomous actor in the relationship with employees. Thus, mutual learning between both humans and AI becomes possible.

AI will continue to evolve in the future presenting both opportunities and challenges. Organizations will need to stay 'in the loop' and adjust both talent staffing systems and knowledge management systems to remain competitive.

TALENT STAFFING AND KNOWLEDGE MANAGEMENT AT THE MAYO CLINIC

The Mayo Clinic in Rochester, Minnesota is an organization that has integrated talent staffing and knowledge management systems. In 1919, Dr. William Mayo explained this integration as the 'spirit of the clinic which incorporates the desire to aid those who are suffering, the desire to advance in medical education by research, by diligent observation, and by the application of knowledge gained from others and, most importantly of all, the desire to pass on to others the scientific candle this spirit has lighted' (Berry & Seltman, 2008: 9).

The Mayo brothers, William and Charles, studied and observed doctors at hospitals and surgical clinics on 'vacations' they took to Europe each year, and then returned to Minnesota sharing what they learned with doctors at their own clinic and with other doctors who traveled to Minnesota to learn from them. As their practice grew, they developed along with administrative personnel at the clinic a sophisticated information system that collected patient records that were whisked around the building and between floors through mechanically engineered document transporters to share knowledge among physicians. Meticulous records, large databases, and a research orientation enabled the two brothers to innovate, learn, and share their knowledge through scientific publications, conferences, and presentations. Now digitized, patient databases are exponentially larger and more detailed than the early days. The clinic now has a Department of Artificial Intelligence and Informatics that according to their website 'promotes collaborative research for advancing the methods, applications and infrastructure in digital medicine with the emphasis on the synergy of people, processes and technology, representing a multidisciplinary unification based on biomedical, computational and social sciences.' They also have a Department of Informatics and Knowledge Management that according to their website 'supports patient care and health care research by effectively leveraging data to generate new knowledge. In turn, this knowledge is used to improve quality and safety, reduce costs, and maintain Mayo's role as a leader in health care innovation.'

The clinic was the first integrated not-for-profit multi-specialty medical group practice bringing together doctors from virtually every major specialty area working collaboratively to care for patients. A strong organizational culture built around a 'patient first' foundation sets the stage for human resource practices that encourage acquiring, creating, and transferring knowledge including: (a) cross-functional and cross-geographic work teams configured and then reconfigured for individual patient needs, (b) rigorous hiring practices with multiple steps to insure fit with their organizational values of respect, integrity, compassion, healing, teamwork, innovation, excellence, and stewardship, (c) hiring half of the graduates from their own medical school, (d) physicians paid on a salary basis rather than number of patients seen or procedures performed, (e) job rotation for administrators, and (f) a participative governance structure much like universities in which physicians serve in leadership roles and then return to practice medicine after their term has ended.

The Mayo Clinic continuously increases the organization's absorptive capacity through thousands of research studies, and thus, helps thousands of individual patients every year. In addition, knowledge flows are facilitated by its own medical school, quality research of staff, and patient education via multiple media worldwide. Talent staffing and knowledge management systems are so deeply embedded in the organization that they form the DNA that has allowed the Mayo Clinic to evolve and change over time while remaining one of the most prestigious medical clinics in the world.

ISSUES IN INTEGRATING TALENT STAFFING AND KNOWLEDGE MANAGEMENT SYSTEMS

The integration of knowledge management and talent staffing systems is still a relatively new area of practice and research. And, it has been made more difficult due to the turf battles over where responsibility for knowledge management should reside. Knowledge management has frequently been viewed as an information technology function in organizations, resulting in an emphasis on codified knowledge acquisition, storage, and transfer. On the other hand, the HR function has been the primary organizational leader in both developing talent staffing systems and transferring much tacit knowledge among employees. Clearly, taking a more holistic approach to knowledge management and talent staffing systems should enable organizations to compete more effectively based on their knowledge assets. However, many challenges must be overcome to realize this goal (see Table 6.1).

In the area of knowledge acquisition and creation, research is beginning to shed light on the decisions of making, buying, or renting knowledge. However, much less is known about what types of configurations, or mixes, of these approaches yield the best outcomes for organizations pursuing specific strategies or operating in specific environments. From a practical standpoint, organizations face the challenge of retaining valued knowledge workers once they are hired. Since these workers typically have high value externally, ways to embed them in an organization (see, for example, Mitchell, Holtom, & Lee, 2001) seem particularly important. And, while some organizations attempt to acquire knowledge wholesale through buying other companies or merging with them, there is no guarantee that the employees (and their knowledge) will remain after the purchase or merger.

In the area of knowledge capture and storage, recent research is beginning to shed light on the two primary methods of codification and personalization (e.g., Haesli & Boxall, 2005). How talent staffing systems can facilitate the capture and storage of knowledge must be viewed from both a current employee's and a leaving employee's perspective. Capturing the knowledge of employees while they are with an organization (be it a long or short time) is critical for increasing an organization's absorptive capacity and potential to gain competitive advantage through knowledge. From a practical standpoint, organizations need to be concerned that employees may leave before their knowledge has been captured (particularly consequential for long-term knowledgeable employees); contingent employees may only do the jobs they are hired for, but not transfer their knowledge to the organization (an opportunity lost); and while strategic alliances may offer ways to capture the knowledge other organizations have acquired, contractual barriers may limit these opportunities.

Finally, in knowledge diffusion and transfer, much has been published and research interest appears to be high. We know more about how to diffuse and transfer knowledge through various means, but we still do not know how to deal with pragmatic problems that may affect competitive advantage and strategic effectiveness. For example, hoarding knowledge is a big problem in many organizations. Individuals face the dilemma of either keeping what

Table 6.1   Issues in integrating knowledge management and talent staffing systems

Knowledge management capabilities and goals	Talent staffing system strategies	Issues
Knowledge acquisition & creation:		
Acquire and create knowledge that provides a basis for competitive advantage; increase absorptive capacity.	Make, buy, or rent individual knowledge through external hires.	Knowledgeable employees are valuable externally and difficult to retain.
	Buy the knowledge of groups of employees through acquisitions and mergers.	Key employees in acquired firms may not remain after acquisition.
	Rent the knowledge of groups of employees with strategic alliances.	
Knowledge capture & storage:		
Capture and store knowledge that can be accessed for solving problems and creating innovations.	Personalization	Employees may leave before their knowledge has been captured.
	Codification	Contingent employees may do the job, but not share the knowledge.
		Contractual barriers may make it difficult to capture knowledge through strategic alliances.
Knowledge diffusion & transfer:		
Diffuse and transfer knowledge between individuals, from individuals to groups (and vice versa), and across teams throughout the organization.	Job rotation	Knowledge hoarding
	Expatriates	Knowledge spillover and loss
	Teamwork	Team fit

they know to themselves (to protect their personal value) or sharing what they know with others (making themselves vulnerable to job loss). Identifying reward structures and organizational climates conducive to knowledge transfer remains a thorny issue.

Additionally, knowledge spillover and loss confront organizations as a difficult challenge. Since employees really are volunteers and can leave at any time, how do you prevent them from taking proprietary knowledge and knowledge that affects competitive advantage with them? Legal and contractual requirements offer only limited protection. Lastly, in transferring knowledge, many organizations are moving to more team-based structures. This presents both problems and opportunities: problems in locating individuals with the knowledge, flexibility, and adaptability to take on many roles, and opportunities to limit knowledge loss and increase the organization's absorptive capacity.

The ancient Egyptian pyramid builders may have solved many of the problems of integrating talent staffing systems with knowledge management. Some of what they learned has been passed on through the codified knowledge they left behind on the pyramid walls. However, we will never know what tacit knowledge they learned and transferred while accomplishing their amazing engineering feats. And, despite our incredible technological advances, we have a long way to go to match their organizational accomplishments. Instead, we must reinvent the wheel (and learn what they probably knew) for a more globally connected world environment that we face today and in the future.

In conclusion, we suggest that talent management (i.e., the 'best' people in the 'best' place) is only part of this process. Rather, we must understand how these people learn, what information and knowledge they possess, and determine how, when, and where to use it strategically. The 'best' people are the ones who learn and adapt quickly as new knowledge and information becomes available. The 'best' places are those where they can have the most impact (Bonner et al., 2022). Has the organization set itself up to capture that learning and disseminate it widely?

Organizations must be constantly adapting their knowledge management to capture, retain, and diffuse that knowledge considering those emerging trends such as artificial intelligence. Likewise, there are organizations such as the Mayo Clinic that can provide an example of what an organization looks like who is prepared to learn from its talent. Although there are significant challenges given the dynamic environment, especially in a post-COVID world, we contend that knowledge management (i.e., what, how, when) should be incorporated with talent management (i.e., who and where) to maximize profits and well-being of all stakeholders (e.g., customers, employees, society).

REFERENCES

Adler, P.S. & Kwon, S.W. (2002). Social capital: Prospects for a new concept. *Academy of Management Review*, **27**: 17–40.

Anand, N., Gardner, H.K. & Morris, T. (2007). Knowledge-based innovation: Emergence and embedding of new practice areas in management consulting firms. *Academy of Management Journal*, **50**(2): 406–428.

Argote, L., Ingram, P., Levine, J.M. & Moreland, R.L. (2000). Knowledge transfer in organizations: Learning from the experience of others. *Organizational Behavior and Human Decision Processes*, **82**(1): 1–8.

Becker, G.S. (1964). *Human Capital*. New York: Columbia University Press.

Berry, L.L. & Seltman, K.D. (2008). *Management Lessons from Mayo Clinic: Inside One of the World's Most Admired Service Organizations*. New York: McGraw-Hill.

Bonner, R.L., Neely, A.R., Stone, C.B., Lengnick-Hall, C.A. & Lengnick-Hall, M.L. (2022). Triaging your human capital: An integrative perspective on strategic human capital asset allocation. *Management Research Review*. https://doi.org/10.1108/MRR-12-2020-0735.

Brelade, S. & Harman, C. (2000). Using human resources to put knowledge to work. *Knowledge Management Review*, **3**(1): 26–29.

Brougham, D. & Haar, J. (2018). Smart technology, artificial intelligence, robotics, and algorithms (STARA): Employees' perceptions of our future workplace. *Journal of Management & Organization*, **24**: 239–257.

Campion, M.A., Cheraskin, L. & Stevens, M.J. (1994). Career-related antecedents and outcomes of job rotation. *Academy of Management Journal*, **37**(6): 1518–1542.

Cohen, W.M. & Levinthal, D.A. (1990). Absorptive capacity: A new perspective on learning and innovation. *Administrative Science Quarterly*, **35**(1): 128–152.

Collings, D.G., Mellahi, K. & Cascio, W.F. (2019). Global talent management and performance in multinational enterprises: A multilevel perspective. *Journal of Management*, **45**(2): 540–566.

Cross, R., Parker, A. & Borgatti, S.P. (2002). A bird's eye view: Using social network analysis to improve knowledge sharing and creation. https://citeseerx.ist.psu.edu/viewdoc/download?doi=10.1.1.428.6296&rep=rep1&type=pdf.

Dalton, D.R. (1997). Employee transfer and employee turnover: A theoretical and practical disconnect? *Journal of Organizational Behavior*, **18**(5): 411–413.

D'Aveni, R.A. (1994). *Hypercompetition: Managing the Dynamics of Strategic Maneuvering*. New York: Free Press.

Davenport, T.H. & Prusak, L. (2000). *Working Knowledge*. Boston, MA: Harvard Business School Press.

DeLong, D.W. (2004). *Lost Knowledge: Confronting the Threat of an Aging Workforce*. Oxford: Oxford University Press.

DeNisi, A.S., Hitt, M.A. & Jackson, S.E. (2003). The knowledge-based approach to sustainable competitive advantage. In Jackson, S.E., DeNisi, A.S. & Hitt, M.A. (eds.), *Managing Knowledge for Sustained Competitive Advantage: Designing Strategies for Effective Human Resource Management*. San Francisco: Jossey-Bass, pp. 3–36.

Fisher, S.R. & White, M.A. (2000). Downsizing in a learning organization: Are there hidden costs? *Academy of Management Review*, **25**(1): 244–251.

Fteimi, N. & Hopf, K. (2021). Knowledge management in the era of artificial intelligence: Developing an integrative framework. University of Bamburg. https://fis.uni -bamberg.de/handle/uniba/49911.

Grant, R.M. (1996). Toward a knowledge-based theory of the firm. *Strategic Management Journal*, **17**: 109–122.

Greer, R.C. (1984). Countercyclical hiring as a staffing strategy for managerial and professional personnel: Some considerations and issues. *Academy of Management Review*, **9**(2): 324–330.

Gregersen, H.B. (2005). Repatriation. In Cartwright, S. (ed.), *The Blackwell Encyclopedia of Management*, 2nd edition. Malden, MA: Blackwell Publishing, p. 319.

Haesli, A. & Boxall, P. (2005). When knowledge management meets HR strategy: An exploration of personalization-retention and codification-recruitment strategies. *International Journal of Human Resource Management*, **16**(11): 1955–1975.

Hansen, M.T., Nohria, N. & Tierney, T. (1999). What's your strategy for managing knowledge? *Harvard Business Review*, **77**(2): 106–116.

Horwitz, F.M., Heng, C.T. & Quazi, H.A. (2003). Finders, keepers? Attracting, motivating and retaining knowledge workers. *Human Resource Management Journal*, **13**(4): 23–44.

Huselid, M.A., Beatty, R.W. & Becker, B.E. (2005). 'A players' or 'A positions'. *Harvard Business Review*, **83**(12): 110–117.

Jackson, S.E., DeNisi, A.S. & Hitt, M.A. (eds.) (2003). *Managing Knowledge for Sustained Competitive Advantage: Designing Strategies for Effective Human Resource Management*. San Francisco: Jossey-Bass.

Kostova, T. & Roth, K. (2003). Social capital in multinational corporations and a micro-macro model of its formation. *Academy of Management Review*, **28**(2): 297–317.

Lengnick-Hall, M.L. & Lengnick-Hall, C.A. (2003). *Human Resource Management in the Knowledge Economy: New Challenges, New Roles, New Capabilities*. San Francisco: Berrett-Koehler.

Leonard, D. & Sensiper, S. (1998). The role of tacit knowledge in group innovation. *California Management Review*, **40**(3): 112–132.

Leonard-Barton, D. (1995). *Wellsprings of Knowledge-building and Sustaining the Sources of Innovation*. Boston, MA: Harvard Business School Press.

Lepak, D.P. & Snell, S.A. (2003). Managing the human resource architecture for knowledge-based competition. In Jackson, S.E., DeNisi, A.S. & Hitt, M.A. (eds.), *Managing Knowledge for Sustained Competitive Advantage: Designing Strategies for Effective Human Resource Management*. San Francisco: Jossey-Bass, pp. 127–154.

Liebeskind, J.P. (1996). Knowledge, strategy, and the theory of the firm. *Strategic Management Journal*, **17**: 93–107.

Matusik, S.F. & Hill, C.W.L. (1998). The utilization of contingent work, knowledge creation, and competitive advantage. *Academy of Management Review*, **23**(4): 680–697.

McFadyen, M.A. & Cannella, A.A., Jr. (2004). Social capital and knowledge creation: Diminishing returns of the number and strength of exchange relationships. *Academy of Management Journal*, **47**: 735–746.

Mendenhall, M.E. (2005). Expatriate Assignment. In Cartwright, S. (ed.), *The Blackwell Encyclopedia of Management*, 2nd edition. Malden, MA: Blackwell Publishing, pp. 126–127.

Mitchell, T.R., Holtom, B.C. & Lee, T.W. (2001). How to keep your best employees: Developing an effective retention policy. *Academy of Management Executive*, **15**(4): 96–108.

Mohrman, S.A. (2005). Knowledge work. In Cartwright, S. (ed.), *The Blackwell Encyclopedia of Management*, 2nd edition. Malden, MA: Blackwell Publishing, p. 218.

Morris, S., Snell, S.A. & Lepak, D.P. (2005). An architectural approach to managing knowledge stocks and flows: Implications for reinventing the HR function. In Burke, R. & Cooper, C. (eds.), *Reinventing HR*. London: Routledge, pp. 31–54.

Newell, S., Robertson, M., Scarborough, H. & Swan, J. (2002). *Managing Knowledge Work*. Basingstoke: Palgrave Macmillan.

Olivera, F. (2000). Memory systems in organizations: An empirical investigation of mechanisms for knowledge collection, storage and access. *Journal of Management Studies*, **37**(16): 811–832.

Polanyi, M. (1966). *The Tacit Dimension*. New York: Anchor Books.

Ronen, S., Friedman, S. & Ben-Asher, H. (2007). Flexible working arrangements: Societal forces and implementation. In Gilliland, S.W., Steiner, D.D. & Skarlicki, D.P. (eds.), *Managing Social and Ethical Issues in Organizations*. Greenwich: Information Age Publishing, pp. 3–51.

Scullion, H. & Collings, D. (2011), *Global Talent Management*. London: Routledge.

Sparrow, P. (2006). Global knowledge management and HRM. In Stahl, G.K. & Bjorkman, I. (eds.), *Handbook of Research in International Human Resource Management*. Cheltenham, UK and Northampton, MA, USA: Edward Elgar, pp. 113–138.

Spender, J.C. (1996). Making knowledge the basis of a dynamic theory of the firm. *Strategic Management Journal*, **17**: 45–62.

Swart, J. & Kinnie, N. (2003). Sharing knowledge in knowledge-intensive firms. *Human Resource Management Journal*, **13**(2): 60–75.

Tang, P.M., Koopman, J., McClean, S.T., Zhang, J.H., Li, C.H., De Cremer, D., Lu, Y., Tung, C. & Ng, S. (2021). When conscientious employees meet intelligent machines: An integrative approach inspired by complementarity theory and role theory. *Academy of Management Journal*, **65**(3).

Teece, D.J. (1998). Capturing value from knowledge assets: The new economy, markets for know-how, and intangible assets. *California Management Review*, **40**(3): 55–79.

Tippins, N.T., Oswald, F.L. & McPhail, S.M. (2021). Scientific, legal, and ethical concerns about AI-based personnel selection tools: A call to action. *Personnel Assessment and Decisions*, **7**(2): 1–22.

von Bertalanffy, L. (1974). *Perspectives on General System Theory*. New York: Basic Books.

Vrontis, D., Christofi, M., Pereira, V., Tarba, S., Makrides, A. & Trichina, E. (2022). Artificial intelligence, robotics, advanced technologies and human resource management: A systematic review. *The International Journal of Human Resource Management*, **33**: 1237–1266.

Wegner, D.M. (1987). Transactive memory: A contemporary analysis of the group mind. In Mullen, B. & Goethals, G.R. (eds.), *Theories of Group Behavior*. Dordrecht: Springer, pp. 185–208.

7. Leveraging firms' absorptive capacity by talent development

Marina Latukha and Maria Laura MacLennan

INTRODUCTION

The overall ability to create and transfer knowledge is one of the main competitive advantages for emerging market firms, which is reflected in ongoing discussions in business and academia about the role of a firm's absorptive capacity (AC) and its drivers (Lane, Salk, & Lyles, 2001; Minbaeva, 2005; Tarique & Schuler, 2010; Ready, Hill, and Thomas, 2014). The increasing role of AC as an important determinant of a company's success stimulates a discussion that aims to identify particular organizational conditions whereby AC may be accelerated and used to improve firm performance (Collings, McDonnell, & Scullion, 2009; Collings, 2014; Flatten et al., 2011; Roberts et al., 2012; Roberts, 2015). AC as a concept has been developing as an extension of knowledge management studies with learning and innovation perspectives. Thus, AC was analyzed from a product innovation and development angle (Murovec & Prodan, 2009; Hansen, 1999; Tsai, 2001), through the exploration of coordination processes to ensure effective knowledge management (Szulanski, 2000; Kostova & Roth, 2002), in relation to organizational results (Cohen & Levinthal, 1990; Tsai, 2001; Kostopoulos et al., 2011; Lewin, Massini, & Peeters, 2011), and a firm's survival (Zahra & George, 2002; Lane, Koka, & Pathak, 2006).

As AC is widely discussed from knowledge development perspectives with a distinction of its dimensions, i.e. acquisition, assimilation, transformation and exploitation, it draws attention to the link between AC and human resource management (HRM) within a firm in order to understand how organizational systems and processes may shape AC. Gold, Malhotra, and Segars (2001) determine elements of knowledge management that are important for knowledge flow and connect them with managerial actions (e.g. acquisition, conversion, application). We may see that such actions can be managed by talents, talent management (TM) practices and talent development initiatives.

Some researchers mention managers' routines as drivers for AC development (Fosfuri & Tribo, 2008; Inkinen, Kianto, & Vanhala, 2015; Lane et al., 2006; Zahra & George, 2002), most of which refer to knowledge management. Those initiatives can be linked to HRM practices highlighting the role of HRM practices in intra-organizational knowledge transfer that has been addressed along with HRM architecture between different employee groups (Foss, 2007; Lepak & Snell, 1999, 2002; Kang, Morris, & Snell, 2007) where those employees, and specifically talented ones, are involved. There is also research on how firms and people deal with knowledge-transfer barriers (Minbaeva et al., 2003; Minbaeva, 2005). As talent management is about attraction, development and retention of best employees (who are considered to be talents), and talent can be treated as a person with outstanding abilities and results (Williams-Lee, 2008) showing potential for further development and possessing key knowledge and competencies (Blass, 2007; Armstrong, 2006; Boxall & Purcell, 2008), some relation to knowledge can be found. TM is going to be crucial for AC as knowledge acquisition, assimilation, transformation and exploitation are linked with individual and organizational competencies (Cohen & Levinthal, 1990; Minbaeva et al., 2003). We assume that talents are immersed in all knowledge processes in an organizational context. Talent is defined as high value-added skills (Lewis & Heckman, 2006), and a 'special' knowledge demanded in a particular organizational context. We can conclude that in order to get unique competencies or potential, a person should have a background received as an intrinsic gift in a field, but at the same time, inherited talent cannot go without certain development, individual motivation to growth, and education. It serves as a background for developing capabilities for knowledge assimilation, transformation and exploitation. This means that sometimes talent can be developed through training, motivation, experience and efforts, in relation to a certain professional area. Collings et al. (2009) argue the importance of key employees (talents) and their abilities to accumulate and share knowledge with others, and as TM refers not only to management but primarily to the development of 'high-performing and high-potential' employees (Collings et al., 2009; Collings, 2014), we also state the role of AC in talent development.

Talent development is considered to be the core element of the TM system (Novations, 2009) as it modifies an organization, its employees, and other stakeholders. It uses planned and unplanned learning, and aims to build, develop, and maintain a firm's competitive advantage. It refers to specific activities that help talented employees to reveal their potential and contribute to organizational results. It includes training and development opportunities that improve the quality of available knowledge and skills and strengthen a firm's appeal as an employer (Schuler, Jackson, & Tarique, 2011). Proper talent development allows an organization to retain talented employees and, at the same time, prepare the right people for the right positions within an organization, developing particular sets of skills and knowledge (Carr, Inkson, & Thorn, 2005; Gilley, Dixon, & Gilley, 2008) contributing to the TM system in a firm. Through such implementation, talent development finds its niche in AC.

Knowledge acquisition and assimilation help organizations to continuously update their knowledge flows and enhance understanding, reflection, and evaluation of valuable external information to ensure strategic flexibility in different contexts (Enkel & Heil, 2014). Knowledge transformation and exploitation configure a recombination and implementation of existing and newly acquired and assimilated knowledge (Volberda, Foss, & Lyles, 2010; Zahra & George, 2002). As employees possess knowledge and the ability to continuously enhance it for strategic initiatives' creation and implementation, they become a key determinant of a firm's success (Kiessling & Harvey, 2006). Since knowledge includes facts, information, descriptions, and skills that are acquired through experience or education by perceiving, discovering, or learning, one can state that talent development and AC are strongly interconnected.

By introducing context-specific learning and development programs, an organization facilitates its intra-organizational communication and knowledge transfer (Ambrosius, 2018). Further development of employees' abilities to acquire new knowledge more efficiently and interpret information obtained from diverse external sources (Szulanski, 1996; Fey et al., 2009; Minbaeva et al., 2003) helps to improve a firm's knowledge assimilation capabilities (Zhou, Fey, & Yildiz, 2020). Moreover, by interacting with the external environment (especially with international markets), a firm builds international human capital, i.e. knowledge of global best practices, global industry standards, and other transportable forms of knowledge and experience that are applicable across multiple firms and countries (Morris, Snell, & Björkman, 2016). By managing collaborations and cross-functional interfaces, a company may widen opportunities for knowledge transformation for individuals in particular, and the firm as a whole (Jansen, Van Den Bosch, & Volberda, 2005), and enable the identification of best practices to further facilitate knowledge exploitation (Lawson et al., 2009). In particular, through cross-functional teams a firm leverages its knowledge sources (Choi, Lee, & Yoo, 2010) and enables its employees to combine sets of existing and newly acquired external knowledge which forms transformative learning (Lane et al., 2006; Lazzarotti, Manzini, & Pellegrini, 2015). By the additional offering of continuous professional development opportunities and providing talented employees with feedback regarding their performance (via performance appraisal systems), a firm motivates high performers to share their experience and utilize valuable assimilated/transformed knowledge in ways that add value (e.g., Chen & Huang, 2009). This process is embedded in the dual nature of AC: on the one hand, it helps a company to create new and identify already existing knowledge from within, and on the other hand, to absorb and assimilate externally available and accessible knowledge (Cohen & Levinthal, 1990; Lewin et al., 2011).

Moreover, knowledge acquisition and transfer, as AC dimensions, are core processes in all developmental practices. Knowledge acquisition refers to the knowledge that a firm can obtain from external sources, such as suppliers, competitors, partners, customers, and external experts (Zahra & George, 2002). Talent development activities, such as formal training programs, become one of the main sources of new knowledge for talented employees. Thus, employees can use these external resources to acquire new information, so-called tacit knowledge (for example, via hands-on experience). Further, this acquired knowledge serves as a basis for the creation of new knowledge that can be visualized and shared with others. At the next stage, knowledge acquired by an employee is assimilated within an organization, i.e., interpreted, comprehended and analyzed. At this stage, knowledge is converted, which means that tacit knowledge undergoes externalization processes to become explicit. Then, new converted knowledge can be further shared by others. If these processes take place within talent development practices, relationship-based developmental experience prevails. The transformation stage can be considered as a combination mode when existing knowledge and newly acquired and assimilated knowledge are combined. At this stage, employees are learning by doing (for example, via job-based developmental practices). Being opposite to the previous stage, the transformation stage is characterized by internalization processes, whereby explicit knowledge becomes part of an individual's knowledge. Therefore, in terms of knowledge management, the transformation stage is somewhat in between the combination and internalization modes. At the exploitation stage employees apply their individually acquired knowledge in practice, simultaneously internalizing it. Tacit to tacit knowledge transfer may also occur when knowledge is shared through experience. This stage also has some features of a socialization mode, as learning that occurs at this stage is more incidental and unconscious.

By identifying these processes, the relations between AC and talent development become evident. However, some research states that diverse country-specific contexts configure a firm's abilities to manage knowledge differently.

Emerging markets still attract the primary attention of business scholars due to their distinguishing features (Beamond, Farndale, & Härtel, 2016; Reis & Quental, 2014; Tansley & Kirk, 2018), with attempts to investigate how the cultural, historical, and economic characteristics of different countries influence organizational processes related to knowledge management and create similarities and differences in TM practices implementation (Cooke, Saini, & Wang, 2014; Gallardo-Gallardo, Thunnissen, & Scullion, 2020; Schuler,

2015). In this ongoing 'war for talent,' emerging market firms continuously look for additional sources of competitive advantage that could help them with knowledge creation and exploitation through attraction and development of the best and brightest talents. The contextual specificity of different countries and its effect on the relationships between AC and talent development might be better seen through an analysis of the most advanced emerging markets such as Russia, China, and Brazil. Though these contexts share some similarities in their development trajectories, they are different enough to capture the effects under investigation (Child & Marinova, 2014). This chapter discusses how AC can be shaped and leveraged by talent development within these three emerging market contexts.

RUSSIA

For many years Russia was isolated from external global knowledge due to its specific historical development, so the majority of Russian companies tended to rely on internally generated knowledge (May et al., 2011; Michailova & Husted, 2003; Outila, Vaiman, & Holden, 2018) and on the established state educational system that historically stimulated knowledge creation in different industries over a long period of time. Russian TM's heritage is derived from the experience of Soviet-era firms, where knowledge acquisition, assimilation, exploitation and transformation were limited due to under-established R&D processes for generating new knowledge (Björkman, Fey, & Park, 2007; Holden & Vaiman, 2013; Michailova, 2000; Outila et al., 2018). In this situation there were many barriers to knowledge exchange with firms' external local and global environments, so conditions for AC were not actualized. However, Dixon and Day's study (2007) suggests that Russian managers have real potential to transform the administrative heritage left by the Soviet Union into a contemporary, more dynamic style of managing business processes that may increase a company's AC.

Recently we observe that Russian companies have the potential to significantly improve their AC by means of paying more attention to particular training and development initiatives at firm level, with an orientation toward teamwork for knowledge sharing purposes. An existing knowledge gap between global competencies and suitable educational background, particularly in the field of management, led to a lack of implementation in an organizational context, and pushed Russian companies to look at foreign players (and in some cases competitors) and start developing AC through a knowledge acquisition strategy (Dixon, Meyer, & Day, 2007; Michailova & Jormanainen, 2011).

In the field of education and training (as a primary source for AC), the early 1990s dramatically changed the vocational education and professional development landscape in Russia (Ardichvili & Dirani, 2005). Due to budget constraints, the Russian government of that time downsized, or merely eliminated many state-sponsored vocational training and professional development programs. As a consequence, foreign companies' subsidiaries created their own training and development facilities. Moreover, new entrants into the Russian labor market had increased possibilities of completing their degrees abroad, or undertaking joint educational or training programs—offered by either Russian or Western universities and professional development centers (Fey & Björkman, 2001)—which undoubtedly helped Russian firms to acquire new knowledge using the experience of people who were employed by foreign firms.

Perhaps as a result of the legacy of an intensive focus on individual merit during the Soviet era or a consequence of the fact that many Russians lack basic business skills—due once again to the ideological rejection of 'capitalist' business education in the Soviet Union (Holden & Vaiman, 2013)—Russian managers today are very fond of continuous employee training and development along Western-inspired lines (Fey & Björkman, 2001), and we are now seeing a rapid growth of business education in Russia. Nevertheless, Holden and Vaiman state that—due to a shorter-term mindset in Russian organizations—talents are often hired for the match of their current expertise with current position requirements, with no consideration for individual development imperatives, even when it is in the future interest of the company: 'most employers in Russia have no patience to develop their star players, because stars are needed now, and not necessarily in the future' (Holden & Vaiman, 2013: 140).

Holden and Vaiman (2013: 142) have identified a 'wariness of talent' in today's business sector in Russia. Russian firms need to catch-up with TM practices (Skuza, Scullion, & McDonnell, 2013) and overcome the isolation of top decision makers, the survival of authoritarian and bureaucratic management patterns (what Holden, 2011 has called 'entrenched bossdom'), the short-term orientation of business decision-making processes (detrimental to longer-term orientations), and lack of business or management-skilled individuals (especially among Soviet-born educated generations).

The need is all the more pressing because 'Russian employees find that their talents are more greatly valued by foreign employers based in Russia than by Russian firms' (Holden & Vaiman, 2013: 130). Indeed, post-Soviet Russian employees—or at least the ones encompassed by TM—expect openness, fairness and transparency, as well as empowerment (Fey & Shekshnia, 2011), and consider it more likely to obtain this in foreign-owned corporations, with Russian managers not always being up to date with the latest ideas in management. Moreover, an ambitious talent expecting fast career progression may face a glass ceiling in many Russian companies which are still headed by their founders and owners and who are unlikely to step down in favor of people outside their inner circle of relatives (Holden & Vaiman, 2013). Such trends influence AC a lot: a lack of intensive developmental perspectives does not contribute to knowledge assimilation and transformation.

Many Russian companies are still affected by historical patterns of growth and organizational features from the past, and are still hampered by some of the characteristics of the Soviet management system including a lack of attention to AC as a special activity that stimulates organizational development, namely employee training practices; leadership development; organizational culture issues (creation of inclusive environment); and knowledge management (Holden & Vaiman, 2013), which together create an AC agenda.

As former Soviet companies did not invest much in employee development, career planning and managerial education (Fey et al., 2009; Holden & Vaiman, 2013), we may observe a blurred background for AC development in the Russian context with some attempts to compensate through intensive training and development activities. Minbaeva et al. (2003) argue that if Russian companies focus on particular TM related training and performance management they can improve AC, as employee abilities are defined by, and employee motivation is determined by performance-based compensation and communications that can possibly be implemented via talent development and retention systems. However, the newly acquired knowledge might not bring the expected value due to the lack of proper mechanisms for knowledge assimilation, transformation and exploitation. TM, particularly talent development may be considered as such mechanisms when companies undertake learning and knowledge sharing sessions, e.g. strategic sessions, project works, development of educational internal platforms and formal training courses where employees may exchange ideas, insights, and generate new competencies. Such actions are possible if leadership and management styles support such participative and involving behavior of employees and do not restrict their engagement in knowledge sharing and individual innovations. Russian companies need to create an environment in which they can effectively communicate and exchange knowledge and ideas (Outila et al., 2018). Dixon and Day (2007) state that Russian companies could overcome the knowledge problem described earlier: they should transform the Soviet Union legacy into up-to-date knowledge by upgrading existing and creating new knowledge that can increase their AC and competitiveness, as such talent development performs the most important role. Being quite dependent on external knowledge, Russian companies have managed to realize the importance of knowledge generation that can be linked to talent development.

CHINA

TM in China began to rise as a hot topic only towards the very end of the 1990s and during the early 2000s with the emergence of private enterprises, limited liability and shareholding corporations (Cooke, 2008). It was stimulated by a rapid growth in the number of foreign-funded business units—a consequence of the 'Open Door' policy. China's integration into the world business environment has stimulated intensive knowledge and competence inflow, stimulated by foreign firms who transferred the full range of advanced managerial practices into the area of HRM and talent management. One of the first studies on TM practices in the private sector in China was undertaken by Björkman and Lu (1999), which stated that nearly half of the investigated foreign-invested firms had adopted their performance appraisal systems to suit the Chinese culture; however, the integration of the 'Western-like' practices (including talent development) was rather challenging due to their limited applicability caused by particular cultural and institutional peculiarities. At the same time, the 1999 study by Lindholm, based on a survey of 600 employees of MNCs operating in China, concluded that employees were satisfied with Western-like performance management systems—among others, evaluation, identification of training needs, and rewards adopted in their company. Furthermore, the TM approaches, including talent development, implemented by foreign MNCs, make them very attractive for potential, ambitious talents, forcing Chinese firms to adapt to this new competition in the war for talent. The competition was quite challenging for Chinese firms, as at that time the majority of them lacked a strategic approach to employees' training and development (Cooke, 2008), hence potentially limiting AC. However, the recent HRM trends, initiated by the largest and most influential Chinese firms, bring about new perspectives. The fact that a new generation of Chinese talents has more social and economic advantages and higher career expectations, pushes Chinese firms to provide well-grounded and complex TM policies and develop talent retention strategies (Veselova & Veselova, 2018).

AC in the Chinese context is discussed mainly through the understanding of knowledge transfer, knowledge integration (Qing, 2008), and the knowledge sharing process (Ma, Qi, & Wang, 2008), which is strongly related to talent development. However, it is assumed that knowledge transfer in Chinese firms is resisted by cultural specificities and beliefs. One of the possible ways to overcome these barriers is considered to be employees' education of not only know-how, but also know-why (Ahlstrom & Nair, 2000), which may require a different perspective for employees' development. It was also found that business and personal ties play a crucial role, in the Chinese context, for organizational learning, knowledge transfer and information exchange (Gao, Xu, & Yang, 2008; Huang, Davison, & Gu, 2008).

After the launch of the 'Open Door' policy, dramatic changes have occurred in Chinese firms' structures and management (Iles, Chuai, & Preece, 2010). The relevance of talent development, initiatives for knowledge sharing and transformation became obvious with the ever increasing demand for talents from the knowledge economy. Currently, there is a steady trend for firms in China to reduce the ratio of expatriates in favor of local labor, which, on the one hand, allows saving on labor costs, and, on the other hand, assumes better localization of operations to ensure knowledge acquisition and assimilation via employees' training and development (Kuhlmann & Hutchings, 2009). The study by Eriksson and colleagues (Eriksson, Qin, & Wang, 2014), analyzing the relationship between firm-level innovation activity, employee turnover and HRM practices, has shown that higher R&D employee turnover is associated with a higher probability of being innovative, but decreases the intensity of innovation activities in innovating firms. Innovating firms are more likely to adopt high-performance HRM practices, and the impact of employees' turnover varies with the number of such practices implemented by a firm (Eriksson et al., 2014). Taking into account the specificity of the Chinese context, a collectivist philosophy and the priority of group interest over the individual, talent development and retention of individual employees could result in a higher return for the whole organization, i.e. its AC. TM practices in China also pertain to a heritage from communist times that is similar to the peculiarities of the Soviet period of business development in Russia, with the focus on a training and development function aimed at knowledge acquisition and assimilation.

In this regard, a study of TM in China, by Hartmann, Feisel, and Schober (2010), presents a number of valuable findings, in particular, that firms lack talents and need them. At the same time, a 'psychological contract' between foreign firms' culture and local employees causes loyalty and retention problems which might be detrimental for a firm's development. However, many Chinese firms still lack TM strategies aimed at dealing with retention problems that prevent knowledge outflow and support knowledge exploitation and transformation capabilities.

BRAZIL

Brazilian culture is often depicted as 'relationist' or 'paternalistic'—words we also find to depict the Chinese work environment: the impact on management is that the supervisor has the personal obligation to protect one's subordinates and even sometimes to provide for the needs of workers and their families (Elvira & Davila, 2005). Following Schneider (2009), Brazilian paternalistic capitalism partly explains the country's institutional development, embedded in inextricable hierarchic systems. This management pattern, founded on hierarchy and respect due to authority, would be a legacy of slavery, the early emergence of a dominant class (initially of landlords) as the basis, and the central role of 'bureaucratic authoritarianism' during the military dictatorship from the 1960s to the 1980s (Carvalho Neto, 2003). However, some researchers temper this statement by observing that Brazilian companies with significant resources (e.g. natural resources, financial power, dominant positions) have used this over the last few years so as to import managerial best practices, either by using the expertise of leading US-based management consultancy firms or by sending their management teams abroad to leading international business schools (Chu & Wood, 2008). Having a huge amount of unqualified specialists also pushes companies to create education systems within an organization.

In recent literature we see some discussion about how Brazilian firms manage AC (Enkel, Gassmann, & Chesbrough, 2009; Celadon & Sbragia, 2015; McCann & Folta, 2008; Maehler et al., 2011), with a specific focus on a combination of external and internal knowledge to develop a firm's innovation capabilities despite being new and underdeveloped (Enkel et al., 2009). It is interesting that Brazilian companies tend to acquire knowledge from external sources globally (suppliers and competitors) (Versiani et al., 2021) along with internal knowledge creation through their own R&D activities—we may see some similarities with Russian companies and conclude that knowledge acquisition is one of the main AC dimensions gaining greater importance in the Brazilian context (Celadon & Sbragia, 2015). For Versiani et al. (2021), the external knowledge source, whether industrial or scientific, may have an influence on the skills development of specific external knowledge in relation to a firm's AC. The diversity of knowledge possessed and used by Brazilian firms has been directly linked to their ability to assimilate externally acquired knowledge and internally generated knowledge, leaving knowledge transformation as an agenda. The correlate of this long-term engagement would normally be the employees' sense of loyalty, giving an excellent chance for knowledge exploitation and transformation over a longer perspective. However, this general commitment may have been affected by the labor market deregulation which occurred in the 1990s and led to frequent workforce downsizing at this time, and later in the second half of the 2000s (Boulhol, 2009), and this might be a cause of the reducing level of AC. As a consequence, many Brazilian workers, including the most qualified ones, feel that their employers have broken the terms of the implicit psychological contract (Appelbaum, Bethune, & Tannenbaum, 1999), which has led to a shift from the one career, one single company, to an itinerant work life and boundaryless careers in Brazil. An interesting trend is that the appreciation of government jobs, reflected in the growing demand for vacancies, is driven by the pursuit of a moderate working day, job stability and good remuneration. However, aspects such as the institution's image, the presence of professional challenges and the encouragement of education, are also relevant. Government jobs are seen as having a stimulating work dynamic, structured work routines, an intense pace of absorption of new knowledge, and have legal protections against dismissals and reductions in working hours when compared to the private sector. We see this as a significant fact potentially affecting talent development perspectives, motivation to training and corporate education from the workforce side, and as an outcome, it serves as one of the determinants of AC.

In overall observation of TM issues in Brazilian companies, we see some efforts in managing talent through performance management, securing skilled and capable people, and dealing with the deficiencies of the education system and the underdeveloped higher education sector which leads to problems of training and skills. In terms of training and development of talent in Brazil, corporate universities are rather well-developed as well as competence mapping, which indeed is used to operate distinctions in training efforts. Based on this, talent development is a highly relevant issue for AC in the Brazilian context (MacLennan & Chueke, 2018) and the concept of 'self-development' becomes quite important. Local firms adopt such practices that stimulate employees to plan and act for their own development that serves as a background for knowledge assimilation and knowledge transformation. Along with that organizations try to take advantage of new technologies and set up partnerships with outside institutions for knowledge acquisition (Fischer & Albuquerque, 2005). Moreover, talent development schemes and initiatives in Brazilian firms are specifically designed to promote the spread of corporate values, develop a culture of management of human resources and excellence in operations, and allow the best use of human capital (under the described circumstances and conditions) but could be more focused to knowledge transformation. From that perspective, trainings and development programs allow Brazilian organizations to make use of both, external knowledge and knowledge from internal R&D, as special conditions are created for individuals from different organizational units to effectively communicate and share experiences (Geary, Aguzzoli, & Lengler, 2017; Fischer & de Albuquerque, 2005). This ultimately boosts the assimilation and transformation of knowledge (Celadon, 2014). However, it is worth mentioning that Brazil faces a problem with high employee mobility and turnover, meaning that companies are not sure that they will get a return on their talent development investment. Local firms' TM strategy, therefore, may become overwhelmingly focused on talent retention, suggesting that the role of talent development in AC development might be limited.

DISCUSSION

By developing its employees, providing them with new knowledge in the process of mentorship, trainings or programs of personal and/or professional development, a firm actually improves not only their abilities to acquire, but also to interpret and understand incoming information (Schuler et al., 2011; Valentin, 2006). Moreover, the involvement of employees in various external training programs develops their mental flexibility, which positively influences their ability to effectively absorb and digest new knowledge. Talented employees are more successful in transferring knowledge and delivering it to other personnel and, moreover, they are quite efficient in motivating other people to improve their performance, so investments in talented individuals result in the improvement of organizational capabilities (Carr et al., 2005; Gilley et al., 2008). Talent development usually encompasses a variety of components, for example training, career development, career management, and organizational development, and training and development. On the one hand, a firm's ability to acquire knowledge is dependent on the intellectual potential of its employees as it is natural that a person will pay attention and direct the attention of their colleagues to the information in the area which is quite familiar to them (Cooke et al., 2014; Lewis & Heckman, 2006; Minbaeva, 2005). Talent development practices can widen personnel's horizons, providing a solid basis for new knowledge acquisition. On the other hand, during the process of talent development a firm can increase a number of potential sources of important information through the setting up of new contacts by its employees, and by networking (Byham, Smith, & Paese, 2002; Conger, 2010; Garavan, Carbery, & Rock, 2012).

To enhance AC using talent development, we claim the necessity of targeting middle and senior managers and the technical/professional talent categories; this includes a spectrum of strategies like conceptual and skill-based development programs, personal growth development programs, feedback-based and action-focused development interventions, designed to enhance generic competencies such as teamwork, problem solving and strategic awareness (Conger, 2010; Garavan et al., 2012). An understanding of the role of talent development practice, involving a variety of developmental functions such as sponsorship, coaching, mentoring, psychosocial support and career advice (Friday, Friday, & Green, 2004) for an individual who takes an active interest and action to advance the career of another individual (Higgins & Kram, 2001), is considered to be of high priority. However, we demonstrate the necessary conditions for talent development to be able to leverage AC in different country settings.

The emerging markets are continuously showing a significant growth over recent years with a rapid development of TM initiatives, including a focus on talent development in those countries. We may ask a question: Are emerging markets similar in their attempts to shape AC by TM, specifically talent development? Yes, partly. In Russia, China, and Brazil the need for talented employees' development is one of the managerial priorities, so the role of TM here is high and constantly increasing. As TM is proved to be a significant determinant of a firm's AC, it stimulates acquisition of intangible assets, creating and developing emerging market firms' competitive advantages. China and Russia are on the next step after the communist period of development where much attention was paid to acquisition and assimilation of knowledge. Brazil didn't have any regime specifics, but in its AC and TM has cultural roots, which allows us to conclude that emerging markets' determinants grounded in historical and cultural development for AC serve rather as barriers than drivers.

From another view, we still are able to find differences and recognize contextual uniqueness. In China, where the presence of foreign multinationals has been longstanding and on a broad basis, talent development practices have spread like wildfire, and are better developed to have power for AC. This tendency also exists in Russia; however, Russian firms are still less advanced in TM, thus, TM practices for AC need further development and adaptation to both economic and labor challenges. Brazilian firms' attempts to shape AC by talent development are linked to the need to leverage the educational level of employees whereas the same agenda for AC mechanisms exists but requires more systematic TM practices and corporate education. Table 7.1 shows the existing AC limits, the AC focus and the necessary conditions from a talent development perspective in Russia, China and Brazil.

We observe that talent development serves firstly as a background for knowledge acquisition in the emerging market contexts; however, it can be used to ensure knowledge assimilation, exploitation, and transformation, developing AC further within the TM concept (Ashton & Morton, 2005; Dewhurst, Hancock, & Ellsworth, 2013; Felin & Hesterly, 2007; Kang et al., 2007; Minbaeva et al., 2003, 2014; Tarique & Schuler, 2010; Scholz, 2012). Considering our discussion about country-specific characteristics we further propose a framework showing the necessary conditions for talent development to enhance AC. The framework is based on a country's historical evolution as a prerequisite for TM systems in the discussed countries (Figure 7.1).

We shed light on the role of TM in AC, namely we observe mechanisms of leveraging AC by talent development, and it extends our understanding of how TM practices in emerging market contexts provide additional value for organizations. Within different contexts we see some similarities and differences in how countries and companies are ready for managing AC that

Table 7.1   *Cross-country analysis of AC status and conditions for AC*

Country	AC limits	Talent development and AC focus	Necessary conditions for AC
Russia	Soviet management system and underdeveloped HRM; lack of business education; lack of management experience among Soviet-born managers; limited access to global knowledge and experience over long period of time; training and development for its compensation.	Filling the knowledge gaps resulting from lack of managerial knowledge by training and development systems at firm level and focus on development and career. *Knowledge acquisition and partly assimilation as the main AC domains*	Well-established talent development system with global knowledge orientation: conditions for development via internships, internal training via corporate universities, leadership development, quick promotions 'from within' contributing to talent retention; team work development to stimulate knowledge sharing and transformation; increasing global collaboration for further knowledge acquisition and exploitation; performance management systems development to ensure AC direction; cultural and environmental characteristics for knowledge assimilation, exploitation and transformation that may retain talents and not lose knowledge and knowledge sharing capabilities developed by talent development.
China	Lack of strategic approach for talent training and development. Active knowledge acquisition strategy through implementation of 'Western-like' practices. Chinese collectivist culture and communist context.	Acquiring knowledge for talent and firms' development mostly externally, internal development as necessity for knowledge assimilation. *Knowledge acquisition, assimilation and transformation as the main AC domains*	The extension of educational approaches from only know-how to know-why outcomes; orientation of training and development system to internal knowledge creation processes and inclusive environment to retain talented employees.

Country	AC limits	Talent development and AC focus	Necessary conditions for AC
Brazil	Paternalistic culture, hierarchy and authority respect; best Western practices awareness and orientation, deficiencies of educational systems (major quality disparities among educational institutions, relatively low quality of primary/ secondary schooling and higher education).	High interest in business-friendly and English-speaking talent profiles and focus on foreign talent recruitment, talent development aims at stimulating employees to plan and act for their own development as well as promoting the spread of corporate values and allowing the best use of human capital; knowledge acquisition from international and global environment; active development of corporate universities; orientation to individual career development tracks. *Knowledge acquisition, partly exploitation and transformation as the main focuses in AC*	Further development of corporate universities and corporate training and development systems; talent retention to keep knowledge within an organization and stimulate knowledge exploitation and transformation; enhancing state educational system with international orientation.

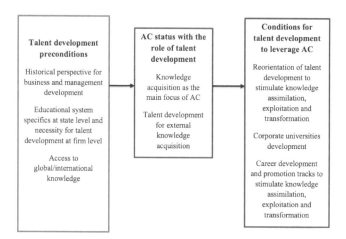

Figure 7.1   Talent development contexts for AC in emerging markets (based on Russia, China and Brazil)

create country-specific talent development focus. Our analysis is important from a managerial perspective as necessary conditions for AC are presented and may serve as an agenda for managers if a firm wants to develop AC. We suggest that talent managers should be aware of talent development initiatives for extending the main AC dimensions.

REFERENCES

Ahlstrom, D. & Nair, A. (2000). The role of know-why in knowledge development within biomedicine: Lessons for organizations. *Asia Pacific Journal of Management*, **17**(2), 331–351.

Ambrosius, J. (2018). Strategic talent management in emerging markets and its impact on employee retention: Evidence from Brazilian MNCs. *Thunderbird International Business Review*, **60**(1), 53–68.

Appelbaum, S.H., Bethune, M. & Tannenbaum, R. (1999). Downsizing and the emergence of self-managed teams. *Participation and Empowerment: An International Journal*, **7**(5), 109–130.

Ardichvili, A. & Dirani, K. (2005). Human capital practices of Russian enterprises. *Human Resources Development International*, **8**(4), 403–418.

Armstrong, M. (2006). *A Handbook of Human Resource Management Practice*. London: Kogan Page.

Ashton, C. & Morton, L. (2005). Managing talent for competitive advantage: Taking a systemic approach to talent management. *Strategic HR Review*, **4**(5), 28–31.

Beamond, M.T., Farndale, E. & Härtel, C.E. (2016). MNE translation of corporate talent management strategies to subsidiaries in emerging economies. *Journal of World Business*, **51**(4), 499–510.

Björkman, I., Fey, C.F. & Park, H.J. (2007). Institutional theory and MNC subsidiary HRM practices: Evidence from a three-country study. *Journal of International Business Studies*, **38**(3), 430–446.

Björkman, I. & Lu, Y. (1999). The management of human resources in Chinese-Western joint ventures. *Journal of World Business*, **34**(3), 306–324.

Blass, E. (2007). *Talent Management: Maximizing Talent for Business Performance*. London: Chartered Management Institute and Ashridge Consulting.

Boulhol, H. (2009). Do capital markets and trade liberalization trigger labor market deregulation? *Journal of International Economics*, **77**(2), 223–233.

Boxall, P. & Purcell, P. (2008). *Strategy and Human Resource Management*. Basingstoke: Palgrave Macmillan.

Byham, W.C., Smith, A.B. & Paese, M.J. (2002). *Grow Your Own Leaders: How to Identify, Develop, and Retain Leadership Talent*. Upper Saddle River, NJ: Financial Times Prentice Hall.

Carr, S.C., Inkson, K. & Thorn, K. (2005). From global careers to talent flow: Reinterpreting 'brain drain'. *Journal of World Business*, **40**(4), 386–398.

Carvalho Neto, A. (2003). A reforma da estrutura sindical Brasileira. Paper presented at VIII Encontro Nacional de Estudos do Trabalho. São Paulo.

Celadon, K. (2014). Knowledge integration and open innovation in the Brazilian cosmetics industry. *Journal of Technology Management & Innovation*, **9**(3), 34–50.

Celadon, K. & Sbragia, R. (2015). Absorptive capacity and open innovation in the Brazilian cosmetics industry. Paper presented at the 9th International Management Conference 'Management and Innovation for Competitive Advantage,' November 5–6, Bucharest, Romania.

Chen, C.J. & Huang, J.W. (2009). Strategic human resource practices and innovation performance: The mediating role of knowledge management capacity. *Journal of Business Research*, **62**(1), 104–114.

Child, J. & Marinova, S. (2014). The role of contextual combinations in the globalization of Chinese firms. *Management & Organization Review*, **10**(3), 347–371.

Choi, S.Y., Lee, H. & Yoo, Y. (2010). The impact of information technology and transactive memory systems on knowledge sharing, application, and team performance: A field study. *MIS Quarterly*, **34**(4), 855–870.

Chu, R. & Wood, T. (2008). Cultura organizacional Brasileira pós-globalização: global ou local? *Revista de Administração Pública*, **42**(5), 969–991.

Cohen, W.M. & Levinthal, D.A. (1990). Absorptive capacity: A new perspective on learning and innovation. *Administrative Science Quarterly*, **35**(1), 128–152.

Collings, D.G. (2014). Integrating global mobility and global talent management: Exploring the challenges and strategic opportunities. *Journal of World Business*, **49**, 253–261.

Collings, D.G., McDonnell, A. & Scullion, H. (2009). Global talent management: The law of the few. *Poznan University of Economics Review*, **9**(2), 5–18.

Conger, J. (2010). Developing leadership talent: Delivering on the promise of structured programs. In Silzer, R. & Dwell, B. E. (eds.), *Strategy-Driven Talent Management: A Leadership Imperative*. San Francisco: Jossey-Bass, pp. 281–311.

Cooke, F.L. (2008). *Competition, Strategy and Management in China*. Basingstoke: Palgrave Macmillan.

Cooke, F.L., Saini, D.S. & Wang, J. (2014). Talent management in China and India: A comparison of management perceptions and human resource practices. *Journal of World Business*, **49**(2), 225–235.

Dewhurst, M., Hancock, B. & Ellsworth, D. (2013). Redesigning knowledge work. *Harvard Business Review*, **91**(1), 58–64.

Dixon, S.E. & Day, M. (2007). Leadership, administrative heritage and absorptive capacity. *Leadership & Organization Development Journal*, **28**(8), 727–748.

Dixon, S.E., Meyer, K.E. & Day, M. (2007). Exploitation and exploration learning and the development of organizational capabilities: A cross-case analysis of the Russian oil industry. *Human Relations*, **60**(10), 1493–1523.

Elvira, M.M. & Davila, A. (2005). *Managing Human Resources in Latin America: An Agenda for International Leaders*. London: Routledge.

Enkel, E., Gassmann, O. & Chesbrough, H. (2009). Open R&D and open innovation: Exploring the phenomenon. *R&D Management*, **39**(4), 311–316.

Enkel, E. & Heil, S. (2014). Preparing for distant collaboration: Antecedents to potential absorptive capacity in cross-industry innovation. *Technovation*, **34**(4), 242–260.

Eriksson, T., Qin, Z. & Wang, W. (2014). Firm-level innovation activity, employee turnover and HRM practices: Evidence from Chinese firms. *China Economic Review*, **30**, 583–597.

Felin, T. & Hesterly, W.S. (2007). The knowledge-based view, nested heterogeneity, and new value creation: Philosophical considerations on the locus of knowledge. *Academy of Management Review*, **32**(1), 195–218.

Fey, C.F. & Björkman, I. (2001). The effect of human resource management practices on MNC subsidiary performance in Russia. *Journal of International Business Studies*, **32**(1), 59–75.

Fey, C., Morgulis-Yakushev, S., Park, H.J. & Björkman, I. (2009). Opening the black box of the relationship between HRM practices and firm performance: A comparison of MNE subsidiaries in the USA, Finland, and Russia. *Journal of International Business Studies*, **40**(4), 690–712.

Fey, C. & Shekshnia, S. (2011). The key commandments for doing business in Russia. *Organizational Dynamics*, **40**(1), 57–66.

Fischer, A.L. & de Albuquerque, L.G. (2005). Trends of the human resources management model in Brazilian companies: A forecast according to opinion leaders from the area. *The International Journal of Human Resource Management*, **16**(7), 1211–1227.

Flatten, T.C., Engelen, A., Zahra, S.A. & Brettel, M. (2011). A measure of absorptive capacity: Scale development and validation. *European Management Journal*, **29**(2), 98–116.

Fosfuri, A. & Tribo, J.A. (2008). Exploring the antecedents of potential absorptive capacity and its impact on innovation performance. *Omega*, **36**(2), 173–187.

Foss, N.J. (2007). The emerging knowledge governance approach: Challenges and characteristics. *Organization*, **14**(1), 29–52.

Friday, E., Friday, S.S. & Green, A.L. (2004). A reconceptualization of mentoring and sponsoring. *Management Decision*, **42**(5), 628–644.

Gallardo-Gallardo, E., Thunnissen, M. & Scullion, H. (2020) Talent management: Context matters. *The International Journal of Human Resource Management*, **31**(4), 457–473.

Gao, S., Xu, K. & Yang, J. (2008). Managerial ties, absorptive capacity, and innovation. *Asia Pacific Journal of Management*, **25**, 395–412.

Garavan, T.N., Carbery, R. & Rock, A. (2012). Mapping talent development: Definition, scope and architecture. *European Journal of Training & Development*, **36**(1), 5–24.

Geary, J., Aguzzoli, R. & Lengler, J. (2017). The transfer of 'international best practice' in a Brazilian MNC: A consideration of the convergence and contingency perspectives. *Journal of International Management*, **23**(2), 194–207.

Gilley, A., Dixon, P. & Gilley, J.W. (2008). Characteristics of leadership effectiveness: Implementing change and driving innovation in organizations. *Human Resource Development Quarterly*, **19**(2), 153–169.

Gold, A.H., Malhotra, A. & Segars, A.H. (2001). Knowledge management: An organizational capabilities perspective. *Journal of Management Information Systems*, **18**(1), 185–214.

Hansen, M.T. (1999). The search-transfer problem: The role of weak ties in sharing knowledge across organization subunits. *Administrative Science Quarterly*, **44**(1), 82–111.

Hartmann, E., Feisel, E. & Schober, H. (2010). Talent management of Western MNCs in China: Balancing global integration and local responsiveness. *Journal of World Business*, **45**(2), 169–178.

Higgins, M.C. & Kram, K.E. (2001). Reconceptualizing mentoring at work: A developmental network perspective. *Academy of Management Review*, **26**(2), 264–288.

Holden, N. (2011). "Not with the mind alone": A critique of "Knowledge transfer between Russian and Western firms: whose absorptive capacity is in question?" by Snejina Michailova and Irina Jormanainen. *Critical Perspectives on International Business*, **7**(4), 350–356.

Holden, N. & Vaiman, V. (2013). Talent management in Russia: Not so much war for talent as wariness of talent. *Critical Perspectives on International Business*, **9**(1–2), 129–146.

Huang, Q., Davison, R.M. & Gu, J. (2008). Impact of personal and cultural factors on knowledge sharing in China. *Asia Pacific Journal of Management*, **25**(3), 451–471.

Iles, P., Chuai, X. & Preece, D. (2010). Talent management and HRM in multinational companies in Beijing: Definitions, differences and drivers. *Journal of World Business*, **45**(2), 179–189.

Inkinen, H., Kianto, A. & Vanhala, M. (2015). Knowledge management practices and innovation performance in Finland. *Baltic Journal of Management*, **10**(4), 432–455.

Jansen, J.J., Van Den Bosch, F.A. & Volberda, H.W. (2005). Managing potential and realized absorptive capacity: How do organizational antecedents matter? *Academy of Management Journal*, **48**(6), 999–1015.

Kang, S.C., Morris, S.S. & Snell, S.A. (2007). Relational archetypes, organizational learning, and value creation: Extending the human resource architecture. *Academy of Management Review*, **32**(1), 236–256.

Kiessling, T. & Harvey, M. (2006). The human resource management issues during an acquisition: The target firm's top management team and key managers. *The International Journal of Human Resource Management*, **17**(7), 1307–1320.

Kostopoulos, K., Papalexandris, A., Papachroni, M. & Ioannou, G. (2011). Absorptive capacity, innovation, and financial performance. *Journal of Business Research*, **64**(12), 1335–1343.

Kostova, T. & Roth, K. (2002). Adoption of an organizational practice by subsidiaries of multinational corporations: Institutional and relational effects. *Academy of Management Journal*, **45**(1), 215–233.

Kuhlmann, T. & Hutchings, K. (2009). Expatriate assignments vs. localization of management in China. *Career Development International*, **15**(1), 20–38.

Lane, P.J., Koka, B.R. & Pathak, S. (2006). The reification of absorptive capacity: A critical review and rejuvenation of the construct. *Academy of Management Review*, **31**(4), 833–863.

Lane, P.J., Salk, J.E. & Lyles, M.A. (2001). Absorptive capacity, learning, and performance in international joint ventures. *Strategic Management Journal*, **22**(12), 1139–1161.

Lawson, B., Petersen, K.J., Cousins, P.D. & Handfield, R.B. (2009). Knowledge sharing in interorganizational product development teams: The effect of formal and informal socialization mechanisms. *Journal of Product Innovation Management*, **26**(2), 156–172.

Lazzarotti, V., Manzini, R. & Pellegrini, L. (2015). Is your open-innovation successful? The mediating role of a firm's organizational and social context. *The International Journal of Human Resource Management*, **26**(19), 2453–2485.

Lepak, D.P. & Snell, S.A. (1999). The human resource architecture: Toward a theory of human capital allocation and development. *Academy of Management Review*, **24**(1), 31–48.

Lepak, D.P. & Snell, S.A. (2002). Examining the human resource architecture: The relationships among human capital, employment, and human resource configurations. *Journal of Management*, **28**(4), 517–543.

Lewin, A.Y., Massini, S. & Peeters, C. (2011). Microfoundations of internal and external absorptive capacity routines. *Organization Science*, **22**(1), 81–98.

Lewis, R.E. & Heckman, R.J. (2006). Talent management: A critical review. *Human Resource Management Review*, **16**, 139–154.

Lindholm, N. (1999). Performance management in MNC subsidiaries in China: A study of host-country managers and professionals. *Asia Pacific Journal of Human Resources*, **37**(3), 18–35.

Ma, Z., Qi, L. & Wang, K. (2008). Knowledge sharing in Chinese construction project teams and its affecting factors: An empirical study. *Chinese Management Studies*, **2**(2), 97–108.

MacLennan, M.L. & Chueke, G.V. (2018). Brazil: Catching up and moving forward. In Latukha, M. (ed.), *Talent Management in Global Organizations*. Cham: Palgrave Macmillan, pp. 277–297.

Maehler, A.E., Marques Curado, C.M., Ávila Pedrozo, E. & Pedro Pires, J. (2011). Knowledge transfer and innovation in Brazilian multinational companies. *Journal of Technology Management & Innovation*, **6**(4), 1–14.

May, R.C., Stewart, W.H., Puffer, S.M., McCarthy, D.J. & Ledgerwood, D.E. (2011). Predictors of individual knowledge acquisition commitment in a post-Soviet setting. *Management International Review*, **51**(5), 697–728.

McCann, B. & Folta, T. (2008). Location matters: Where we have been and where we might go in agglomeration research. *Journal of Management*, **34**(3), 532–565.

Michailova, S. (2000). Contrasts in culture: Russian and Western perspectives on organizational change. *The Academy of Management Executive*, **14**(4), 99–112.

Michailova, S. & Husted, K. (2003). Knowledge-sharing hostility in Russian firms. *California Management Review*, **45**(3), 59–77.

Michailova, S. & Jormanainen, I. (2011). Knowledge transfer between Russian and Western firms: Whose absorptive capacity is in question? *Critical Perspectives on International Business*, **7**(3), 250–270.

Minbaeva, D. (2005). HRM practices and MNC knowledge transfer. *Personnel Review*, **34**(1), 125–144.

Minbaeva, D., Pedersen, T., Björkman, I., Fey, C.F. & Park, H.J. (2003). MNC knowledge transfer, subsidiary absorptive capacity, and HRM. *Journal of International Business Studies*, **34**(6), 586–599.

Minbaeva, D., Pedersen, T., Björkman, I. & Fey, C.F. (2014). A retrospective on MNC knowledge transfer, subsidiary absorptive capacity, and HRM. *Journal of International Business Studies*, **45**(1), 52–62.

Morris, S., Snell, S. & Björkman, I. (2016). An architectural framework for global talent management. *Journal of International Business Studies*, **47**(6), 723–747.

Murovec, N. & Prodan, I. (2009). Absorptive capacity, its determinants, and influence on innovation output: Cross-cultural validation of the structural model. *Technovation*, **29**(12), 859–872.

Novations (2009). *Talent Development Issues Study*. New York: Novations Group.

Outila, V., Vaiman, V. & Holden, N. (2018). Macro talent management in Russia: Addressing entangled challenges in managing talent on the country level. In Vaiman, V. & Collings, D.G. (eds.), *Macro Talent Management in Emerging and Emergent Markets*. Abingdon: Routledge, pp. 25–45.

Qing, X. (2008). The culture relativity in the knowledge flow. *Chinese Management Studies*, **2**(2), 109–121.

Ready, D.A., Hill, L.A. & Thomas, R.J. (2014). Building a game-changing talent strategy. *Harvard Business Review*, **92**(1–2), 62–68.

Reis, R. & Quental, C. (2014). Global talent management in Brazil: Jeitinho as a managerial talent. In Ariss, A. (ed.), *Global Talent Management*. New York: Springer, pp. 123–140.

Roberts, N. (2015). Absorptive capacity, organizational antecedents, and environmental dynamism. *Journal of Business Research*, **68**(11), 2426–2433.

Roberts, N., Galluch, P.S., Dinger, M. & Grover, V. (2012). Absorptive capacity and information systems research: Review, synthesis, and directions for future research. *MIS Quarterly*, **36**(2), 625–648.

Schneider, B. (2009). Hierarchical market economies and varieties of capitalism in Latin America. *Journal of Latin American Studies*, **41**(3), 553–575.

Scholz, T.M. (2012). Talent management in the video game industry: The role of cultural diversity and cultural intelligence. *Thunderbird International Business Review*, **54**(6), 845–858.

Schuler, R.S. (2015). The 5-C framework for managing talent. *Organizational Dynamics*, **1**, 47–56.

Schuler, R.S., Jackson, S.E. & Tarique, I. (2011). Global talent management and global talent challenges: Strategic opportunities for IHRM. *Journal of World Business*, **46**(4), 506–516.

Skuza, A., Scullion, H. & McDonnell, A. (2013). An analysis of the talent management challenges in a post-communist country: The case of Poland. *The International Journal of Human Resource Management*, **24**(3), 453–470.

Szulanski, G. (1996). Exploring internal stickiness: Impediments to the transfer of best practice within the firm. *Strategic Management Journal*, **17**(S2), 27–43.

Szulanski, G. (2000). The process of knowledge transfer: A diachronic analysis of stickiness. *Organizational Behavior & Human Decision Processes*, **82**(1), 9–27.

Tansley, C. & Kirk, S. (2018). You've been framed: Framing talent mobility in emerging markets. *Thunderbird International Business Review*, **60**(1), 39–51.

Tarique, I. & Schuler, R.S. (2010). Global talent management: Literature review, integrative framework, and suggestions for further research. *Journal of World Business*, **45**(2), 122–133.

Tsai, W. (2001). Knowledge transfer in intraorganizational networks: Effects of network position and absorptive capacity on business unit innovation and performance. *Academy of Management Journal*, **44**(5), 996–1004.

Valentin, C. (2006). Researching human resource development: Emergence of a critical approach to HRD enquiry. *International Journal of Training & Development*, **10**(1), 17–29.

Versiani, A., Cruz, M., Rezende, S. & Castro, J. (2021). Absorptive capacity, innovation, and external sources of knowledge: The Brazilian power sector. *Revista de Administração Mackenzie*, **22**(5), 1–31.

Veselova, A. & Veselova, L. (2018). China: Managing the global talent market. In Latukha, M. (ed.), *Talent Management in Global Organizations*. Cham: Palgrave Macmillan, pp. 15–39.

Volberda, H.W., Foss, N.J. & Lyles, M.A. (2010). Absorbing the concept of absorptive capacity: How to realize its potential in the organization field. *Organization Science*, **21**(4), 931–951.

Williams-Lee, A. (2008). Accelerated leadership development tops the talent management menu at McDonald's. *Global Business and International Excellence*, **27**(4), 15–31.

Zahra, S.A. & George, G. (2002). Absorptive capacity: A review, reconceptualization, and extension. *Academy of Management Review*, **27**(2), 185–203.

Zhou, A.J., Fey, C. & Yildiz, H.E. (2020). Fostering integration through HRM practices: An empirical examination of absorptive capacity and knowledge transfer in cross-border M&As. *Journal of World Business*, **55**(2), 100947.

8. Employee knowledge hiding: the roles of protean career orientation, HR system and relational climate

Anne Roefs, Saša Batistič and Rob F. Poell

INTRODUCTION

Despite various efforts to encourage knowledge sharing among talented employees in organizations, hiding knowledge from peers still occurs. Knowledge hiding happens when workers intentionally refrain from sharing knowledge requested by a colleague. Organizations need to understand why and when their workers hide knowledge, for their talent management practices to be effective. This chapter will illustrate the concept of knowledge hiding and address how personal characteristics (e.g., Protean career orientation) as well as organizational practices (e.g., HR system and relational climate) can affect knowledge hiding. Implications for (talent) management policies will be provided as well.

WHAT IS KNOWLEDGE HIDING?

With the rise in working from home and the gig economy, where people move more freely from role to role, knowledge sharing becomes increasingly important for organizations. Knowledge sharing refers to 'the process of sharing valuable information and ideas among individuals in an organization' (Cabrera & Cabrera, 2002). It decreases the risk of having single points of knowledge and benefits speed and continuity of business processes (e.g., through ease of finding information and more efficient handovers). Talent management hinges on knowledge transfer among talented employees, for their own sake and for that of the organization. Since it has long been established that knowledge sharing is critical to organizational performance (Ipe, 2003) and that successful knowledge management initiatives depend on employee knowledge sharing (Wang & Noe, 2010), what motivates employees to share or withhold knowledge should be an important consideration. This brings us to the topic of knowledge hiding.

Knowledge hiding is often understood as the opposite of knowledge sharing, but this is not necessarily the case. Knowledge hiding can be defined as 'an intentional attempt by an individual to withhold or conceal knowledge that has been requested by another person' (Connelly et al., 2012: 65). This highlights the difference in motivations behind knowledge hiding and a mere lack of knowledge sharing. It also shows how the challenge of Human Resource (HR) and Talent Management is increasingly to better understand employees, rather than just provide tools such as knowledge sharing platforms. In this chapter we adhere to inclusive rather than exclusive views of Talent Management (Swailes, Downs, & Orr, 2014), meaning we believe 'talent' is a characteristic of every employee to be identified and developed rather than considering only a few employees talented and deserving of special treatment. Therefore, our understanding of Talent Management is very close to that of HR Management: 'the recognition and acceptance that all employees have talent together with the ongoing evaluation and deployment of employees in positions that give the best fit and opportunity (via participation) for employees to use those talents' (Swailes et al., 2014: 533).

Managers often assume that knowledge hiding does not occur in their organizations. Therefore, apart from understanding one's employees, it is also important to question commonly held assumptions within organizations. There are many reasons why knowledge hiding happens in organizations, which can be divided into three categories illustrated below.

1.   Organization-related reasons, for instance: a competitive environment, unfavorable norms or policies, and a poor motivational climate. When an organization has a culture of secrecy and not sharing, employees tend to adopt that culture (Connelly et al., 2012). Consider the following example scenario: Tom and Jamal are both account managers at a bank. Tom prides himself on being the top performer on the team and the rewards that come with it: account managers receive variable payment based on their performance scores, which are in turn largely based on the value of their managed portfolio compared to that of their peers. The key to Tom's success is his know-how when it comes to cross-selling. Jamal recently joined the team and asks Tom for advice, since they have roughly the same number of accounts in similar sectors, but a marked difference in portfolio value. Tom takes a look at Jamal's portfolio and suggests Jamal is simply unlucky. Tom plays dumb. He actually sees plenty of options but prefers to maintain the difference in perceived performance to maximize his own reward.

2. Job-related reasons, for example: time pressure, knowledge complexity and protection of important information. Sometimes however, an employee may just want to secure confidentiality or otherwise protect the interests of a third party (Connelly et al., 2012). The following example scenario can be illustrative: Rajesh and Regina are management consultants at a large consultancy firm. Rajesh is currently trying to land a project. The faster he can get his proposal to the client, and the better he can showcase the firm's manufacturing experience in it, the better the odds of sealing the deal. He asks Regina to share previous project proposals, reports and cases with him, since she has worked extensively in manufacturing. Regina is managing two projects, both with upcoming deadlines, and is short on time to secure new projects for herself, let alone help others to do so. She would need to anonymize cases and is unsure how much would end up being useful to Rajesh. Claiming confidentiality, she rationalizes refusing to share materials or disclose details that may help him, saving herself time.

3. Inter & intra-personal reasons, such as: poor intentions, revenge, seeking power, and a lack of trust (Staples & Webster, 2008). Think of the following example scenario: Ellen works as an operations specialist for a transport company and has been on the look-out for a promotion for some time now. She works in a team responsible for coordination, planning and control of incoming and outgoing goods. Her colleague Tarik is having difficulties processing the inventory in the ERP system and asks Ellen for help, as she is known as somewhat of an expert when it comes to IT systems. Ellen suspects that her manager will soon leave the company and expects that both Tarik and herself are suitable candidates for the job. She aims to remain the expert on systems they work with, to have a better chance at getting the job. Because of this, she doesn't want to help Tarik and decides to evade his request. She promises to explain later, as she is currently busy. In fact Ellen has no intention to do so and will feign forgetting about it.

Either positively or harmfully intended, and whether it is due to organization, job or someone's coworker, the reasons for hiding knowledge can vary, as can the methods (evasive hiding, rationalized hiding, or playing dumb) (Connelly et al., 2012). Organization-level factors can affect factors at job level and, in turn, factors at individual level. For instance, due to a competitive environment and strict individual targets in their jobs, employees may hide their knowledge to maintain power and status. HR and Talent Management can mainly influence factors on the contextual, organizational level; these do, however, have an impact on the other levels as well. Nevertheless, how much effort is warranted to expose and tackle knowledge hiding?

Knowledge hiding can have serious financial implications for companies, as the scenarios described above can illustrate.

- If Ellen gets the job, she may not be the best candidate and the company gets someone who strategically hides knowledge in a more influential position. On average, a bad hire can cost an organization 30% of the employee's first-year earnings (Cardenas, 2014).
- If the lack of knowledge hiding seen between Rajesh and Regina is common within the firm, it could cost the firm its competitive edge. Let's assume it has a proposal win rate of 33% (the industry average; Simmons, n.d.) and an annual revenue of 1 billion dollars. Every 1% on top of that 33% proposal win rate translates to roughly 30 million dollars in annual revenue. What percentage could be gained by eliminating the adverse effects of knowledge hiding, such as the decreased relevance of showcased experience and the increased lead times to write proposals?
- The tendency to keep knowledge for cross-selling to oneself is likely a common theme within the bank in the example, because this behavior is inadvertently rewarded. This can hurt the bank's overall portfolio, as cross-selling is known to increase customer loyalty.

The consequences of knowledge hiding can be substantial. Besides financial implications, it also brings risks of damaging relationships and causing distrust among employees (Connelly & Zweig, 2015). It can lead to reciprocation: colleagues refusing to share knowledge with those who hid knowledge (Postolache, 2017a). This can seriously undermine the creativity and effectiveness of teams and entire organizations (Wu et al., 2009). Discouraging knowledge hiding behaviors results in several benefits: retention of know-how (Postolache, 2017a), sharing best practices across the organization (North, Reinhardt, & Schmidt, 2004), better and faster decision making (Postolache, 2017b), and more innovation and growth (Tsai, 2001).

These benefits underline the importance of knowledge transfer. Organizations are facing challenges from the gig economy and the digital age, where temporary positions are common and employees increasingly work remotely (sometimes at the expense of team spirit). Companies risk losing valuable knowledge and moving slower than competitors that share knowledge more effectively internally. HR and Talent Management can play a role in preventing knowledge hiding and its adverse consequences. Before going into the question of how organizations can do this, however, we need to understand more about the factors that play a role in employee knowledge hiding.

THE ROLES OF PROTEAN CAREER ORIENTATION, HR SYSTEM AND RELATIONAL CLIMATE

Recent studies have shown a number of factors that provoke knowledge hiding, such as knowledge-based psychological ownership, territoriality, job insecurity, job complexity, and distrust (Connelly et al., 2012; Huo et al., 2016; Peng, 2013; Serenko & Bontis, 2016). Factors proposed to reduce the degree of knowledge hiding are the existence of a positive organizational knowledge culture (Serenko & Bontis, 2016), knowledge sharing climate (Connelly et al., 2012), and HR systems (Batistič & Poell, 2022). This chapter focuses on the roles of a protean career orientation, the HR system and the relational climate in the organization.

Since the decline of the traditional organizational career, academics are increasingly discussing the protean career as an emerging career perspective (Briscoe, Hall, & DeMuth, 2006). Originating from Hall's (1976) protean career concept, a protean career orientation (PCO) is described as 'an individual's proclivity to enact a career focused on achieving subjective success through autonomous career management' (Direnzo, Greenhaus, & Weer, 2015: 538). It could be argued that protean-oriented employees are not likely to hide their knowledge, as doing so could lead to increased distrust among, and less external assistance from colleagues (Černe et al., 2014), resulting in an obstacle on the road to subjective career success. One could also, however, reason that PCO triggers knowledge hiding intentions, as protean-oriented employees are highly self-reliant (Briscoe & Hall, 2006) and likely to protect their human capital in order to achieve success in their careers.

Besides the personal characteristic that is PCO, two aspects of the organizational context might affect employee knowledge hiding: a commitment-based HR system and a communal-sharing relational climate in the organization. In commitment HR systems, HR practices for obtaining, retaining, and developing employees are intended to develop a long-term, trusting relationship between the organization and the employee (Lepak & Snell, 1999, 2002). In communal-sharing climates, relationships between employees are based on feelings of solidarity, belonging and trust (Fiske, 1992). HR systems and organizational climates are among the most influential dimensions of organizational context with regard to their effects on employee attitudes and behaviors (Ferris et al., 1998; Kuenzi & Schminke, 2009). Both the commitment HR system and the communal-sharing climate are likely to reduce the prevalence of knowledge hiding, as we will explain in more detail below.

Protean Career Orientation

The decline of the traditional career has resulted in less loyalty, greater mobility and less certainty in economic and employment relationships (Briscoe & Hall, 2006). The protean career concept has since framed the thinking of academics and career practitioners (Briscoe & Hall, 2006). In this nontraditional career orientation, employees are directed at achieving subjective career success through self-directed vocational behavior (Briscoe et al., 2006; Hall, 2004). The focus of protean individuals is on subjective, psychological success, i.e. job satisfaction, self-awareness, adaptability, and learning, as opposed to objective career success factors such as income, promotions, and job status (Hall & Chandler, 2005). Two main aspects constitute the concept of PCO: values-driven predispositions and self-directed career management (Briscoe et al., 2006). The former reflects the extent to which employees' career decisions are driven by personally meaningful as opposed to extrinsic, socially imposed values and goals (Direnzo et al., 2015; Hall, 2004). The latter describes the extent to which employees feel independent and in charge of their own career (Briscoe et al., 2006).

Direnzo et al. (2015) argue that PCO is similar to an attitude. In addition to a cognitive and evaluative element, PCO holds a behavioral component: an action tendency to behave in certain ways (Direnzo et al., 2015). Knowledge hiding may be an example of such a behavior. To illustrate, employees holding a PCO are more independent in their career management and less inclined to seek external direction and assistance as compared to colleagues with a traditional career perspective (Briscoe et al., 2006). Employees with this tendency of relying upon themselves may therefore not realize the benefits of engaging in social behaviors with colleagues. In the end, protean-oriented individuals may even decide to hide their knowledge for their coworkers, as they could believe that helping others does not directly contribute to the goal of achieving success in their own career.

Furthermore, when protean-oriented employees acquire and create knowledge themselves in favor of their own career development, they may feel they have personal control over this knowledge. These employees are likely to develop a strong knowledge-based psychological ownership (Peng, 2013; Serenko & Bontis, 2016) and may treat their ideas, information and knowledge as their territories (Peng, 2013). To construct, maintain and restore their territories, employees engage in marking behaviors, e.g. public announcements of one's idea, as well as defending behaviors, e.g. holding knowledge privately (Brown, Lawrence, & Robinson, 2005). Especially when employees regard their knowledge as a valuable asset, they might be motivated to hide it.

In the strategic HRM literature, human capital can be highlighted as an organizational resource that helps firms achieve competitive advantage, and ultimately superior firm-level performance (Boon et al., 2018). It can be argued that striving for competitive advantage also occurs at the individual level. An employee can be in possession of human capital that is valuable for his or her individual job performance or career development. When this human capital is rare, not possessed by many other employees and difficult to imitate (Hall, 1992), it can help the employee gain competitive advantage over his or her coworkers. In this way, the employee may regard his or her human capital as a tool to achieve psychological career success and may therefore decide to withhold it from others. Therefore, protean-oriented employees may be more likely to protect and hide their knowledge compared to peers with a traditional career orientation.

Commitment-Based HR System

The attributions that employees make about the reasons why management adopts HR practices are assumed to have consequences for their attitudes and behaviors (Nishii, Lepak, & Schneider, 2008). Employees with commitment-focused HR attributions experience that the HR practices of their employer (e.g. training, staffing, scheduling, pay, and benefits) are intended to stimulate service quality and employee well-being. On the contrary, employees hold control-focused HR attributions when they believe that the HR practices are aimed to be cost-driven and focused on control, e.g. cost reduction and exploiting employees (Fontinha, Chambel, & De Cuyper al., 2012). Although knowledge hiding may have positive intentions or outcomes in some contexts, it is usually a negative perspective on an individual's knowledge contribution (Peng, 2013). This is why we focus here on organizational contexts in which employees are discouraged to engage in knowledge hiding behaviors.

Commitment HR systems provide employees with incentives directed at increasing their well-being and extending their organizational career (Mossholder et al., 2011). In return, they are likely to experience a felt obligation to reciprocate in positive and beneficial ways (Nishii et al., 2008). Because aspects of interdependence, trust, and information sharing are highly valued in commitment systems (Mossholder, Richardson, & Settoon, 2011), intentional knowledge hiding is likely to be regarded as a harmful act in this particular system. Furthermore, commitment focused organizations select the right people for jobs and provide socialization activities when they first join (Conway, 2004). These activities promote social behaviors like knowledge sharing, peer support, and helping (Mossholder et al., 2011) and may encourage protean-oriented employees to also rely on their coworkers for moving their career forward.

Additionally, commitment systems strongly emphasize training and development to enhance the skills and knowledge of employees (Batistič et al.,

2016). When an organization offers training and development to the workforce widely, feelings of knowledge-based psychological ownership may weaken. Knowledge will become a collective good within the organization, which may result in a lower necessity for protean individuals to keep their knowledge privately. Finally, commitment oriented firms aim for fair rewards that adequately reflect the employees' contribution (Conway, 2004), and employees are considered to perform well when they accept the firm's interests and norms, such as knowledge sharing, as their own (Mossholder et al., 2011). Hence, they would be discouraged from withholding their knowledge, as doing so may hinder them from achieving their protean career ambitions.

Communal-Sharing Relational Climate

Climate perceptions at work help employees understand what behaviors are expected and rewarded (Černe et al., 2014). Relational climates are an example of such perceptions, which include market pricing, equality matching, communal sharing, and authority ranking (Fiske, 1992). These relational forms describe interpersonal activities, such as how people understand and motivate each other in their relationships (Mossholder et al., 2011). We will focus here on the communal-sharing climate, as this climate is expected to be the best for minimizing knowledge hiding. Furthermore, this particular climate has been studied before as complementing a commitment HR system (Batistič et al., 2016; Mossholder et al., 2011).

In communal-sharing climates, feelings of solidarity predominate, and personal welfare of others is considered significant above self-concerns (Mossholder et al., 2011). Interactions between employees are based on feelings of belonging and trust (Batistič et al., 2016) and can be compared to relationships that exist among family or clan members (Ouchi, 1980). Protean-oriented employees usually depend on themselves in their career path; however, in a communal-sharing climate they may be motivated to also care for their colleagues' well-being. This may result in protean individuals becoming aware of the benefits of being involved in knowledge sharing processes. Close relationships in communal-sharing climate generate instrumental benefits, such as receiving task-relevant knowledge from colleagues, and expressive benefits, such as emotional support from colleagues in career decisions (Mossholder et al., 2011). Therefore, instead of only relying upon themselves, protean individuals may decide to share their ideas and information with colleagues. If such behaviors are reciprocated by colleagues, it can assist them in moving their career forward.

Furthermore, because of the desire of frequent interaction in the dense community of communal-sharing climates (Mossholder et al., 2011), knowledge hiding behaviors are not likely to be appreciated. Such counterproductive work behaviors may cause reciprocation of negative knowledge behavior by col-leagues (Serenko & Bontis, 2016). When coworkers exclude the initial knowl-edge hider from knowledge sharing sessions, achieving psychological success in his or her career may be hindered. Finally, work in a communal-sharing climate is carried out following the principle that members of the community contribute what they can without tracking inputs (Clark, 1984). Not recording individual inputs may result in less competition among employees. This would make it irrelevant for the protean individual to hide his or her knowledge with the aim of outperforming colleagues.

Evidence from Organizational Practice

In a previous empirical study, we found some evidence for the roles of protean career orientation, commitment HR system and communal-sharing climate in employee knowledge hiding (Roefs, 2019). A total of 310 respondents based in 50 teams from 23 companies filled out a survey on these topics. They were from a diverse range of industries in the public as well as the private sectors, including health care, public transport, digital marketing, and municipalities. Details on the methods and results can be found in Roefs (2019).

In contrast to what was expected, protean-oriented employees least often hide their knowledge when they operate in a work context characterized by a low commitment HR system and a low communal-sharing climate. A rationale for this outcome could be that employees working in a context with low commitment HR system and low communal-sharing climate may have the feeling of 'being in the same boat.' Employees who perceive that the HR practices of their firm are not aimed at commitment might believe that management regards workers purely as a resource to be exploited to the benefit of the organization (Grant & Shields, 2002). They see HR practices as yet another management initiative in order to secure greater control over, and greater efficiency from employees (Grant & Shields, 2002). Furthermore, when employees work in a context that is low in communal-sharing climate, they may feel that the firm does not invest in team structures where employees fit and belong together based on collective needs (Mossholder et al., 2011).

Taking both contextual factors together, when employees perceive the firm exploits them and do not consider social bonds and collective welfare in teams, they may realize they are in the same unpleasant situation. Rather than competing, individuals may help each other to overcome the problems caused by management. As also evident in the employee gossip and employee cyni-cism literature (Chiaburu et al., 2013; Michelson, Van Iterson, & Waddington, 2010), this beneficial consequence of poor management practices could result in lower levels of knowledge hiding. Furthermore, a context with low communal-sharing climate encourages employees to stand out from the group and to express non-conforming opinions (Batistič et al., 2016). Being honest about one's unwillingness to share knowledge would therefore be eased in this context. This argumentation was especially true for employees with a protean career orientation. Being part of the same difficult situation could motivate protean-oriented employees to help one another in achieving their notion of psychological career success. In this case, it is evident that the strengths of the context seem to offset the needs of the individual (Cable & Edwards, 2004).

IMPLICATIONS FOR THEORY AND PRACTICE

The results of our own empirical study suggest an important insight for HR and Talent Management regarding the impact of work context. The attributions that employees make about the HR system and relational climate in their work environment apparently influence how often they hide their knowledge for peers. In a work atmosphere where *low states* of commitment HR system and communal-sharing climates are present, employees would *least often* hide their knowledge when they enact protean-oriented careers. Conversely, when *high levels* of commitment HR system and communal-sharing climate are predominant, individuals would *most often* display knowledge hiding behaviors when they hold a protean career orientation. Individual differences such as protean career orientation can therefore influence knowledge hiding behaviors, but only when individuals interpret the organizational context in a particular way (in this case the interplay of commitment HR system and communal-sharing climate). This prevalent interaction between the (inter)personal dynamics of how employees influence each other towards collective goals ('person' or leadership characteristics) and the organizational systems and processes that attempt to influence employees in a systematic way ('environment' or HRM aspects) has been outlined before in earlier research (Cable & Edwards, 2004; Leroy et al., 2018).

Our own outcomes highlight the important role of front-line managers in properly implementing the HR and Talent Management practices (Leroy et al., 2018) and appropriately stimulating relational climates (Mossholder et al., 2011). When their aim is to reduce knowledge hiding behaviors, managers should generate a work environment with low commitment HR system and low communal-sharing climate, and subsequently aim for attracting, developing and retaining employees with a protean career orientation. It must be noted, however, that aiming for low levels of this system and climate can be counterintuitive and might have other, more negative, results, such as lower levels of employee commitment, employee satisfaction, organizational citizenship behavior, and customer satisfaction (Nishii et al., 2008). A combination of low commitment HR system and low communal-sharing climate thus has the potential of discouraging knowledge hiding behaviors, but may also reduce advantages, such as organizational commitment and employee and customer satisfaction. This confirms the idea that managers should reconsider the holistic view that only one HR system and one relational climate can lead to the best results (Černe, Batistič, & Kenda, 2018). Hence, organizations should consistently consider a deliberate tradeoff when selecting HR systems and climates as part of their business and talent strategy.

More generally speaking, the reasons and methods for knowledge hiding differ between organizations and teams, and so do the consequences. Managers who are wondering whether, why and how knowledge hiding occurs in their organization can collect data to provide initial answers. Two approaches spring to mind here.

1. Gathering new data: one way to measure whether and how knowledge hiding takes place in the workplace is through a survey. Academic literature provides us with several existing and reliable questionnaires for some key topics managers may want to measure. Examples include:
   i. Knowledge hiding questionnaire: a 12-item scale developed by Connelly et al. (2012). The questionnaire opens with a personal knowledge hiding experience. An example statement that follows is: 'In this instance, I offered him/her some other information instead of what he/she really wanted.'
   ii. HR practices as an organizational factor: how do employees perceive the HR practices (service quality, cost reduction, employee well-being, etc.)? A 20-item scale on HR attributions by Nishii et al. (2008) is available. One of the statements is: 'The organization pays its employees what it does so that employees will feel valued and respected—to promote employee well-being.'
   iii. Climate as an organizational factor: a 33-item scale measuring relational models by Haslam and Fiske (1999), examining how employees evaluate the organizational climate (communal sharing, equality matching, authority ranking and market pricing). An example item is: 'People in the team share many important responsibilities jointly, without assigning them to anyone alone.'
2. Using available data: a risk of introducing new questionnaires is survey fatigue among employees (i.e., the number of survey requests leads to decreased or skewed participation and decreased reliability of outcomes). Alternatively, managers can consider data already available in their organizations and likely related to effects (and outcomes) of knowledge hiding or sharing. To identify promising data sources, it is a good idea to involve stakeholders across the organization and consult them to guide data analysis and indicator development. This approach can also be taken to enrich or phase out a survey, by identifying existing data related to survey

outcomes. Managers should keep in mind what is needed to monitor effectiveness as they implement policies to encourage knowledge sharing and discourage knowledge hiding. Even though HR's influence is strongest at the organizational level, it may be that the desired effects occur (and should be monitored) mostly at the personal or job-related level.

Based on ideas about how to measure and monitor effects, what policies can HR and Talent Management consider? Applying the cynical look possibly implied by our own key empirical finding (employees are *discouraged* to hide knowledge when working in an environment that is distrustful or non-caring and characterized by control-focused HR practices) is one option. Under these circumstances, employees can feel like they are all in the same boat, with the company as a 'common enemy.' They gain most by helping each other overcome the problems caused by management, resulting in a lower tendency to hide knowledge. Purely relying on these results to minimize knowledge hiding, one could choose policies that foster a hostile working environment. Obviously, that could result in other, more negative consequences: disgruntled employees, lower customer satisfaction, etc. There is always a tradeoff to consider with HR policies as part of a business strategy.

What *are* viable solutions to consider, then? We offer the following three:

- Organizational-level policies: the easiest option for HR and Talent Management is to implement policies aimed at the organizational level. For example, thinking of the scenario with Tom and Jamal, organizations could consider a team-based remuneration policy. Meant as an incentive for employees to maximize performance and profits for the company, individual performance-based pay can encourage maximizing one's own reward by hiding knowledge, at the expense of company performance.
- Job-level procedures: employees need time to share their know-how with each other. In the scenario with the consultancy firm, Regina may want to help out Rajesh, but as she is struggling with her own deadlines, she doesn't feel able to. Organizations can use surveys and other data to periodically examine work processes and workload to establish a working environment that enables mutual cooperation and assistance.
- Individual-level actions: even with the right policies and procedures, individuals such as Ellen may have a tendency to withhold knowledge for personal gain. As a company you can reduce such behavior by implementing leadership assessments for management positions, encouraging fostering interpersonal trust. Additionally, organizations could offer training to improve adaptability skills, self-management, organizational citizenship (i.e., going the extra mile and acting altruistically) and thus minimize knowledge hiding (Han et al., 2016).

CONCLUSION

Questioning commonly held beliefs in organizations can pay off. Knowledge hiding occurs in any organization. Despite many efforts to enhance knowledge sharing (e.g., using IT systems and knowledge management policies), employees may still feel encouraged to withhold their know-how from peers. From a talent management perspective, this is a potential cost to talented workers and the organization that should be avoided. To address this issue, we need to look beyond providing employees with systems and policies that support desired behavior. After all, why would talented employees bother about these tools? Do they even have the space and time to do so? Do the HR and Talent Management practices in place and the relational climate in the organization send out a consistent message to these employees about what is really valued in terms of knowledge sharing? Managers will need to deal with such issues and we hope this chapter has provided them with some inspiration and guidance to do so.

REFERENCES

Batistič, S., Černe, M., Kaše, R. & Zupic, I. (2016). The role of organizational context in fostering employee proactive behavior: The interplay between HR system configurations and relational climates. *European Management Journal*, **34**(5), 579–588.

Batistič, S. & Poell, R.F. (2022). Do HR systems and relational climates affect knowledge hiding? An experiment and two-source multi-level study. *Journal of Business Research*, **147**, 82–96.

Boon, C., Eckardt, R., Lepak, D.P. & Boselie, P. (2018). Integrating strategic human capital and strategic human resource management. *International Journal of Human Resource Management*, **29**(1), 34–67.

Briscoe, J.P. & Hall, D.T. (2006). The interplay of boundaryless and protean careers: Combinations and implications. *Journal of Vocational Behavior*, **69**(1), 4–18.

Briscoe, J.P., Hall, D.T. & DeMuth, R.L.F. (2006). Protean and boundaryless careers: An empirical exploration. *Journal of Vocational Behavior*, **69**(1), 30–47.

Brown, G., Lawrence, T.B. & Robinson, S.L. (2005). Territoriality in organizations. *Academy of Management Review*, **30**(3), 577–594.

Cable, D.M. & Edwards, J.R. (2004). Complementary and supplementary fit: A theoretical and empirical integration. *Journal of Applied Psychology*, **89**(5), 822–834.

Cabrera, A. & Cabrera, E.F. (2002). Knowledge-sharing dilemmas. *Organization Studies*, **23**(5), 687–710.

Cardenas, R. (2014). What's the real cost of a bad hire? http://www.hrexchangenetwork.com/hr-talent-acquisition/articles/what-s-the-real-cost-of-a-bad-hire.

Černe, M., Batistič, S. & Kenda, R. (2018). HR systems, attachment styles with leaders, and the creativity–innovation nexus. *Human Resource Management Review*, **28**(3), 271–288.

Černe, M., Nerstad, C.G.L., Dysvik, A. & Škerlavaj, M. (2014). What goes around comes around: Knowledge hiding, perceived motivational climate, and creativity. *Academy of Management Journal*, **57**(1), 172–192.

Chiaburu, D.S., Peng, A.C., Oh, I., Banks, G.C. & Lomeli, L.C. (2013). Antecedents and consequences of employee organizational cynicism: A meta-analysis. *Journal of Vocational Behavior*, **83**(2), 181–197.

Clark, M.S. (1984). Record keeping in two types of relationships. *Journal of Personality and Social Psychology*, **47**(3), 549–557.

Connelly, C.E. & Zweig, D. (2015). How perpetrators and targets construe knowledge hiding in organizations. *European Journal of Work and Organizational Psychology*, **24**(3), 479–489.

Connelly, C.E., Zweig, D., Webster, J. & Trougakos, J.P. (2012). Knowledge hiding in organizations. *Journal of Organizational Behavior*, **33**(1), 64–88.

Conway, E. (2004). Relating career stage to attitudes towards HR practices and commitment: Evidence of interaction effects? *European Journal of Work and Organizational Psychology*, **13**(4), 417–446.

Direnzo, M.S., Greenhaus, J.H. & Weer, C.H. (2015). Relationship between protean career orientation and work-life balance: A resource perspective. *Journal of Organizational Behavior*, **36**(4), 538–560.

Ferris, G.R., Arthur, M.M., Berkson, H.M., Kaplan, D.M., Harrell-Cook, G. & Frink, D.D. (1998). Toward a social-context theory of the human resource management–organization effectiveness relationship. *Human Resource Management Review*, **8**(3), 235–264.

Fiske, A.P. (1992). The four elementary forms of sociality: Framework for a unified theory of social relations. *Psychological Review*, **99**(4), 689–723.

Fontinha, R., Chambel, M.J. & De Cuyper, N. (2012). HR attributions and the dual commitment of outsourced IT workers. *Personnel Review*, **41**(6), 832–848.

Grant, D. & Shields, J. (2002). In search of the subject: Researching employee reactions to human resource management. *The Journal of Industrial Relations*, **44**(3), 313–334.

Hall, D.T. (1976). *Careers in Organizations*. Pacific Palisades, CA: Goodyear.

Hall, D.T. (2004). The protean career: A quarter-century journey. *Journal of Vocational Behavior*, **65**(1), 1–13.

Hall, D.T. & Chandler, D.E. (2005). Psychological success: When the career is a calling. *Journal of Organizational Behavior*, **26**(2), 155–176.

Hall, R. (1992). The strategic analysis of intangible resources. *Strategic Management Journal*, **13**(2), 135–144.

Han, S.H., Seo, G., Yoon, S.W. & Yoon, D. (2016). Transformational leadership and knowledge sharing: Mediating roles of employee's empowerment, commitment, and citizenship behaviors. *Journal of Workplace Learning*, **28**(3), 130–149.

Haslam, N. & Fiske, A.P. (1999). Relational models theory: A confirmatory factor analysis. *Personal Relationships*, **6**(2), 241–250.

Huo, W., Cai, Z., Luo, J., Men, C. & Jia, R. (2016). Antecedents and intervention mechanisms: A multi-level study of R&D team's knowledge hiding behavior. *Journal of Knowledge Management*, **20**(5), 880–897.

Ipe, M. (2003). Knowledge sharing in organizations: A conceptual framework. *Human Resource Development Review*, **2**(4), 337–359.

Kuenzi, M. & Schminke, M. (2009). Assembling fragments into a lens: A review, critique, and proposed research agenda for the organizational work climate literature. *Journal of Management*, **35**(3), 634–717.

Lepak, D.P. & Snell, S.A. (1999). The human resource architecture: Toward a theory of human capital allocation and development. *Academy of Management Review*, **24**(1), 31–48.

Lepak, D.P. & Snell, S.A. (2002). Examining the human resource architecture: The relationships among human capital, employment, and human resource configurations. *Journal of Management*, **28**(4), 517–543.

Leroy, H., Segers, J., Van Dierendonck, D. & Den Hartog, D. (2018). Managing people in organizations: Integrating the study of HRM and leadership. *Human Resource Management Review*, **28**(3), 249–257.

Michelson, G., Van Iterson, A. & Waddington, K. (2010). Gossip in organizations: Contexts, consequences, and controversies. *Group & Organization Management*, **35**(4), 371–390.

Mossholder, K.W., Richardson, H.A. & Settoon, R.P. (2011). Human resource systems and helping in organizations: A relational perspective. *The Academy of Management Review*, **36**(1), 33–52.

Nishii, L.H., Lepak, D.P. & Schneider, B. (2008). Employee attributions of the 'why' of HR practices: Their effects on employee attitudes and behaviors, and customer satisfaction. *Personnel Psychology*, **61**(3), 503–545.

North, K., Reinhardt, R. & Schmidt, A. (2004). The benefits of knowledge management: Some empirical evidence. Paper presented at the OKLC Conference, Innsbruck, Austria.

Ouchi, W.G. (1980). Markets, bureaucracies, and clans. *Administrative Science Quarterly*, **25**(1), 129–141.

Peng, H. (2013). Why and when do people hide knowledge? *Journal of Knowledge Management*, **17**(3), 398–415.

Postolache, A. (2017a). Part 1: Introduction to Deep Smarts and World Bank case study. http://www.quandora.com/introduction-deep-smarts-world-bank-case-study.

Postolache, A. (2017b). 5 benefits of knowledge sharing within an organization. http://www.quandora.com/5-benefits-knowledge-sharing-organization.

Roefs, A. (2019). Exploring the cross-level effects on knowledge hiding of protean career orientation, commitment HR system and communal sharing climate: A three-way interaction model. Master's thesis in Human Resource Studies, Tilburg University, Netherlands.

Serenko, A. & Bontis, N. (2016). Understanding counterproductive knowledge behavior: Antecedents and consequences of intra-organizational knowledge hiding. *Journal of Knowledge Management*, **20**(6), 1199–1224.

Simmons, C. (n.d.). Are win rates a valuable measure of success? https://24hrco.com/images/articles/html/ChrisSimMay10.html.

Staples, D.S. & Webster, J. (2008). Exploring the effects of trust, task interdependence and virtualness on knowledge sharing in teams. *Information Systems Journal*, **18**(6), 617–640.

Swailes, S., Downs, Y. & Orr, K. (2014). Conceptualising inclusive talent management: Potential, possibilities and practicalities. *Human Resource Development International*, **17**(5), 529–544.

Tsai, W. (2001). Knowledge transfer in intraorganizational networks: Effects of network position and absorptive capacity on business unit innovation and performance. *Academy of Management Journal*, **44**(5), 996–1004.

Wang, S. & Noe, R.A. (2010). Knowledge sharing: A review and directions for future research. *Human Resource Management Review*, **20**(2), 115–131.

Wu, W., Lin, C., Hsu, B. & Yeh, R. (2009). Interpersonal trust and knowledge sharing: Moderating effects of individual altruism and a social interaction environment. *Social Behavior and Personality: An International Journal*, **37**(1), 83–93.

9. The unrealized value of global workers: the need for global talent management

Anthony McDonnell, Stefan Jooss and Kieran M. Conroy

INTRODUCTION

Global work is an essential feature in many multinational enterprises (MNEs), providing a mechanism to coordinate business activities globally and use resources more strategically (Cascio & Boudreau, 2016). Research has recognized the importance of advancing our understanding around global work experiences and organizational efforts to manage such work (Reiche, Lee, & Allen, 2019) and to better align global talent management strategies and knowledge management processes with this type of work (Harzing, Pudelko, & Reiche, 2016). The benefits derived from global work range from being able to expand business operations to more strategic use of resources and greater access to specialized talent (Reiche et al., 2019). The type of benefits that may be derived and the challenges involved, however, are likely to vary depending on the type of global work arrangements being used. Much of the literature has focused on traditional forms of global work such as long-term or traditional expatriates or, in more recent times, self-initiated expatriates (Kraimer, Bolino, & Mead, 2016). In this chapter we focus more on a broader suite of global work arrangements that in broad terms encompass all situations where employees collaborate with each other in a culturally diverse context and who are also often geographically distant from one another (Hinds, Liu, & Lyon, 2011).

Global talent management considers the attraction, selection, development, and retention of high-performing employees in pivotal roles globally (Collings, Mellahi, & Cascio, 2019). In this chapter, we take the perspective that a substantial cadre of global workers are in pivotal roles within MNEs due to the wide strategic boundary spanning activities they undertake amongst a multiplicity of actors and business units. They play critical business roles in terms of control and coordination along with being key recipients and/or purveyors of knowledge. Given that knowledge is increasingly seen as a critical organizational asset, its effective management can be viewed as business critical (Kiessling & Harvey, 2006). The most valuable knowledge is often embedded within people's experiences and thus formalizing and sharing it can be a challenge (Whelan & Carcary, 2011). The nature of global workers' roles means that there is much scope for them to gain considerable knowledge across the boundaries that they traverse. How these workers are managed therefore takes on prominence if organizations are going to realize benefits. Moreover, they possess substantial autonomy over their roles which provides opportunity for significant variability in performance, and as a result, contribution to organizational objectives and success (Collings & Mellahi, 2009). Therefore, they represent a particular type of talent within MNEs.

In this chapter, we first define global work arrangements, provide an overview of the various forms of global workers, and conceptualize global talent management with a focus on pivotal positions around these arrangements. Second, we unpack the global workers' role as key boundary spanners in organizations. We show how various forms of global workers create value for MNEs through their boundary spanning activity, particularly in relation to knowledge management. Third, we depict the tensions faced by these individuals, along with the management of such global workers, highlighting a mismatch in demands and resources and a lack of oversight from corporate HR functions.

GLOBAL WORK ARRANGEMENTS

Global work arrangements encompass a range of individuals where international working is a key feature of roles including traditional expatriates, short-term assignees, flexpatriates, international business travellers (IBTs), rotational assignees, international commuters, global domestics, and global virtual workers (see e.g., Jooss, McDonnell, & Conroy, 2021b; Reiche et al., 2019; Shaffer et al., 2012). These forms of global work can be distinguished based on their purpose, duration, location, compensation, the extent of corporate HR involvement, and the associated advantages and drawbacks, among others. For example, traditional expatriates are individuals who relocate for a period of 12 months or more to one destination, often being accompanied by their family and receiving an expatriate package with a range of benefits. For these global workers, HR and mobility functions are involved in managing the international assignment (i.e., preparation, support, repatriation). In contrast, significantly less HR involvement and oversight is found when managing shorter or more flexible forms of global work such as international business travel, flexpatriation, and short-term assignees (see Jooss et al., 2021b).

IBTs are individuals 'for whom business travel is an essential component of their work' (Welch & Worm, 2006: 284 cited in Collings, Scullion, & Morley, 2007: 206). This generally ranges from a few days to up to three weeks of international travel. IBTs do not relocate to the various countries that they visit and maintain their home country responsibilities during their short stay abroad. Flexpatriates are individuals 'who travel for brief assignments, away from their home base and across cultural or national borders, leaving their family and personal life behind' (Mayerhofer et al., 2004: 1371). While traditional expatriates generally just relocate to one country, flexpatriates are assigned to multiple and potentially highly diverse countries which requires adaptability in their working approach. International commuters are individuals who commute 'from a home country to a place of work in another country, usually on a weekly or bi-weekly basis, while the family remains at home' (Mayerhofer et al., 2004: 1375). Rotational assignees operate internationally on a shift cycle (Shortland, 2018). An intensive period of work abroad, often in hardship and offshore locations, is followed by a time off period back in the home country (Collings et al., 2007). Short-term international assignees are assigned to one or a small number of countries for up to one year (Shaffer et al., 2012). In this case, generally, the family does not relocate, and compensation remains the home country responsibility.

Global domestics are individuals who have key responsibilities at a more regional or global level that entail interactions with others from a range of countries. However, in their role, they are not required to physically move but remain in the home country (Shaffer et al., 2012). Finally, in recent years, and accelerated by the COVID-19 pandemic, global virtual work has become fundamental to how firms coordinate and collaborate internationally (Hafermalz & Riemer, 2020). Global virtual workers do not interact in person but through technology-mediated means (Hinds, Liu, & Lyon, 2011). When the pandemic hit, and as countries implemented various restrictions around travel, MNEs have had to eradicate or reduce most of their other forms of global work which they predominantly had relied on pre-COVID. Instead, MNEs tried to imitate 'spaces of collocation' and face-to-face interaction for global workers across country borders through virtual means (Faulconbridge et al., 2020; Reiche et al., 2019). Many individuals had to conduct the global nature of their roles, for the first time, in a fully virtual context (Carnevale & Hatak, 2020). While not every one of the aforementioned work arrangements entail individuals performing positions of a business critical or pivotal nature, we argue that many are. Either way, in line with the different perspectives and approaches of talent management in existence, we argue that these global workers deserve further attention when talking about talent and the value that they may bring to an organization. Moreover, the portfolio of options for global working provides opportunities to individuals to gain international experience which has long been argued as being critical to those harbouring ambitions to join top management teams (Lublin, 1996). A key challenge is that we have little understanding on the sheer scale of the utilization of such different forms of global workers given many of these forms tend to fall outside organizational reporting and support systems except for long-term international assignees (Suutari et al., 2013).

GLOBAL TALENT MANAGEMENT: GLOBAL WORKERS AND PIVOTAL POSITIONS

We conceptualize global talent management as talent management at a global scale. While there is no set agreement on the meaning or conceptualization of talent management, four approaches are commonly depicted (Collings & Mellahi, 2009): a people approach, practices approach, strategic talent pool approach, and pivotal positions approach. We briefly outline each now.

First, the people approach refers to talent management as a categorization of people. Here, the focus tends to be on individuals that have competencies that are hard to find or difficult to replace and associated concepts are a portfolio of people with differentiating investments, a performance-potential matrix, and a focus on intellectual skills as part of the knowledge economy (Sparrow & Makram, 2015). The people approach is also closely related to the categorization of employees into A, B, and C players where the most investment is into A players, a small number of elite employees, and where poor performers are slowly exited from the organization. This approach further discusses innate versus developmental skills and while some authors see the differentiated investment as a core focus, others have centred on the debate between inclusive and exclusive approaches to talent. As part of the latter, inclusive approaches consider talent management for all employees while exclusive approaches focus on a subset of the employee population (Dries, 2013).

Second, the practices approach considers talent management as the presence of key practices. This approach acknowledges the importance of well-crafted practices encompassing a set of activities, programmes, processes, and systems (Al Ariss, Cascio, & Paauwe, 2014). For example, recruiting and selecting talent requires an analysis of the labour market, benchmarking exercises, and employer branding. Once talent has joined a company, onboarding, development, performance and rewards practices must be in place to retain these employees. In addition, processes to identify and develop key internal talent must be established including succession planning, talent reviews, career management, and internal mobility (Sparrow & Makram, 2015).

Third, the strategic pools approach centres around human capital as a collective. Talent pools are ultimately a grouping or clustering of talent (either people or positions) and the focus lies on those wider labour pools that promise significant impact upon investment and improvement of organizational capabilities and performance (Boudreau & Ramstadt, 2007) As a central aspect of this approach, strategic workforce planning strongly considers business strategy and talent strategy alignment, translation of organizational capabilities needs into talent needs, and targeting of specific cohorts of centrality (Sparrow & Makram, 2015). Related to this approach is the question of value of human capital considering both impact on organizational performance and feasibility of executive strategic plans, as well as risk optimization and management (Cascio & Boudreau, 2012).

Finally, the positions approach focuses on the identification of pivotal positions. As a response to the critique by Pfeffer (2001) on the locus of value creation, this approach centres on positions rather than people in the first instance. Instead of segmenting the workforce by A, B, and C players, Huselid, Beatty, and Becker (2005) refer to A, B, and C positions; A positions being those that have a direct strategic impact and exhibit high performance variability among those in the position, representing upside potential. These A positions are also characterized by high autonomous decision-making, performance being the primary determinant of compensation, and creating value by substantially enhancing revenue. Given their scope of responsibility, consequences of mistakes may be very costly but missed revenue opportunities are an even greater loss for the organization (Huselid et al., 2005). These pivotal positions are ultimately defined by their centrality to organizational strategy in combination with the extent to which a change in the quality or quantity of people in these positions generates significant outcomes (Boudreau & Ramstad, 2007; Collings & Mellahi, 2009). Notably, this not only considers planning around present pivotal positions but also those positions that may become pivotal in the future, highlighting the dynamic nature required under this approach (Cascio & Boudreau, 2016). Once these pivotal positions are identified, organizations ought to invest disproportionately in those positions and ensure they are staffed with the best people because it is these positions which offer the greatest return of potential at an organizational level (Huselid & Becker, 2011).

While without uniform agreement, the positions approach has gained considerable traction in the literature (McDonnell & Wiblen, 2021). For this chapter, we adopt this positions approach, whilst acknowledging that a combination of the above approaches is likely to exist in some organizations. We continue with making the argument that global workers are likely to have a considerable strategic impact through their wide boundary spanning activities central to many of their positions within the MNE.

GLOBAL WORKERS AS KEY BOUNDARY SPANNERS

Global work scholars have yet to fully adopt a boundary spanning perspective. Research on boundary spanning traditionally explores how organizations innovate more effectively by navigating the boundaries that exist, and adapting to the frictions these create, with the external environment (Aldrich & Herker, 1977). Boundaries are evident within and between organizations and are characterized by differences, novelty, ambiguity, and complexity (Carlile, 2002). Studies consider boundary spanning from a variety of perspectives such as boundary spanning roles, motivations, behaviours, and activities that individuals perform (Birkinshaw, Ambos, & Bouquet, 2017; Minbaeva & Santangelo, 2018). More recently, scholars have begun to look at global boundary spanning, particularly in the context of MNEs that coordinate and orchestrate knowledge flows within globally distributed workforces. Global boundary spanning is defined as a 'set of communication and coordination activities performed by individuals within an organization and between organizations to integrate activities across multiple cultural, institutional and organizational contexts' (Schotter et al. 2017: 404).

For global workers in an MNE context, emphasis is given to understanding how boundaries disrupt the flow of knowledge, development of relationships, and bridging of cultural differences (Conroy, McDonnell, & Jooss, 2020). A major criticism of this perspective is it often fails to identify the parameters of who may be classified as a boundary spanner, with seemingly any individual, role, or activity considered a boundary spanning concern. As Schotter et al. (2017: 413) suggest, although 'individual actors play an important role in the effectiveness of boundary spanning ... not every individual may be equally effective in this role'.. We argue that boundary spanning offers a useful theoretical base to conceptualize the pivotal positions, behaviours, and activities of global workers, but assert that the nature and scope of their role impacts how effective a global worker is at navigating cross-border interfaces. This also brings the relevance of global approaches to talent management to mind. Another related criticism involves identifying exactly what boundaries are being traversed as global boundaries which should be classified by varying degrees of novelty, uncertainty, and foreignness (Mäkelä et al., 2019). We suggest that global workers are exposed to various intra-firm boundaries in MNEs such as unit boundaries between HQ and subsidiaries, functional boundaries between departments, or hierarchical boundaries between management layers. Inter-firm boundaries also exist where global workers interact and exchange knowledge while building social capital with global and local organizations. Exploring how global workers coordinate knowledge flows across these boundaries may advance our understanding of their pivotal positions.

The various types of global workers in MNEs such as traditional expatriates, inpatriates, third country nationals, IBTs, and virtual workers, to name a few, all potentially confront a myriad of cross-national boundaries and, in doing so, may enact various boundary spanning positions and activities. Most scholars underestimate that, given the broad scope and comprehensive nature of their responsibilities, global workers are most at risk of conflicting circumstances across diverse multiple boundaries. This also means that there is likely to be much variation in the performance of individuals performing such roles which, in turn, impacts on the value conferred on the organization.

Research on traditional expatriates suggests that they fulfil important boundary spanning positions by transferring HQ-specific knowledge to local subsidiaries that may be crucial for managing boundary interfaces and overcoming liabilities of foreignness in external environments (Harzing, 2001). Boundary spanning activities of expatriates may be particularly important in peripheral locations when knowledge is imprisoned in local networks and not easily extracted or intelligible (Furusawa & Brewster, 2019). Traditional expatriates may act as corporate ambassadors in informing and updating HQ on important changes in the local subsidiary, which offsets the degree of bounded rationality for corporate executives in managing across global boundaries. These are also important figureheads in building relational ties across organizational boundaries with external stakeholders in the local context and engaging in multi-faceted boundary spanning activities the longer they stay in the local subsidiary (Au & Fukuda, 2002). Johnson and Duxbury (2010) argue that expatriates coordinate in such a way that opens the boundary to enable cross-boundary knowledge flows while also guarding or closing the boundary to protect or buffer from any potentially harmful interferences externally. Other boundary spanning activities of these expatriates may include shaping the agendas of external agents, gathering local intelligence, signalling corporate commitment and improving the subsidiary's legitimacy or reputation locally (Johnson & Duxbury, 2010). The main body of research on global workers focuses on traditional expatriates and how they can be supported in adjusting to managing across cultural boundaries. Applying a boundary spanning lens, Liu and Meyer (2020) looked at how expatriates facilitate reverse knowledge transfer in the context of international acquisitions for Chinese MNEs as well as the significance of collaborative-team based HRM practices in motivating increased boundary spanning behaviour.

In addition to expatriates, inpatriates also occupy pivotal boundary spanning positions when they undertake international assignments from the local subsidiary to the home country of the HQ (Collings et al., 2010). Although receiving less attention as critical linking agents across home–host country boundaries, inpatriates are deployed in crucial boundary spanning positions as both senders of subsidiary-specific knowledge to the HQ through reverse knowledge transfer and receivers of corporate knowledge that is distributed to the local subsidiary upon repatriation (Harzing et al., 2016). Inpatriates reach across the intra-firm boundaries in the MNE and seek to build social capital with corporate decision makers, usually with a view to furthering their career or influencing decisions for the benefit of the local subsidiary (Harvey, Novicevic, & Speier, 2000; Sarabi, Froese, & Hamori, 2017). Reiche (2011) is one of the few to explore the boundary spanning role of inpatriates and argues that they are important knowledge carriers that may enhance the absorptive capacity of HQ. Harvey's research has also been to the fore on inpatriates looking at how this process leads to broadening of the cultural diversity of HQ top management teams, particularly in US MNEs (Harvey & Buckley, 1997). Mentoring of inpatriates by HQ staff can improve their assimilation into the corporate ranks as outsiders increase the transfer of reverse knowledge (Harvey et al., 2005) while improving trust and firm-specific learning during and retention after the assignment (Reiche, Kraimer, & Harzing, 2011). Yet, despite the challenges that inpatriates face in managing across the intra-firm boundary between the HQ and the subsidiary, there is limited research that explores the HR practices in place to support their boundary spanning activities. We also know very little about the boundary spanning positions of inpatriates in terms of managing inter-organizational boundaries in interfacing with external stakeholders in the HQ's home country context. Given their relocation status situates them in a given host country context (expatriates stationed at the subsidiary and inpatriates seconded to HQ), it could be argued that both expatriates and inpatriates confront rather static boundaries in a home–host setting. Moreover, there is also the case of third country nationals which have also received limited attention in this domain but which can perform key boundary spanning roles (notable exception being Barmeyer, Stein, & Eberhardt, 2020).

Global workers that engage in extensive travel across the MNE, without ever fully relocating, are likely to confront a multiplex of boundaries as they traverse a diversified network of subsidiaries. As such those global workers classified as IBTs also occupy pivotal boundary spanning positions but the boundary activities they engage in are much more transient and fleeting. Unlike traditional expatriates, parent country nationals and inpatriates who are rooted a single location, IBTs are confronted with greater spatial and temporal diversity in navigating a broad range of boundaries. For instance, IBTs spend only a limited amount of time in any given market meaning they are under pressure to continuously build relationships and exchange knowledge across different boundaries (Bozkurt & Mohr, 2011). It could be argued that an important boundary spanning activity of IBTs may be the recombination of globally dispersed and discrete pockets of knowledge (Hovhannisyan & Keller, 2015). Recombination involves the melding or synthesis of two or more previously isolated yet complementary bundles of knowledge in a way that produces value across the MNE (Lee, Narula, & Hillemann, 2021). As IBTs are one of the few global workers that travel to a wide variety of locations, they have the potential to identify and connect disparate knowledge pockets leading to the creation of valuable knowledge bundles. IBTs may operate in central bridging positions between parent country expatriates and inpatriates, collecting and carrying large amounts of explicit knowledge but also translating and transferring more complex tacit knowledge between diverse units (Duvivier, Peeters, & Harzing, 2019). However, in order to become more effective in their boundary spanning positions, IBTs will likely need to engage in increased levels of travel, yet this creates physical and psychological pressures for these global workers. Although there are increasing numbers of studies that consider the perils of international business travel (Jooss, Conroy, & McDonnell, 2021a), scholars have yet to fully appreciate the unique boundary spanning activities that these global workers engage in as well as how they are supported in this process.

There is no doubt that due to COVID-19 more global workers will engage in less relocation-based assignments as well as pared back global travel schedules due to realization that a lot of global work can be conducted virtually (PwC, 2020). Global virtual work, however, is not without boundary considerations and sharing rich tacit knowledge across a technology-mediated context is often more difficult due to a lack of visual and sensory cues that create the structure of social capital development (Nurmi & Hinds, 2020). Although facing greater geographical and physical distance in a virtual setting, global workers can still establish perceived proximity or feelings of closeness by increasing frequency, depth, and interactivity of communication (Wilson et al., 2008). The reality is that most global workers managing across virtual boundaries will be operating as a part of a globally distributed team. Global work is no longer performed independently or sequentially, or indeed in a purely face-to-face context, but requires interdependent and coordinated action and the development of routines that are both corporeally and virtually embedded across the MNE (Ancona & Caldwell, 1992). Much of the work from Marrone (2010) on team boundary spanning as well as studies on global virtual teams (Jimenez et al., 2017) can and should be applied to extend our understanding of global workers and their boundary spanning positions.

Despite the above considerations on how various global workers perform important linking roles within, across, and outside MNE boundaries as part of these critical roles, there is limited evidence on how the challenges these individuals confront are managed and supported, particularly in the case of all forms other than traditional expatriates. Next, we explore the challenges or tensions involved in the management of such global talent.

TENSIONS IN MANAGING GLOBAL WORKERS

While the literature has highlighted several positive individual impacts for global workers such as exposure to new cultures and destinations, personal growth and development, and career advancement (Dimitrova, 2020), global work is characterized by a high level of complexity and therefore accompanied by multiple demands. Cultural, linguistic, spatial, and temporal distances make the coordination of work but also the management of these people a challenging task (Edwards et al., 2016). Using the job demands-resources model (Demerouti et al., 2001), Shaffer and colleagues (2012) present an overview of a range of demands including personal demands, work demands, and non-work demands. While personal demands encompass aspects such as stress and coping and identity transformation, work demands consider career transition concerns and structural and perceptual barriers. Non-work demands relate mainly to work-family conflicts, friendships, and personal life. In a similar vein, Jooss et al. (2021a) discuss physical, psychological, and social demands that global workers face. These demands are a result of high physical mobility, cognitive flexibility, and non-work disruption (Shaffer et al., 2012), particularly for those global workers that engage in significant global boundary spanning across a multiplicity of changing contexts. For example, IBTs and flexpatriates especially encounter such demands given their role which requires a significant amount of travel and high level of flexibility, adapting to new environments. In addition, these global workers often have to manage both home and host country work responsibilities, leading to a significant workload often beyond their formal job description. While it is known that many organizations do incorporate the need for global travel in job descriptions the granularity of what this means appears less often understood and to have a material impact on those undertaking these roles by way of support. The reality appears to be that the global dimension of positions where they involve more flexible forms of global working (e.g., flexpatriates) are treated almost solely as domestically based employees (Pate & Scullion, 2018). This may in part be due to often glamorized perspectives towards those that undertake extensive international travel, rather than adopting a more critical lens to the challenges and potentially detrimental aspects that this can bring.

Given the boundary spanning aspect to many of these positions, greater emphasis needs to be placed on ensuring that these global workers remain motivated and are retained by organizations (Dimitrova, 2020). To achieve this, we argue that effective talent management approaches are needed to be put in place that accounts for the unique work context that global workers face, and which ultimately will influence the contribution made to the MNE. In this regard, we argue that current talent management processes do not fully capture either the value of global workers as boundary spanners or the proliferating demands created through the nature of their work (Jooss et al., 2021b). Recent empirical work illustrates why such a lack of oversight and strategic management can be problematic (Jooss et al., 2021a). The authors found a substantial job demands-resources mismatch faced by global workers. Global workers have a high level of autonomy around how they carry out their global work which many individuals used to engage in job crafting actions. However, these job crafting actions inadvertently intensified rather than eased the demands-resources mismatch that these workers faced. Increasing demands without an appropriate support infrastructure will arguably lead to strain and hinder the effective performance of their boundary role, for example, in relation to knowledge sharing practices. We therefore call for greater oversight by corporate HR function to, in the first instance, critically assess what boundary spanning activities require physical mobility across borders versus potential to engage virtually. To maintain motivation and retain global workers, talent management practices must be cognisant of the demands that are involved when roles have significant global dimensions and direct appropriate resources to these workers.

CONCLUSION

In this chapter, we have argued that the role of global workers, due to the boundary spanning role undertaken, represents individuals which can have disproportionate impact on the value added to the organization. Moreover, we have argued that the inherent value of global workers in boundary spanning roles often appears under-utilized and under-appreciated within MNEs. For example, global workers may be central to the identification of new location investment decisions, collecting valuable contextualized information, developing social capital, accumulating and sharing knowledge, and so forth (Jooss et al., 2021b). This may in part be due to the overwhelming focus of global talent management on senior organizational leaders and/or traditional expatriates with others less-considered (Collings et al., 2019).

On an individual level, the chapter also highlights that much concern exists around the failure to identify and adequately address the significant demands of these workers (Jooss et al., 2021a) and how this can limit the value creation of these individuals despite potentially being in such pivotal positions (Morris, Snell, & Bjorkman, 2016). Connecting the *people and practices approach* to talent management with the *pivotal positions approach* to talent management, organizations need to ensure that global workers in pivotal positions are not only identified as individuals in such roles, but also provide the necessary framework to operate successfully. This requires reflection at various stages of the talent management process including recruiting, selecting, developing, engaging, and retaining these individuals as well as wider consideration of sustainable global work models. Beyond traditional expatriation, there appears to be too little consideration of global workers and the unique pressures and challenges they face in being able to realize the true value that those in such positions can confer on the organization. Such approaches appear to be inconsistent with the commonly cited arguments about one of the greatest challenges that MNEs are dealing with being sufficiently strong global talent pipelines (Al Ariss et al., 2014; Cascio & Boudreau, 2016).

Moreover, the effective management of the individual global worker also needs to be extended to a wider organizational knowledge management level if value is to be realized. This is because the 'strategic value of knowledge embedded in individual know-how, actions and collective experiences and expertise suggests that effectively managing the top performing knowledge workers is necessary for enhancing organizational performance and competitiveness' (Whelan & Carcary, 2011: 683). Global workers depending on their role remit have the ability to source internal (i.e. wider MNC) and external knowledge. Talent management can play a key mediating role in knowledge sourcing and the translation into better organizational performance (Chadee & Raman, 2012). However, cases where knowledge management and talent management are considered in a holistic way by organizations appear more likely to be rare than common. However, this has been given little attention by researchers (notable exception being Chadee & Raman, 2012).

Given the issues that have been highlighted in this chapter, it is unsurprising that there is a lack of evidence behind firms managing their talent on a global scale effectively, as well as realizing the potential value from such key employees. Even where job descriptions recognize the key role of global working in positions, MNEs appear to fail to effectively recognize the importance of this dimension, how it can create value for the organization, and how it presents considerable challenges to these employees (Jooss et al., 2021a). While differentiation lies at the heart of talent management (McDonnell & Wiblen, 2021), it appears that there are insufficient HR architectures in place to support and manage global workers which appropriately recognize the additional challenges and idiosyncrasies that exist in this context. Whether this is best addressed through a global talent management function or global mobility function, or where responsibility is incorporated within the corporate HR function, is open to question. More importantly, there is a need for explicit recognition and management of global workers and all the constituent elements of such roles to enable the maximum contribution to be realized. Taking it further, there is a need to consider the architecture required to foster the possible value from knowledge that such global workers can source and transfer.

REFERENCES

Al Ariss, A., Cascio, W.F. & Paauwe, J. (2014). Talent management: Current theories and future research directions. *Journal of World Business*, **49**(2), 173–179.

Aldrich, H. & Herker, D. (1977). Boundary spanning roles and organization structure. *Academy of Management Review*, **2**(2), 217–230.

Ancona, D.G. & Caldwell, D.F. (1992). Bridging the boundary: External activity and performance in organizational teams. *Administrative Science Quarterly*, **37**(4), 634–665.

Au, K.Y. & Fukuda, J. (2002). Boundary spanning behaviors of expatriates. *Journal of World Business*, **37**(4), 285–296.

Barmeyer, C., Stein, V. & Eberhardt, J.M. (2020). Third-country nationals as intercultural boundary spanners in multinational corporations. *Multinational Business Review*, **28**(4), 521–547.

Birkinshaw, J., Ambos, T.C. & Bouquet, C. (2017). Boundary spanning activities of corporate HQ executives insights from a longitudinal study. *Journal of Management Studies*, **54**(4), 422–454.

Boudreau, J.W. & Ramstad, P.M. (2007). *Beyond HR: The New Science of Human Capital*. Boston, MA: Harvard Business School Press.

Bozkurt, Ö. & Mohr, A.T. (2011). Forms of cross-border mobility and social capital in multinational enterprises. *Human Resource Management Journal*, **21**(2), 138–155.

Carlile, P.R. (2002). A pragmatic view of knowledge and boundaries: Boundary objects in new product development. *Organization Science*, **13**(4), 442–455.

Carnevale, J.B. & Hatak, I. (2020). Employee adjustment and well-being in the era of COVID-19: Implications for human resource management. *Journal of Business Research*, **116**, 183–187.

Cascio, W.F. & Boudreau, J.W. (2012). *A Short Introduction to Strategic Human Resource Management*. Cambridge: Cambridge University Press.

Cascio, W.F. & Boudreau, J.W. (2016). The search for global competence: From international HR to talent management. *Journal of World Business*, **51**(1), 103–114.

Chadee, D. & Raman, R. (2012). External knowledge and performance of offshore IT service providers in India: The mediating role of talent management. *Asia Pacific Journal of Human Resources*, **50**, 459–482.

Collings, D.G., McDonnell, A., Gunnigle, A. & Lavelle, J. (2010). Swimming against the tide: Outward staffing flows from multinational subsidiaries. *Human Resource Management*, **49**(4), 575–598.

Collings, D.G. & Mellahi, K. (2009). Strategic talent management: A review and research agenda. *Human Resource Management Review*, **19**(4), 304–313.

Collings, D.G., Mellahi, K. & Cascio, W.F. (2019). Global talent management and performance in multinational enterprises: A multilevel perspective. *Journal of Management*, **45**(2), 540–566.

Collings, D.G., Scullion, H. & Morley, M.J. (2007). Changing patterns of global staffing in the multinational enterprise: Challenges to the conventional expatriate assignment and emerging alternatives. *Journal of World Business*, **42**(2), 198–213.

Conroy, K.M., McDonnell, A. & Jooss, S. (2020). Navigating complex frontiers: International business travellers as global boundary spanners in MNEs. *Academy of Management Proceedings*, **2020**(1), 12455.

Demerouti, E., Bakker, A.B., Nachreiner, F. & Schaufeli, W.B. (2001). The job demands-resources model of burnout. *Journal of Applied Psychology*, **86**(3), 499–512.

Dimitrova, M. (2020). Of discovery and dread: The importance of work challenges for international business travelers' thriving and global role turnover intentions. *Journal of Organizational Behavior*, **41**(4), 369–383.

Dries, N. (2013). The psychology of talent management: A review and research agenda. *Human Resource Management Review*, **23**(4), 272–285.

Duvivier, F., Peeters, C. & Harzing, A.-W. (2019). Not all international assignments are created equal: HQ-subsidiary knowledge transfer patterns across types of assignments and types of knowledge. *Journal of World Business*, **54**(3), 181–190.

Edwards, T., Sánchez-Mangas, R., Lavelle, J., Minbaeva, D. & Jalette, P. (2016). Global standardization or national differentiation of HRM practices in multinational companies? A comparison of multinationals in five countries. *Journal of International Business Studies*, **47**(8), 997–1021.

Faulconbridge, J., Jones, I., Anable, J. & Marsden, G. (2020). Work, ICT and travel in multinational corporations: The synthetic work mobility situation. *New Technology, Work and Employment*, **35**(2), 195–214.

Furusawa, M. & Brewster, C. (2019). The determinants of the boundary-spanning functions of Japanese self-initiated expatriates in Japanese subsidiaries in China: Individual skills and human resource management. *Journal of International Management*, **25**(4), 100674.

Hafermalz, E. & Riemer, K. (2020). Interpersonal connectivity work: Being there with and for geographically distant others. *Organization Studies*, **41**(12), 1627–1648.

Harvey, M.G. & Buckley, M.R. (1997). Managing inpatriates: Building a global core competency. *Journal of World Business*, **32**(1), 35–52.

Harvey, M., Novicevic, M.M., Buckley, M.R. & Fung, H. (2005). Reducing inpatriate managers' 'liability of foreignness' by addressing stigmatization and stereotype threats. *Journal of World Business*, **40**(3), 267–280.

Harvey, M.G., Novicevic, M.M. & Speier, C. (2000). An innovative global management staffing system: A competency-based perspective. *Human Resource Management*, **39**(4), 381–394.

Harzing, A.-W. (2001). Of bears, bumble-bees, and spiders: The role of expatriates in controlling foreign subsidiaries. *Journal of World Business*, **36**(4), 366–379.

Harzing, A.-W., Pudelko, M. & Reiche, B.S. (2016). The bridging role of expatriates and inpatriates in knowledge transfer in multinational corporations. *Human Resource Management*, **55**(4), 679–695.

Hinds, P., Liu, L. & Lyon, J. (2011). Putting the global in global work: An intercultural lens on the practice of cross-national collaboration. *Academy of Management Annals*, **5**(1), 135–188.

Hovhannisyan, N. & Keller, W. (2015). International business travel: an engine of innovation? *Journal of Economic Growth*, **20**(1), 75–104.

Huselid, M.A., Beatty, R.W. & Becker, B.E. (2005). 'A players' or 'A positions'? The strategic logic of workforce management. *Harvard Business Review*, **83**(12), 110–117.

Huselid, M.A. & Becker, B.E. (2011). Bridging micro and macro domains: Workforce differentiation and strategic human resource management. *Journal of Management*, **37**(2), 421–428.

Jimenez, A., Boehe, D.M., Taras, V. & Caprar, D.V. (2017). Working across boundaries: Current and future perspectives on global virtual teams. *Journal of International Management*, **23**(4), 341–349.

Johnson, K.L. & Duxbury, L. (2010). The view from the field: A case study of the expatriate boundary-spanning role. *Journal of World Business*, **34**(1), 29–40.

Jooss, S., Conroy, K.M. & McDonnell, A. (2021a). Discretion as a double-edged sword in global work: The perils of international business travel. *Human Resource Management Journal*. In press.

Jooss, S., McDonnell, A. & Conroy, K. (2021b). Flexible global working arrangements: An integrative review and future research agenda. *Human Resource Management Review*, **31**(4), 100780.

Kiessling, T. & Harvey, M. (2006). The human resource management issues during an acquisition: The target firm's top management team and key managers. *International Journal of Human Resource Management*, **17**(7), 1307–1320.

Kraimer, M.L., Bolino, M.C. & Mead, B. (2016). Themes in expatriate and repatriate research over four decades: What do we know and what do we still need to learn? *Annual Review of Organizational Psychology and Organizational Behavior*, **3**, 83–109.

Lee, J.M., Narula, R. & Hillemann, J. (2021). Unraveling asset recombination through the lens of firm-specific advantages: A dynamic capabilities perspective. *Journal of World Business*, **56**(2), 101193.

Liu, Y. & Meyer, K.E. (2020). Boundary spanners, HRM practices, and reverse knowledge transfer: The case of Chinese cross-border acquisitions. *Journal of World Business*, **55**(2), 100958.

Lublin, J. (1996). An overseas stint can be a ticket to the top. *Wall Street Journal*, 29 January.

Mäkelä, K., Barner-Rasmussen, W., Ehrnrooth, M. & Koveshnikov, A. (2019). Potential and recognized boundary spanners in multinational corporations. *Journal of World Business*, **54**(4), 335–349.

Marrone, J.A. (2010). Team boundary spanning: A multilevel review of past research and proposals for the future. *Journal of Management*, **36**(4), 911–940.

Mayerhofer, H., Hartmann, L.C., Michelitsch-Riedl, G. & Kollinger, I. (2004). Flexpatriate assignments: A neglected issue in global staffing. *The International Journal of Human Resource Management*, **15**(8), 1371–1389.

McDonnell, A. & Wiblen, S. (2021). *Talent Management: A Research Overview*. London & New York: Routledge.

Minbaeva, D. & Santangelo, G.D. (2018). Boundary spanners and intra-MNC knowledge sharing: The roles of controlled motivation and immediate organizational context. *Global Strategy Journal*, **8**(2), 220–241.

Morris, S., Snell, S. & Bjorkman, I. (2016). An architectural framework for global talent management. *Journal of International Business Studies*, **47**(6), 723–747.

Nurmi, N. & Hinds, P.J. (2020). Work design for global professionals: Connectivity demands, connectivity behaviors, and their effects on psychological and behavioral outcomes. *Organization Studies*, **41**(12), 1697–1724.

Pate, J. & Scullion, H. (2018). The flexpatriate psychological contract: A literature review and future research agenda. *The International Journal of Human Resource Management*, **29**(8), 1402–1425.

Pfeffer, J. (2001). Fighting the war for talent is hazardous to your organization's health. *Organizational Dynamics*, **29**(4), 248–259.

PwC (2020). *COVID-19: The Impact for Global Mobility and the Mobile Workforce.* PwC Global Mobility Pulse Survey Results. London: PwC. https://www.pwc.com/gx/en/legal/assets/covid-19-pulse-survey-results.pdf.

Reiche, B.S. (2011). Knowledge transfer in multinationals: The role of inpatriates' boundary spanning. *Human Resource Management*, **50**(3), 365–389.

Reiche, B.S., Kraimer, M.L. & Harzing, A.W. (2011). Why do international assignees stay? An organizational embeddedness perspective. *Journal of International Business Studies*, **42**(4), 521–544.

Reiche, B.S., Lee, Y. & Allen, D.G. (2019). Actors, structure, and processes: A review and conceptualization of global work integrating IB and HRM research. *Journal of Management*, **45**(2), 359–383.

Sarabi, A., Froese, F.J. & Hamori, M., (2017). Is inpatriate assignment experience a ticket to the top of a foreign subsidiary? The moderating effect of subsidiary context. *Journal of World Business*, **52**(5), 680–690.

Schotter, A.P., Mudambi, R., Doz, Y.L. & Gaur, A., (2017). Boundary spanning in global organizations. *Journal of Management Studies*, **54**(4), 403–421.

Shaffer, M.A., Kraimer, M.L., Chen, Y.P. & Bolino, M.C. (2012). Choices, challenges, and career consequences of global work experiences: A review and future agenda. *Journal of Management*, **38**(4), 1282–1327.

Shortland, S. (2018). What seals the deal? How compensation and benefits affect women's decisions to accept expatriation in the oil and gas industry. *Personnel Review*, **47**(3), 765–783.

Sparrow, P. & Makram, H. (2015). What is the value of talent management? Building value-driven processes within a talent management architecture. *Human Resource Management Review*, **25**(3), 249–263.

Suutari, V., Brewster, C.J., Riusala, K. & Syrjäkari, S. (2013). Managing non-standard international experience: Evidence from a Finnish company. *Journal of Global Mobility*, **1**(2), 118–138.

Welch, D.E. & Worm, V. (2006). International business travellers: A challenge for IHRM. In Stahl, G.K. & Björkman, I. (eds.), *Handbook of Research in International Human Resource Management*. Cheltenham, UK and Northampton, MA, USA: Edward Elgar Publishing, pp. 283–301.

Whelan, E. & Carcary, M. (2011). Integrating talent and knowledge management: Where are the benefits? *Journal of Knowledge Management*, **15**(4), 675–687.

Wilson, J.M., Boyer O'Leary, M., Metiu, A. & Jett, Q.R. (2008). Perceived proximity in virtual work: Explaining the paradox of far-but-close. *Organization Studies*, **29**(7), 979–1002.

10. Upward global knowledge management: a review and preliminary field validation of the host country national local liaison role model

Charles M. Vance, Marian van Bakel, Torben Andersen and Vlad Vaiman

INTRODUCTION

The prevailing international management literature continues to have a predominant top-down focus on the influence of company and regional headquarter strategic planning, as well as the work of assigned expatriates in achieving foreign operation success (e.g., see An, Choe, & Kang, 2021; Stendahl, Schriber, & Tippmann, 2021; Reuber, Tippmann, & Monaghan, 2021; Zhong, Zhu, & Zhang, 2021). This general trend also is true in the literature more specifically related to international knowledge management (e.g., see Stoermer, Davies, & Froese, 2021; Arias-Pérez, Velez-Ocampo, & Cepeda-Cardona, 2021; Nair, Kishore, & Demirbag, 2021; Dahou, Hacini, & Burgoyne, 2019). This predominant top-down focus in the international management literature falls at the relative neglect of needed attention toward the influence and potential input from local lower-level employees, including host country nationals (HCNs) and foreign employees managed at local host country subsidiary operations (van Bakel, 2019; Toh & DeNisi, 2003, 2005). Although the recent COVID-19 pandemic has forced attention toward increased local leadership staffing of foreign operations and supervised remotely by virtual expatriate management arrangements (Haak-Saheem, 2020; Caligiuri et al., 2020; Collings & Sheeran, 2020), emphasis traditionally has been placed on effective staffing and training approaches for company-assigned expatriate managers as MNC liaison agents of control, neglecting attention toward the development needs, performance expectations, and staffing opportunities involving the lower levels of the global workforce, who also contribute to international operation success (Ando, 2021; Vance, 2006, 2011; Suutari, 2002; Kamoche, 1997).

With particular regard to knowledge management (KM), there is growing recognition that companies that consider and involve all employees as worthy talent in KM practices, rather than only a few select players (i.e., headquarters senior executives and MNC-assigned expatriates leading host country operations) possess a potential advantage over competing firms (Cucino et al., 2021; Bello-Pintado & Bianchi, 2021; Chen, Lam, & Zhu, 2021; Hannola et al., 2018; Takeuchi & Nonaka, 2004; van Bakel et al., 2022). HCN managers and other local administrative staff and support staff who work with an expatriate typically are engaged in the sharing of information and knowledge with both the expatriate and other lower-level local employees. With their two-way flow of knowledge and information, these HCNs also play a key liaison role for the benefit of company operations. In fact, this bottom-up flow of information facilitated by the HCN liaison role, transmitted through the expatriate, may provide vital information for decision-making in other MNC subsidiary operations as well as at regional and central MNC headquarters.

Work by Vance and colleagues (Vance, Vaiman, & Andersen, 2009; Vance et al., 2014) has examined this potentially critical HCN liaison role between assigned expatriates and the local surrounding work environment, including other local employees. In this chapter, we will briefly review the key components of this proposed HCN liaison (HCNL) role, and then review preliminary field research to begin to validate this model. Finally, we will propose needed areas for further research in understanding and employing appropriate HR practices involving HCNLs for improved KM and organizational performance.

HCNL ROLE MODEL DESCRIPTION

The HCNL role is enacted within a position held by a HCN, or perhaps another local employee (i.e., a localized third country national), within a firm's local workforce. This local employee provides a communications and information flow link between one or more local employee groups and one or more expatriates, thus serving as a liaison agent, or sometimes even a co-producer of highly relevant and important knowledge, promoting two-way information flow and potential influence (Schwartz & Jacobson, 1977). This role can be formally assigned, such as with an expatriate's local administrative assistant, who regularly interacts with both lower-level employees and an expatriate, serving as the official gateway for two-way information flow. Or this role can be an informal one, such as in the case of an experienced and widely trusted HCN who provides the expatriate with useful advice and enlightenment regarding the local workforce, as well as explains and clarifies expatriate messages and behavior for local employees to facilitate their understanding and commitment. Of course, an assigned expatriate also can be a peer or even subordinate to the HCNL, as when expatriates have a narrow, technology transfer focus in their work, or are assigned primarily for their global competence development (McPhail, et al, 2012; Vance et al., 2009).

Vance et al. (2014) identified and described five major components of the HCNL role: cultural interpreter, communication manager, information resource broker, talent manager, and internal change agent. These components, with their associated specific behavioral manifestations or functions, can potentially facilitate and support effective knowledge management leading to desired performance of both the local workforce and the expatriate. Although isolated for focus and clarification, these HCNL role components and their associated behavioral functions are not mutually exclusive; they are inter-related and can influence each other. In addition, it is possible that multiple HCNs in concert can contribute to the different components that make up the overall HCNL role. We now will examine each component and associated behavioral function of the model, as depicted in Table 10.1.

Table 10.1 Five HCN liaison role components and associated behavioral functions

HCN liaison role components	Corresponding behavioral functions
Cultural Interpreter	• Equivocal Communication Clarifier • Cultural Guide • Conflict Mediator
Communication Manager	• Language Translator • Communication Moderator • Communication Facilitator • Communication Mediator
Information Resource Broker	• Information Boundary Spanner • Organizational Memory Source • Informal Organization Knowledge Source
Talent Manager	• Talent Identifier • Trainer/Coach • Mentor
Internal Change Agent	• Change Co-Planner • Change Executor • Workforce Alignment Facilitator

Cultural Interpreter

Intercultural differences present a serious challenge to MNCs in all areas of KM (Goswami, Agrawal, & Goswami, 2021; Anantatmula, 2010). Despite common language fluency, deep culturally based perspectives can differ significantly and lead to misunderstanding and conflict (Holden & Glisby, 2010). To help address these challenges, the HCNL who is well familiar with the cultures of the local workforce and the expatriate can serve as a *cultural interpreter*. In this role component, the HCNL can perform at least three different behavioral functions: equivocal or ambiguous communication clarifier, cultural guide, and conflict mediator.

Equivocal communication clarifier

In this first function as cultural interpreter, the HCNL serves to clarify for either HCN employees (both peer and lower-level) or expatriates any ambiguous or uncertain communications (both verbal and non-verbal) occurring within the host operation or surrounding environment. Due to an expatriate's lack of exposure to and work experience in the host country, he or she may benefit from explanations provided by the HCNL's interpretation of otherwise puzzling or potentially misunderstood meaning of local messages and communications associated with work operations.

Cultural guide

In their role component as cultural interpreters, HCNLs may also serve proactively as cultural guides to facilitate and direct expatriates' effective adjustment to the new host country work environment by helping them understand the cultural basis driving local activities and events, and to avoid and maneuver through potential local cultural landmines. In addition, they may help guide other local employees in their effective understanding of both MNC company culture and the culture of the parent country where the headquarters is based, providing an improved understanding of both expatriate behavior and information emanating from parent country headquarters.

Conflict mediator

Both assigned expatriates and local employees try to make sense of what is happening around them as they view through often quite different cultural lenses. Based on these divergent cultural perspectives, cross-cultural interactions may easily lead to confusion, resentment, and conflict. Culturally based expectations about work performance (e.g., speed, quality, form of communication) may also differ between expatriates and HCNs. Resulting confusion, frustration, resentment, and conflict often result in severely curtailed information sharing and knowledge transfer due to decreased trust and goodwill in supporting effective collaboration. With their understanding of both local employee and expatriate cultural perspectives, HCNLs may serve as a mediator between both parties to uncover and elucidate culturally based sources of misunderstanding, and constructively resolve inevitable conflict to build a work environment of mutual trust.

Communication Manager

The complexity and heterogeneity inherent in many foreign subsidiary environments, often involving multiple different languages and cultural backgrounds, can pose a significant challenge to an MNC's effective global KM (Festa et al., 2021). Early in the process of developing market entry, MNCs often place the task of communications management within the purview of a local human resources or communication professional (Robertson, 2005). This HR or communication professional assigned as an HCNL communication manager addresses individual and organizational communications issues and needs within the local workforce (including local employees and expatriates), and the local external marketplace (e.g., local regulatory and recruitment agencies). In contributing to effective knowledge transfer within the host country operation and surrounding local external environment, this HCNL serves as a communication manager. This liaison role component includes such behavioral functions as language translator, communication moderator, communication facilitator, and communication mediator.

Language translator
The effective transfer of knowledge and implementation of new practices into the foreign subsidiary, where local employees clearly understand and embrace the new practices, is greatly influenced by the degree to which these new practices are translated into the local language and systems of meaning (Becker-Ritterspach, Saka-Helmhout, & Hotho, 2010). In addition, the reverse flow of accurate information of competitive value from members of the local workforce and the general local environment is essential for effective expatriate decision-making and transfer of accurate, useful knowledge back to headquarters and to other MNC subsidiaries. Thus, especially where assigned expatriates do not have fluency in the prevailing language(s) of the host country operation, including local dialects and figures of speech, the HCNL who is fluent in the expatriate and prevailing MNC language can serve a valuable function as language translator to facilitate the two-way flow of accurate information.

Communication moderator
In addition to direct translation of communications, the HCNL also may assist by correcting or moderating two-way communications as they are relayed between members of the host country workforce and expatriates to ensure effective information reception. For example, in translating an expatriate's

communication to local employees, an astute HCNL might hear a phrase or word choice that, if translated literally and directly, could create unnecessary stress or resentment among local employees. The HCNL may wisely slightly alter and translate the message in a way that communicates the expatriate's intended message, but in a much more acceptable fashion for the local employees. Similar to altering the *content* of a message to make it more palatable for the workforce recipient, the HCNL may decide to change the *timing* of the delivery of the message, such as delay the knowledge transfer to the expatriate or to the local workforce until they are best able to understand and accept the information. Whatever the moderating influence on communications and knowledge transfer, there should be an overall positive impact on workforce performance improvement and productivity.

Communication facilitator

An HCNL may not have a direct responsibility over communications, yet still often is in an important position to promote and facilitate free-flowing, multi-directional knowledge sharing and communications within the foreign operation, as well as across organizational boundaries within the local host country environment. Key to this knowledge sharing facilitation success is the development of a general climate of trust, and an expectation that honest and open communication with the expatriate will be valued. The HCNL also can provide encouragement and coaching to other HCNs for effectively sharing knowledge directly with the expatriate and communicating issues and concerns. The HCNL also can provide suggestions to the expatriate on how to optimize his or her accessibility (both physical and psychological) to other HCN employees to facilitate their direct communications.

Communication mediator

The HCNL may also serve in a useful mediator or relay function to support the effective knowledge transfer in multiple directions. Especially when a common language is not shared between the expatriate and the local workforce, the HCNL who shares fluency in the expatriate's language can valuably receive, process, and pass on intended knowledge and information between the expatriate and the local workforce. When local employees, for whatever reason, are hesitant to communicate directly with the expatriate (e.g., the need to share bad performance news or negative feedback to the expatriate), the HCNL who is trusted among the local workforce may solicit and obtain the information from HCNs and pass it along anonymously to the expatriate.

Information Resource Broker

Research involving the convergence of KM and network theory examines the vital role of organizational leaders and professionals as knowledge and information resource brokers (Larsson, Segerstéen, & Svensson, 2011; Lu & Reve, 2011). The HCNL is in a position to serve as an important broker or resource for providing many forms of information and knowledge for both expatriate and other workforce members. We now will examine in particular the HCNL's contribution as an information resource broker for the expatriate through the behavioral functions of information boundary spanner, organizational memory source, and informal organization knowledge source.

Information boundary spanner

As competitive forces increase in local markets there is a concomitant growing need to have access to accurate knowledge to be responsive to local market interests (Ziyi & Nguyen Quyen, 2020). The HCNL who is very familiar with valid sources of information, crossing formal and informal individual and organizational boundaries, about the local business environment (including local resources, customs, government regulations and avoidable bureaucratic obstacles) can be invaluable to the expatriate and company headquarters in obtaining vital market information for the basis of making sound business decisions. This information and knowledge boundary spanning contribution is particularly important in countries where there are highly complex and structured routes for obtaining market knowledge, and in emerging economies where institutional arrangements are often diffuse and informal.

Organizational memory source

Some firms express a clear ethnocentric control strategy, where they assign home country expatriates for 3–5 years to provide leadership in foreign operations. However, the HCN professionals reporting to these periodically changing expatriates typically remain with the foreign operation in a similar mid-level or technical position for a much longer duration. Due to the continuing challenge of repatriate retention, valuable knowledge obtained through an expatriate assignment experience, both tacit and explicit, may be lost to competing organizations (Froese et al., 2021; Davoine, Barmeyer, & Rossi, 2018). Although it is hoped that returning expatriates will pass on as much helpful information as possible to those replacing them as well as to strategic planners at headquarters, much valuable experience-based local market knowledge may not be transferred, especially tacit knowledge that is exchanged more informally through regular personal interactions. The HCNL remaining within the MNC therefore represents an important source of organizational memory and workplace know-how continuity. Their explicit and tacit knowledge obtained through past experience and learning within the local subsidiary can subsequently help illuminate current challenges and activities for new expatriates and can provide valuable input to headquarters for the valid and customized training and preparation of future expatriates to be assigned there (Vance & Ensher, 2002).

Informal organization knowledge source

Considerable experience-generated knowledge related to local performance success, including what to avoid and how to efficiently get work accomplished in an organization, often remains informal and never formally encoded into company policy and procedure documents (Hoe & McShane, 2010). Related to the previous behavioral function of organizational memory source, the HCNL can be a valuable fount of this informal organization knowledge, providing it to the new expatriate as needed. A new expatriate would be prudent in seeking information early about local internal individual and group relationship dynamics, informal rules, and important characteristics of the local organizational culture to avoid unnecessary work performance disruption and conflict. The HCNL can be an important source of such informal information to help promote the new expatriate's on-site learning. And associated with the communication mediator function, the HCNL also can be a valuable source for sharing local employee 'grapevine' information and informal feedback that can be useful to the expatriate in assessing the internal organizational climate, and in adjusting and formulating new plans.

Talent Manager

The increasing emphasis upon talent management—the attraction, development, deployment, and retention of human talent—within our global knowledge economy (e.g., Abeuova & Muratbekova-Touron, 2019; Davoine et al., 2018; Morris, Snell, & Björkman, 2016) also applies to activities of HCN liaisons in their upstream and downstream work interactions. These talent management activities can involve upstream work interactions with expatriates, professionals at company headquarters, and professionals in other country operations of the firm; and downstream work interactions with local employees and individuals within the surrounding host country business environment (Vance, 2006). This talent manager component of the HCNL role includes talent identifier, trainer/coach, and mentor behavioral functions.

Talent identifier

Competitive advantage goes to MNCs that are effective in identifying potential leadership talent located in the home country and company headquarters as well as in foreign subsidiaries (Tyskbo, 2021). With their familiarity with the local business environment and labor market, HCN liaisons can be invaluable in identifying and recruiting local talent (from both within and outside the firm) for meeting the immediate workforce requirements of the local host country operation. And with their solid understanding of the MNC's strategic plans and performance needs in the local host country, region, and overall global operations, the HCN liaison is also in a very favorable position to identify from direct subordinates, or from discussions with other local managers, potential HCN talent for promotion and assignment to MNC headquarters, such as for inpatriate assignment aimed at further development (Moeller, Harvey, & Williams, 2010), or to serve in an expatriate capacity in another foreign operation of the firm.

Trainer/coach
The HCNL also can serve as an on-site coach in developing the skills and abilities of both expatriates and HCNs, through personal interactions providing advice and immediate direction and feedback to facilitate effective performance. Besides the previously described cultural guidance for enhancing cross-cultural understanding, the HCNL also can provide formal company/local operation orientation and specific job training, as well as less formal on-the-job coaching to facilitate knowledge transfer and effective skill development among expatriates and local workforce members (Wang & Chan, 2006; Vance & Paik, 2005). Through regular direct interaction with expatriates and lower-level HCNs alike, the HCNL's on-the-job coaching can be especially valuable for the transfer of tacit knowledge, which is difficult to codify and impart by means of more formal information sharing and training (Holden & Glisby, 2010). This developmental focus of the HCNL as trainer/ coach can include purposeful socialization and orientation efforts for new HCN employees to ensure that they understand and embrace the key common priorities and values of the MNC and host country operation (Toh & DeNisi, 2007). Although training for new expatriates will likely be much less formal than for the newly hired HCN employees, the expatriates' need for immediate acquisition of new understanding and insights can nevertheless be significant. Besides the sharing of job-related and technical knowledge, the continuing coaching support inherent in the close HCNL–expatriate relationship can help facilitate the expatriate's positive interaction adjustment (van Bakel, Gerritsen, & Van Oudenhoven, 2011).

Mentor
In addition to knowledge sharing and skill development related to the trainer/ coach function focusing on immediate performance, the HCNL may serve as a mentor with an ongoing working relationship of credibility and trust to assist both individual employees and expatriates in promoting their professional

growth and future career development opportunities (van Bakel et al., 2022). In this mentoring capacity, the HCNL can provide helpful advice and a strong role model to less-experienced peer and lower-level HCNs who are interested in future career advancement within the local workplace and beyond within other MNC operations. In a form of reverse mentoring (Harvey et al., 2009), HCNLs can provide expatriates with useful on-site guidance that has immediate and longer-term career development value (Carraher, Sullivan, & Crocitto, 2008). This HCNL on-site ongoing mentoring support, having both immediate and potential longer-term career development impact, may extend beyond initial adjustment to facilitate throughout the expatriate assignment, which in turn may also have future positive repatriation and other future career opportunities for the expatriate (Selmer, 2000). In addition, there is strong evidence that the future career enhancement aspect of mentoring provided by HCNLs can reduce local employee turnover, particularly critical in hot labor markets (Grant, 2008; Reiche, 2007).

Internal Change Agent

The effective management of change increasingly presented by the growing forces of globalization is imperative for organizations in both developed and emerging economies (Arazmjoo & Rahmanseresht, 2020; Hong et al., 2019). In addition, national cultures can differ in their readiness to accept and adapt to innovation and change (Carsten & Schomaker, 2019), and workforce acceptance of change in policies and procedures is critical for implementing new MNC strategies. The HCNL can serve as a helpful internal change agent partner with the expatriate to effectively manage the process of change within the local operation with workforce commitment. Three important behavioral functions within this final HCN liaison role component include change co-planner, change executor, and workforce alignment facilitator.

Change co-planner

A firm's initially completely outsourced business operations abroad may move to a joint venture or other form of partnership arrangement, and eventually to a completely owned subsidiary. Effective change in local operations and activities is essential to support such development, and ideally should be part of an ongoing strategic planning process. However, a common complaint is that those at company headquarters who are making strategic decisions involving the change of foreign operations status and work arrangements are unfamiliar with the reality of the overall host country business environment and its unique operational challenges. However, local experienced HCNs in their liaison role can serve as helpful co-planners to provide relevant and valid input to enhance strategic decision making, and to help formulate local details of for effective change implementation. Based on their close knowledge of the local business environment, HCNL knowledge sharing can be extremely valuable in recognizing opportunities for growth and emerging threats, recommending changes for addressing these opportunities and threats, and providing detailed input on the timing, pace, and direction of change efforts.

Change executor
Key to successful strategic management following planning is the effective execution and implementation of change. An expatriate, often based on headquarter directives, may have a clear and even reasonable picture of an important new direction and related specific performance goals for a foreign operation, but often will be ill-equipped to alone formulate specific implementation plans for bringing about desired changes. A wise expatriate will communicate strategic plans and performance goals, and then permit a competent and experienced HCNL to work out local details, ideally with other HCN involvement, to execute or implement the change in a way that best fits local conditions of the host country workforce and external business environment.

Thus, the HCN professional may serve in a vital liaison role in implementing strategy and guiding effective change. However, various studies related to power distance and HCN autonomy in problem solving and decision-making (e.g., Khan & Maalik, 2011; Vasugi, Kaviatha, & Prema, 2011), note challenges in getting managers and professional employees in many emerging economies to take direct responsibility for key business decisions and implementation details, preferring these leadership functions to be handled by the official expatriate leader. From the authors' experience, even higher-level HCNs often seem to prefer precise and detailed instructions and job descriptions with little uncertainty and ambiguity, requiring personal initiative and discretion. Therefore, HCN management training and workplace coaching in change management and implementation skills are critical here to help HCNLs overcome potential culturally-based impediments to their assertion of power to facilitate change and effect strategy implementation, which traditionally were leadership responsibilities reserved for assigned expatriates.

Workforce alignment facilitator
A critical change agent function that the HCNL can perform is helping overcome potential and predictable HCN workforce resistance to a proposed change (Balogun, Jarzabkowski, & Vaara, 2011; Hawes & Chew, 2011). The HCNL may help build trust and commitment (constituting critical emotional alignment) and decrease workforce resistance by effectively communicating to local employees about the purpose and nature of the intended change, and how all will be affected. Since frequent, honest communications are critical for building employee trust and overcoming resistance to proposed change

efforts (Sabeen et al., 2021), the HCNL can be a rich source and communicator of pertinent information, often with greater local credibility than the assigned expatriate, to regularly keep employees informed before and during the change process. This increased understanding and trust regarding the change effort can help the local employees also contribute as knowledgeable and committed participants, lending their detailed knowledge and experience-based ideas and suggestions in the often-complex process of change implementation.

Another aspect of the internal alignment facilitator function is linked with the previous discussion of training, where the HCNL promotes within the local workforce an understanding of and commitment to common organizational cultural values and priorities held by the local subsidiary unit and the MNC as a whole (Cicekli, 2011). This development of increased common identity and mindset through shared company values and priorities alignment increases the ability to receive and share information that is vital to the successful change and development within the MNC, both locally and beyond (Persson, 2006; Vance & Paik, 2005). In addition, this cultural values and mindset alignment may help reduce and minimize resistance and increase local employee readiness for future change in a more consistent and organized manner (House et al., 2002; Krumbholz & Maiden, 2001).

INITIAL FIELD VALIDATION OF THE HCNL MODEL

In concept, the HCNL model points to significant potential benefits for improving overall knowledge sharing and transfer within the host country operation and throughout the MNC. Effective HCNL role development also may increase MNC performance capability by building MNC leadership talent, and common identity and mindset within the workforce at foreign operations. The HCNL may also be particularly helpful in promoting expatriate on-site learning and adjustment (McPhail et al., 2012; Johnson et al., 2003). However, as called for by Vance et al. (2014), this proposed model of the HCNL role should be examined in the field to validate the role components and to gain a clearer picture of its operational characteristics. To contribute to this field validation effort, we will examine recent qualitative research from a master's thesis facilitated and supervised by the second author of this chapter (Lührs, 2021).

The target group for this field study consisted of traditionally company-assigned expatriates (AEs) and self-initiated expatriates (SIEs) with Austrian, German, and Swiss citizenship, most of whom had been working in the US from about one to five years. These SIEs and AEs, mostly male and 30–50 years of age, were working in various industries in the US at American companies, and at foreign operations of MNCs from their home countries and from third countries. The HCNs serving in liaison roles with these expatriates were at different organizational levels, including their superiors, subordinates, and peers. Semi-structured recorded interviews were conducted in person and online with 20 expatriates contacted through convenience sampling. These interviews explored if and how these expatriates experienced the above five HCNL role components in their work in the MNCs in the US. The recorded interviews were afterward transcribed and coded using the thematic analysis approach by Braun and Clarke (2006). The results confirmed that the Germanic expatriates experienced all five of the role components of the HCNL model. Additional insights were gained associated with this particular field research involving the relatively close cultural distance or similarity of the expatriates and the HCNLs (Ronen and Shenkar, 2013). We now will examine a brief sampling of expatriate comments confirming and illustrating their actual experience with the previously discussed behavioral functions within each of the five HCNL role components (refer to Table 10.1).

HCNL Role Field Validation: Cultural Interpreter

Equivocal communication clarifier

In the field interviews, most of the expatriates emphasize the importance of decreasing, through HCNL assistance, their uncertainty by learning and clarifying anti-discrimination laws and regulations, including associated with sexual harassment, and particularly within the context of job candidate treatment in job interviews. For example, expatriate Stefan provided examples of what kinds of questions that should be avoided: 'The hiring process is very formal … you cannot ask gender, where you're from, where you live, how old are you—all this stuff is not allowed.' Most expatriates, following predeparture training in the home country, received HR-related guidance at the beginning of their stay from company HR professionals and other local colleagues functioning as HCN liaisons. Other differing cultural expectations that were reported as often communicated by HCNLs involved work behavior associated with planning and innovativeness. For example, the way in which Americans typically approach new projects with relatively little detailed planning and a penchant toward action followed by correction was also a frequent source of learning for the Germanic expatriates. As expatriate Markus reflected, 'Here everything is probably not 100% but only five, but you have it immediately.'

Cultural guide

Some expatriates were assigned an HCN as an official mentor who took over the behavioral function of the cultural guide. Many expatriates found HCN mentors on their own in their work environments to help guide and explain cultural differences. Others received HCN cultural guidance more informally, as stated by Sebastian: '… just through conversations people have helped me ... make sense of the culture here [...].' These HCN cultural guides also notably helped the expatriate to better understand cultural activities and events. Expatriate senior analyst Dennis declared that he felt welcomed by and learned from his colleagues as they invited his family to a Thanksgiving dinner. Expatriates also received HCN guidance on numerous matters through their regular informal interactions. Sabrina, a German HR manager for North America, mentioned that she received guidance from a local American middle manager who initially shared an office with her, on writing checks, going golfing and bowling, and other typical American activities. Several expatriates mentioned learning much about the meaning and importance of collegiate and professional American sports.

Conflict mediator
HCN liaisons served to reduce and resolve conflicts arising due to cultural differences between the expatriate and the local workforce. Through an official company guidance process of 360-degree feedback, Alexander received anonymous, candid feedback and guidance from his HCN team in areas in which he could improve his management style and rapport with local employees. From this feedback process, Matthias, a medical doctor, also experienced something similar. He noted, 'You get bad reviews if you leave too early. Even though you get your work done ... I had this [a] couple of times that they say your work ethic is not great.' This is how his HCN associates gave him feedback about what behavior he should change to avoid conflicts. The Germanic expatriates tended to reflect agreement that their American colleagues needed such official feedback process because they were very polite and were not very proactive in giving negative, corrective feedback to the expatriates who typically were in higher positions.

HCNL Role Field Validation: Communication Manager

Language translator
Expatriates frequently reported that HCNs supported them by translating messages for the local workplace, and particularly in getting nuances of the language correct to express the intended meaning since the expatriates spoke English. In learning from his local colleagues' modeling, Stefan said that he used '... a lot of slang and phrases and everything, and I adapted them in my life.' Tobias also mentioned learning language through HCN modeling, such as in conducting job interviews with HCNs from HR. He stated, 'You kind of watch what others are doing and asking, and then you adapt.' Daniel, who had worked as an expatriate elsewhere, indicated that he received support from HCNs to improve his use of English as commonly spoken locally: 'I mean, we Europeans tend to learn British English and British slang, versus the American

English and American slang ... our flow in speech is more formal than it is in a US work environment. So, I got some feedback there.' Due to the above observed politeness and reluctance to give expatriate corrective feedback, Sabrina mentioned that she needed to regularly push colleagues to correct her language mistakes. Andreas agreed, expressing gratitude for his American manager who

> would actually call it out ... like hey that's so funny the way you pronounce that. He would actually just like take it with humor when there was like a funny situation or when I would pronounce something wrong or use a word in the wrong context, and I told him very early on like I want you to do that—like so many of my colleagues don't do that, and I've been using it wrong for so long and nobody's ever dared to say that to me.

Communication moderator
Seven expatriates mentioned that from the beginning of their stay in the US they would send for feedback and possible adjustment a draft of an important formal communication or legal document to a local HCN colleague or their American manager before sending it out to a larger audience of employees or customers. Alexander, who had already been in the US for more than two years, said, 'I write the draft, and they crossline [identify] everything what sounds strange to them.' This approach was similar to that taken by Stefan, who wanted to avoid having his English sound like 'Google translate,' and he regularly asked local HCN colleagues to look at his messages and provide corrective feedback to ensure that nothing 'is twisted up or not understandable.' Dennis similarly sends his communication to his American manager before sending it to senior leaders 'to make sure it fits the right tone and drives the message home.'

Communication facilitator
The expatriates also received advice from their HCN colleagues that facilitated the expatriates' ability to communicate directly with the local workforce. One aspect mentioned several times in the interviews was HCN coaching to help expatriates provide more positive vibes in feedback and cheerful communication for optimal workforce impact—a form of communication tone to which the Germanic expatriates were not particularly accustomed. Sabrina admitted that she initially had difficulty with this positive feedback culture. She explained, 'So here if somebody is doing a random regular job, they kind of expect Oh, good job and that's awesome how you did it and all these kinds of positive vibes which I had a really hard time, in the beginning, to make that sound as I meant it.' Sebastian described his similar experience where he received feedback from his manager on how to communicate more effectively, 'I called like features in our app horrible, and then my manager was like, oh, someone

worked on this. Don't hurt their feelings.' Expatriate Andreas also commented on helpful communication facilitation from his American manager:

> you're being very realistic and sometimes maybe a little bit overly pessimistic about things. And I did have quite a few of those conversations where he would actually tell me, like, unless you can present me with a viable solution, or at least, make a proposal, don't come to me and complain about something.

Communication mediator

In general, likely due to the expatriates' relatively strong command of English and close cultural distance with the American workforce (Ronen and Shenkar, 2013), they preferred to communicate directly with local workers and reported only occasional need for HCNs to assist with communication mediation. However, Matthias described one situation when such mediation was helpful: 'I had one time, they told me my notes are too messy. And my coordinator came to me and said, hey, you should improve your notes.'

HCNL Role Field Validation: Information Resource Broker

Information boundary spanner

The expatriates often reported receiving information from locals about the local environment to help them navigate personal and professional matters. For example, some expatriates received support from their HR managers on where and how to rent an apartment or house, or apply for an American Social Security number. Stefan reported, 'They said, hey, like this is the area you should live in, and this is the street.' Melanie described the helpful medical contact information and back-up support related to her pregnancy and eventual childbirth (e.g., personal phone numbers to call if anything was needed) that she received from local employees—even those she hardly knew. Tobias highlighted the very useful preparation of one HCNL serving in a relocation service role: '... she's American, but she lived in Germany for quite some time. So, she's fluent in both languages ... and knows what it feels like to live in Germany and then come over to the US.'

Besides supplying helpful information in meeting expatriate personal needs, HCNLs also provided helpful information related to the work environment. Alexander reported relying on his local HCN colleagues for providing local business information: 'I really rely on them. Whatever I want to do here, I consult them first, saying hey we have an issue we need a painting supplier, who do you know? Ask your network for recommendations. This is how it works.' Patrick, who was head of digital platforms in the food industry, also received helpful information from his firm's American legal counsel to understand differences between the US and European legal systems. Markus reported relying on the American senior vice president for sales to better understand American customers and received coaching on appropriate negotiation strategies.

Organizational memory source

Several expatriates indicated that they talked to their HCN colleagues and members of the HR department for useful information about the history of the local operation that improved their understanding and sense-making in their current work. Kathrin mentioned, 'I talked to colleagues and ... they showed us the history of the plant here and the different other plants that we have across the US. ... they told me a lot about it and how it used to be back then, what it looked like, what changed recently. Yeah, it was a lot of informal chats about these things.' Andreas indicated that he received information from the past that helped him be successful in his job. He noted that '... even today, I still sometimes learn about things from the people I'm still in contact with, where they then tell me like, Oh, yeah, this is what really happened.'

Informal organizational knowledge source

Tobias received helpful information about the informal organization chart during his lunch breaks with his HCN colleagues. He explained, 'You have the official organization chart and then you get support, who is married to whom? Who is the nephew of whom? Who is related in some other way?' Daniel had lunch with his American mentor and one of the senior managers every two weeks to extend his network in a 'non-formal setting.' He described receiving information about informal policies with, 'They don't give you a guidebook, so to speak, they give you the framework and then once in a while they give you feedback on things, which might be appropriate or not appropriate.' Regarding her informal source of organizational knowledge, Katrin noted that it was important to '... just follow what people do here.'

HCNL Role Field Validation: Talent Manager

Talent identifier

In this behavioral function, the HCNL supports the expatriate in finding external or internal talent for the organization. Michael mentioned receiving help from his HCN colleagues to identify possible new external job candidates. Several expatriates mentioned that their companies desired to decrease the number of expatriates in the future (and increase the proportion of HCNs), due to the significant expenses and visa challenges.

Trainer/coach

Phillip remembered being taught by his American manager that he should focus more on things they can do rather than what they cannot do. Andreas experienced similar coaching from his American manager, stating, 'You can't make it sound too negative, because then you will lose people support ... the American thinking here is more like Yes, we can do it.' Benjamin recalled learning from his American boss to build on his success, and to actively sell himself and his achievements. In addition, he learned from his local peer colleagues about soft skills for effective communication with his colleagues—something that he was previously lacking. Markus also learned from his colleagues to not be so 'formal and stiff' like he was in Germany. He added about his learning from his local social interactions at work, 'People are not afraid of making mistakes, people are not afraid of making something wrong, the mentality is just do it. If you do it wrong, then you know, you can correct it.'

Mentor

The HCNL as mentor provides guidance that has a positive impact on expatriate career development. Sebastian remarked about the career guidance he received, 'I had a more senior software engineer, who I had weekly conversations with. He supported me on how to become a more senior software engineer and pick up more challenging projects.' Andreas received significant support from his manager, who encouraged him to take over a crucial project. Andreas acknowledged, 'I accepted, and because of that decision, I am where I am today ... that's how I got my job.' Tobias described a collective HCN mentoring influence on his career success, where the support of his American team was essential. He noted, '... the people you work together—they have a high impact on your personal career. That is how you learn in interaction with other people.'

Besides developing further within the company, expatriates also received guidance for obtaining career preparation and development outside of the company. Markus was encouraged and supported by his manager to obtain further formal education. He stated, 'I'm studying MBA in Boston, and he approved that and pushed me to do that and gives me ... the time off to do that, and the company pays for it.' Sebastian also received recruiter and job-placement support from local HCN colleagues in finding another job after being laid off by his first company. He noted, '... that was the way they helped me; they gave me access to their professional network.' Sandra, who moved to the US with her husband, received support in finding a new job from one of her husband's HCN colleagues. He directed her to a viable organization where she should apply, and even helped her complete her job application.

HCNL Role Field Validation: Internal Change Agent

Change co-planner
The HCN can support the expatriate in planning company change and adapting to fit demands and opportunities in the local environment. In implementing change projects, most of the expatriates mentioned that it is crucial to early on involve local colleagues in the planning. As Sabrina remarked, 'A change process never works if just one person wants to have it. So, we normally try to integrate at least everyone that is involved in the process as early as possible.' Michael remarked on his experience with change through goal achievement, 'Whenever you try to achieve a goal, you ask your employees, how do we best do it?' Besides local colleagues, local American management also supported expatriates in the planning of the change. Alexander stated, 'I had support from different levels, talking to my boss, talking to my peers getting feedback from them how do we perform? How can you work?'

Change executor
Related to assisting expatriates in executing or implementing the planned change, Christian observed, 'As soon as they felt like, well it's, not that [Christian] wants to create more work, it's actually to make life easier. As soon as that little click happened, they were very willing to help out.' Sebastian also received guiding support from multiple HCNs in implementing change due to their feedback on his change proposals. As he described this process, 'I write a proposal, then I share it with my team, and then I share it with a broader audience, and then we implement that particular change. So, people give feedback on that, right?' Andreas emphasized the small implementation decisions contributed by local colleagues during the process that made the change successful.

Workforce alignment facilitator
The HCNL performing this behavioral function supports the expatriate in overcoming natural and typical local workforce resistance to change. In the interviews, this workforce alignment facilitation support typically came from HCNs who were in upper and middle management. Expatriate Daniel was often successful in gaining support from local management, who emphasized to local workers the need for change. Sabrina described her American CFO as effective in addressing possible resistance through her good relationship with the workforce. She described this CFO as acting as a 'typical mother of the company ... and she has a really good way to convince people in a very positive way.'

DISCUSSION

In this chapter we have examined the important HCN local liaison role that contributes in multiple ways to effective knowledge transfer between the host country workforce and top management in the foreign operation. We have demonstrated here that this HCN liaison role can have a positive impact through knowledge sharing on expatriate and HCN work performance, with ultimate positive impact on performance at the local operation and potentially enhanced quality of knowledge flowing back to company headquarters and throughout the MNC. We also contend that our proposed HCNL model may help move MNCs beyond their traditional international management focus upon expatriates to being more inclusive of other important sources of global talent within the MNC. This multidimensional HCN liaison role between expatriate and the HCN workforce and local host country environment is a significant improvement upon the traditional, rather simplistic and imperialistic notion of the MNC's home country expatriate as filling the sole liaison role between company headquarters and the foreign operation. We are not negating this traditionally recognized expatriate liaison role. On the contrary, these differing expatriate and HCN liaison roles may work in tandem to enhance overall knowledge sharing and knowledge management within the host country operation and throughout the MNC.

It was observed in the interviews that within the HCNL role component of communications manager, many of the expatriates preferred to communicate directly with the local workforce, with less perceived benefit of a HCN liaison role. In fact, due to the expatriates' generally strong English language fluency and relatively close cultural distance with the American workforce (Ronen and Shenkar, 2013), it is notable that there still was field validation in all of the behavioral functions of all five HCNL model components. Further field research is needed, however, particularly in developing countries involving greater cultural and linguistic distance where the need for the HCNL role and its various component behavioral functions may be more pronounced. This research is needed to provide a clearer picture about which of these components and behavioral functions tend to be most frequently used in the HCN liaison role and under which conditions (including age of the host country operation, international experience of the expatriate and the HCNLs, primary purpose of the expatriate assignment, etc.), and which components can have the greatest influence on knowledge transfer and in contributing to expatriate performance and overall foreign operation productivity.

With particular regard to cultural distance, there is evidence that the degree of homophily or perceived similarity and trust between expatriates and HCNs can influence HCN and expatriate absorptive capacity in receiving information, and HCN motivational disposition to share information (Vance & Paik, 2005). Thus, where expatriates have assignments involving significant interaction with HCNs in countries representing great cultural distance, there likely will be greater challenges and obstacles to an unrestrained, two-way flow of useful knowledge and information. HCNs who are highly trusted and have strong credibility within their local work environment, and who have a strong understanding of the expatriate and MNC culture and their strategic objectives, will likely provide valuable contributions toward optimal knowledge sharing and promote increased productivity under these conditions of great cultural distance.

MNC knowledge management activities and processes have experienced a significant shift, in some cases permanent, due to adjustments and learning from the recent COVID-19 pandemic (Provitera & Ghasabeh, 2022). A major impact of the pandemic has been an increased general utilization of virtual workforce operations and management, and virtual expatriate management arrangements in particular (Haak-Saheem, 2020; Caligiuri et al., 2020; Collings & Sheeran, 2020). Although the field research described here did not focus specifically on effects of the ongoing pandemic, future research should examine how this powerful pandemic experience may have permanently affected the HCNL model presented here in post-COVID-19 practice.

Therefore, further exploratory and prescriptive field research will be very helpful in increasing our understanding of current effective HCN staffing, training, coaching, compensation, and other human resource practices that support the various components and functions of the HCNL role. This prescriptive research should help in building effective HR practices and approaches for identifying and selecting job candidates who can best fulfill the various behavioral functions within the overall HCNL role. Moreover, these behavioral functions, validated across various conditions of country development and cultural distance, may serve as a useful guide for HCN training to ensure that the HCNLs develop the necessary skill sets to effectively fulfill this important liaison role.

REFERENCES

Abeuova, D. & Muratbekova-Touron, M. (2019). Global talent management: Shaping the careers of internationally educated talents in developing markets. *Thunderbird International Business Review*, **61**(6), 843–856.

An, Y.H., Choe, S. & Kang, J. (2021). Ways to win: Strategic choices, institutions and performance in sub-Saharan Africa. *Multinational Business Review*, **29**(3), 374–396.

Anantatmula, V.S. (2010). Impact of cultural differences on knowledge management in global projects: Very informal newsletter on library automation. *Cross-Cultural Research*, **40**(3), 239–253.

Ando, N. (2021). Human capital, cultural distance and staffing localization. *Multinational Business Review*, **29**(3), 420–439.

Arazmjoo, H. & Rahmanseresht, H. (2020). A multi-dimensional meta-heuristic model for managing organizational change. *Management Decision*, **58**(3), 526–543.

Arias-Pérez, J., Velez-Ocampo, J. & Cepeda-Cardona, J. (2021). Strategic orientation toward digitalization to improve innovation capability: Why knowledge acquisition and exploitation through external embeddedness matter. *Journal of Knowledge Management*, **25**(5), 1319–1335.

Balogun, J., Jarzabkowski, P. & Vaara, E. (2011). Selling, resistance and reconciliation: A critical discursive approach to subsidiary role evolution in MNEs. *Journal of International Business Studies*, **42**(6), 765–786.

Becker-Ritterspach, F., Saka-Helmhout, A. & Hotho, J. (2010). Learning in multinational enterprises as the socially embedded translation of practices. *Critical Perspectives on International Business*, **6**(1), 8–37.

Bello-Pintado, A. & Bianchi, C. (2021). Workforce education diversity, work organization and innovation propensity. *European Journal of Innovation Management*, **24**(3), 756–776.

Braun, V. & Clarke, V. (2006). Using thematic analysis in psychology. *Qualitative Research in Psychology*, **3**(2), 77–101.

Caligiuri, P.M., De Cieri, H., Minbaeva, D., Verbeke, A. & Zimmermann, A. (2020). International HRM insights for navigating the COVID-19 pandemic: Implications for future research and practice. *Journal of International Business Studies*, **51**(5), 697–713.

Carraher, S., Sullivan, S. & Crocitto, M. (2008). Mentoring across global boundaries: An empirical examination of home- and host-country mentors on expatriate career outcomes. *Journal of International Business Studies*, **39**(8), 1310–1326.

Carsten, D. & Schomaker, R.M. (2019). Cultural impacts on national innovativeness: Not every cultural dimension is equal. *Cross-Cultural Research*, **53**(2), 186–214.

Chen, M.Y., Lam, L.W. & Zhu, J. (2021). Should companies invest in human resource development practices? The role of intellectual capital and organizational performance improvements. *Personnel Review*, **50**(2), 460–477.

Cicekli, E. (2011). Antecedents of normative integration in multinational companies: A conceptual model. *International Journal of Management*, **28**(4), 177–183.

Collings, D.G. & Sheeran, R. (2020). Research insights: Global mobility in a post-Covid world. *Irish Journal of Management*, **39**(2), 77–84.

Cucino, V., Del Sarto, N., Di Minin, A. & Piccaluga, A. (2021). Empowered or engaged employees? A fuzzy set analysis on knowledge transfer professionals. *Journal of Knowledge Management*, **25**(5), 1081–1104.

Dahou, K., Hacini, I. & Burgoyne, J. (2019). Knowledge management as a critical success factor in developing international companies' organizational learning capability. *Journal of Workplace Learning*, **31**(1), 2–16.

Davoine, E., Barmeyer, C. & Rossi, C. (2018). Retaining repatriate knowledge at the crossroads between global knowledge management and global talent management. *Management International Review*, **22**, 142–165.

Festa, G., Rossi, M., Kolte, A. & Situm, M. (2021). Territory-based knowledge management in international marketing processes: The case of 'made in Italy' SMEs. *European Business Review*, **32**(3), 425–442.

Froese, F.J., Stoermer S., Reiche, S.B. & Klar, S. (2021). Best of both worlds: How embeddedness fit in the host unit and the headquarters improve repatriate knowledge transfer. *Journal of International Business Studies*, **52**(7), 1331–1349.

Goswami, A.K, Agrawal, R.K. & Goswami, M. (2021). Influence of national culture on knowledge management process: Literature review and research agenda. *Benchmarking*, **28**(4), 1186–1212.

Grant, E.A. (2008). How to retain talent in India. *Sloan Management Review*, **50**(1), 6–7.

Haak-Saheem, W. (2020). Talent management in Covid-19 crisis: How Dubai manages and sustains its global talent pool. *Asian Business & Management*, **19**(3), 298–301.

Hannola, L., Richter, A., Shahper, R. & Stocker, A. (2018). Empowering production workers with digitally facilitated knowledge processes: A conceptual framework. *International Journal of Production Research*, **56**(14), 4729–4743.

Harvey, M., McIntyre, N., Thompson Heames, J. & Moeller, M. (2009). Mentoring global female managers in the global marketplace: Traditional, reverse, and reciprocal mentoring. *The International Journal of Human Resource Management*, **20**(6), 1344–1361.

Hawes, C. & Chew, E. (2011). The cultural transformation of large Chinese enterprises into internationally competitive corporations: Case studies of Haier and Huawei. *Journal of Chinese Economic and Business Studies*, **9**(1), 67–83.

Hoe, S.L. & McShane, S. (2010). Structural and informal knowledge acquisition and dissemination in organizational learning: An exploratory analysis. *The Learning Organization*, **17**(4), 364–386.

Holden, N.J. & Glisby, M. (2010). *Creating Knowledge Advantage: The Tacit Dimensions of International Competition and Cooperation*. Copenhagen: Copenhagen Business School Press.

Hong, P.C., Kallarakal, T.K., Moina, M. & Hopkins, M. (2019). Managing change, growth and transformation: Case studies of organizations in an emerging economy. *The Journal of Management Development*, **38**(4), 298–311.

House, R., Javidan, M., Hanges, P. & Dorfman, P. (2002). Understanding cultures and implicit leadership theories across the globe: An introduction to project GLOBE. *Journal of World Business*, **37**(1), 3–10.

Johnson, E.C., Kristof-Brown, A.L., Van Vianen, A.E.M., De Pater, I.E. & Rigsby, M.M. (2003). Expatriate social ties: Antecedents and consequences of relationships with comparable others and host country nationals. *International Journal of Selection and Assessment*, **11**(4), 277–288.

Kamoche, K. (1997). Knowledge creation and learning in international HRM. *International Journal of Human Resource Management*, **8**(3), 213–225.

Khan, T. & Maalik, M. (2011). Impact of culture on employees' trust in management: Evidence from Pakistani banking sector. *Interdisciplinary Journal of Contemporary Research in Business*, **3**(2), 1032–1054.

Krumbholz, M. & Maiden, N. (2001). The implementation of enterprise resource planning packages in different organizational and national cultures. *Information Systems*, **26**(3), 185–204.

Larsson, M., Segerstéen, S. & Svensson, C. (2011). Information and informality: Leaders as knowledge brokers in a high-tech firm. *Journal of Leadership & Organizational Studies*, **18**(2), 175–191.

Lu, R. & Reve, T. (2011). Guanxi, structural hole and closure. *Journal of Strategy and Management*, **4**(3), 275–288.

Lührs, L. (2021). The HCNL roles experienced by Germanic expatriates in the US and the impact of the COVID-19 pandemic. Master's thesis, Southern Denmark University.

McPhail, R., Fisher, R., Harvey, M. & Moeller, M. (2012). Staffing the global organization: Cultural nomads. *Human Resource Development Quarterly*, **23**(2), 259–276.

Moeller, M., Harvey, M. & Williams, W. (2010). Socialization of inpatriate managers to the headquarters of global organizations: A social learning perspective. *Human Resource Development Review*, **9**(2), 169–193.

Morris, S., Snell, S. & Björkman, I. (2016). An architectural framework for global talent management. *Journal of International Business Studies*, **47**(6), 723–747.

Nair, S.R., Kishore, G.P. & Demirbag, M. (2021). Reaping benefits from knowledge transfer: The role of confidence in knowledge. *Journal of Knowledge Management*, **25**(5), 1059–1080.

Persson, M. (2006). The impact of operational structure, lateral integrative mechanisms and control mechanisms on intra-MNE knowledge transfer. *International Business Review*, **15**(5), 547–569.

Provitera, M.J. & Ghasabeh, M.S. (2022). Redefining knowledge management in the wake of the post-pandemic crisis. *Training and Development Excellence Essentials*, **03**, ProQuest.

Reiche, B. (2007). The effect of international staffing practices on subsidiary staff retention in multinational corporations. *International Journal of Human Resource Management*, **18**(4), 523–536.

Reuber, A.R., Tippmann, E. & Monaghan, S. (2021). Global scaling as a logic of multinationalization. *Journal of International Business Studies*, **52**(6), 1031–1046.

Robertson, E. (2005). Placing leaders at the heart of organizational communication. *Strategic Communication Management*, **9**(5), 34–37.

Ronen, S. & Shenkar, O. (2013). Mapping world clusters: Clusters formation, sources and implications. *Journal of International Business Studies*, **44**, 867–897.

Sabeen, H.B., Kiyani, S.K., Dust, S. & Zakariya, R. (2021). The impact of ethical leadership on project success: The mediating role of trust and knowledge sharing. *International Journal of Managing Projects in Business*, **14**(4), 982–998.

Schwartz, D.F. & Jacobson, E. (1977). Organizational communication network analysis: The liaison communication role. *Organizational Behavior and Human Performance*, **18**(1), 158–174.

Selmer, J. (2000). Usage of corporate career development activities by expatriate managers and the extent of their international adjustment. *International Journal of Commerce & Management*, **10**(1), 1–23.

Stendahl, E., Schriber, S. & Tippman, E. (2021). Control changes in multinational corporations: Adjusting control approaches in practice. *Journal of International Business Studies*, **52**(3), 409–431.

Stoermer, S., Davies, S. & Froese, F.J. (2021). The influence of expatriate cultural intelligence on organizational embeddedness and knowledge sharing: The moderating effects of host country context. *Journal of International Business Studies*, **52**(3), 432–453.

Suutari, V. (2002). Global leader development: An emerging research agenda. *Career Development International*, **7**(4), 218–233.

Takeuchi, H. & Nonaka, I. (eds.) (2004). *Hitotsubashi on Knowledge Management*. Singapore: John Wiley & Sons.

Toh, S.M. & DeNisi, A.S. (2003). Host country national reactions to expatriate pay policies: A model and implications. *Academy of Management Review*, **28**(4), 606–621.

Toh, S.M. & DeNisi, A.S. (2005). A local perspective to expatriate success. *Academy of Management Executive*, **19**(1), 132–146.

Toh, S.M. & DeNisi, A.S. (2007). Host country nationals as socializing agents: A social identity approach. *Journal of Organizational Behavior*, **28**(3), 281–301.

Tyskbo, D. (2021). Competing institutional logics in talent management: Talent identification at the HQ and a subsidiary. *The International Journal of Human Resource Management*, **32**(10), 2150–2184.

Van Bakel, M. (2019). It takes two to tango: A review of the empirical research on expatriate-local interactions. *International Journal of Human Resource Management*, **30**(21), 2993–3025.

Van Bakel, M., Gerritsen, M. & Van Oudenhoven, J.P. (2011). Impact of a local host on the success of an international assignment. *Thunderbird International Business Review*, **53**(3), 391–402.

Van Bakel, M., Vaiman, V., Vance, C.M. & Haslberger, A. (2022). Broadening international mentoring: Contexts and dynamics of expatriate and HCN intercultural mentoring. *Journal of Global Mobility*, **10**(1), 14–35.

Vance, C.M. (2006). Strategic upstream and downstream considerations for effective global performance management. *International Journal of Cross-Cultural Management*, **6**(1), 37–56.

Vance, C.M. (2011). Enhancing absorptive capacity and management knowledge transfer through host country workforce training: Lessons from Sacagawea and Squanto. In P. Benson (ed.), *Emerging Themes in International Management of Human Resources*. Charlotte, NC: Information Age Publishing, pp. 3–22.

Vance, C.M., Andersen, T., Vaiman, V. & Gale, J. (2014). A taxonomy of potential contributions of the host country national local liaison role in global knowledge management. *Thunderbird International Business Review*, **56**(2), 173–191.

Vance, C.M. & Ensher, E.A. (2002). The voice of the host country workforce: A key source for improving the effectiveness of expatriate training and performance. *International Journal of Intercultural Relations*, **26**(4), 447–461.

Vance, C.M. & Paik, Y. (2005). Forms of host-country national learning for enhanced MNC absorptive capacity. *Journal of Managerial Psychology*, **20**(7), 590–606.

Vance, C., Vaiman, V. & Andersen, T. (2009). The vital liaison role of host country nationals in MNC knowledge management. *Human Resource Management*, **48**(4), 649–659.

Vasugi, S., Kaviatha, F. & Prema, R. (2011). An empirical investigation on employee empowerment practices in Indian software industries. *Interdisciplinary Journal of Contemporary Research in Business*, **2**(11), 668–674.

Wang, X. & Chan, C.C.A. (2006). The multiplier effect of investment in training in China. *International Journal of Management*, **23**(2), 234–243.

Zhong, Y., Zhu, J.C. & Zhang, M.M. (2021). Expatriate management of emerging market multinational enterprises: A multiple case study approach. *Journal of Risk and Financial Management*, **14**(6), 252.

Ziyi, W. & Nguyen Quyen, T.K. (2020). Local responsiveness strategy of foreign subsidiaries of Chinese multinationals: The impacts of relational-assets, market-seeking FDI, and host country institutional environments. *Asia Pacific Journal of Management*, **37**(3), 661–692.

Index